DIGITAL FORENSICS AND INVESTIGATION: FROM DATA TO DIGITAL EVIDENCE

DIGITAL FORENSICS AND INVESTIGATION: FROM DATA TO DIGITAL EVIDENCE

Anne Wade

SOCIETY Publishing

www.societypublishing.com

Digital Forensics and Investigation: From Data to Digital Evidence

Anne Wade

Society Publishing

2010 Winston Park Drive,

2nd Floor

Oakville, ON L6H 5R7

Canada

www.societypublishing.com

Tel: 001-289-291-7705
001-905-616-2116
Fax: 001-289-291-7601
Email: orders@arclereducation.com

ISBN: 978-1-77361-351-2 (Hardcover)

ABOUT THE AUTHOR

Dr. Anne Wade has been a researcher and an instruction in the Criminal Justice field for 27 years. She is currently an Associate Professor at a Community College in North Carolina. She holds an Ed.D. in Educational Leadership and a Ph.D. in Public Safety Leadership/Criminal Justice. Her research interests are in Criminology, Victimology, and the Human Services. She is married to Wesley Wade. She is an artist, writer, research, teacher, and trainer.

TABLE OF CONTENTS

LIST OF FIGURES

LIST OF TABLES

PREFACE

Digital tools such as hard drives and smartphones have recently been used to extract core information from terrorists. An iPhone was used to capture the famous celebrity, Michael Jackson in his final moments. We will keep talking about the role of digital forensics in our modern world because it has brought a lot of ease to every facet of life and various industries. It has helped deliver justice by catching criminals. Cyber activity has become a significant part of our lives and obviously, we cannot do without it because the world has changed due to science and technology. This is in addition to the fact that research is conducted daily to improve the lives of people all around the world. According to the EC Council, about 85% of businesses and government agencies have detected a security breach.

Over the past few years, practitioners and researchers have made significant advances in digital forensics. Our understanding of technology has improved and we have gained the necessary experience to refine our practices. We have overcome major technical challenges, giving practitioners greater access to digital evidence. New forensic techniques and tools are created almost daily to support forensic acquisition of volatile data, inspection of remote systems, and analysis of network traffic.

Purpose and Readership

Various books on "forensics" from diverse authors are very specific and tend to ignore core aspects of digital forensics. This book specially corrects this mistake by covering most core aspects that readers need to understand when dealing with forensic investigation. It is organized in such a way that the hierarchy of various forensics topics is highlighted. The case studies give readers a realistic view and a sense of the technical, legal, and practical challenges that arise in real computer investigations. Tables and figures are included for comparison and better understanding. A bibliography is listed at the end of this book for further studies and research.

This book is intended to help crime investigators in various government agencies and security personnel to understand the concept of digital forensics comprehensively, access the benefits of various sources of digital evidence, evaluate and integrate some of the important principles of digital evidence into investigations, and decode the relationship between digital evidence and open source tools. It is written to meet the needs of digital forensic investigators, information security engineers, security analysts, cybercrimes investigators, firewall engineers, forensic scientists, attorneys, law enforcement, computer professionals, and other professionals in the Information and communication technology (ICT) industry.

Organization of the Book

This book is divided into 10 chapters. Chapter one gives a comprehensive analysis of digital forensics. The first section of this chapter introduces the readers to the concept of forensic examination. The second section discusses the origin of digital evidence; the third section highlights the principles of digital evidence while the last section gives insight on anti-forensics. Chapter two enables the readers to get an understanding of the current investigative processes in forensic investigation. However, the various models that were established by researchers and investigators are explained. Chapter three informs the reader about the role of network and Internet in forensic investigation. It is divided into two parts. The first part (pages 52–58) gives information about the types and examples of network used in obtaining network-based evidence while the second part (pages 58–64) gives information about the use of the Internet, email, and social network in network forensics. Pages 64–71 elaborate file analysis, the elements involved, and protection against intrusions. Chapter four explains the types of operating systems in digital forensics with their mode of operation. Chapter five explains fundamental concept of cloud computing, types of deployment models, and analysis of the challenges and opportunities in cloud forensics. Chapter six attempts to provide an overview of the methods commonly used to obtain data from mobile phones in a forensic routine. Mobile forensic tools and processes of retrieving data from various types of handheld device are also discussed. Chapter seven attempts to give a systematic overview of system security requirements and highlights the potential means to satisfy them. The purpose of this chapter is to provide a well-grounded framework within which readers can make proper purchase and execution decisions. Chapter eight discusses "digital forensics and legal proceedings." It discusses the operational and legal issues related to digital evidence. The forensic applications of new scientific discoveries have most been dramatically seen in the criminal trial court will also be covered. This book addresses the aforementioned forms of scientific forensic evidence that have sufficient validity used in a criminal proceeding.

Chapter nine addresses cyberstalking as a major form of cybercrime. This topic is treated separately as it is more extensive than any other type of cybercrime. This chapter gives a pointer into the unusual behaviors of cyberstalkers, tactics associated with cyberstalking crimes, and legislative intervention measures. Some case studies are shared to enable readers to have a glimpse of what is being discussed in reality. Chapter 10 explains content-related cybercrime under three different subheadings or sections, namely child pornography, hate speech, and cyberterrorism. This chapter also highlights some case studies and legal framework undertaken by international organizations in a bid to tackle cybercrimes militating against the global society.

CHAPTER 1

INTRODUCTION TO DIGITAL FORENSICS

"There is a positive aspect to the increasing use of technology by criminals—the involvement of computers in crime has resulted in an abundance of digital evidence that can be used to apprehend and prosecute offenders."

—Eoghan Casey

CONTENTS

Digital forensics is a relatively new science that is gradually becoming popular as cyber criminals utilize networks and computers to execute their unscrupulous activities. Terrorists are using high-level technology through the Internet to recruit, communicate and execute their deadly operations. Hence, there is a burden on the shoulders of global government agencies which are tackling cybercrimes and the related menace that has crept into the society. A professional in digital forensics must have the skill set which includes a deep understanding of hardware and software, forensic science, computer networks, and government laws. This chapter enlightens the reader about the concept of digital forensics and the methodologies involved as well as various models and frameworks that are adopted in crime investigations.

1.1 AN OVERVIEW OF DIGITAL FORENSICS

With the development of science and technology coupled with the daily use of computers in our everyday lives, it has become expedient to include the contents of computers as part of official evidence. Laptops, servers, and desktops are familiar to us because we use them often; however, there are other means by which forensic evidence can be stored. Other devices that can perform similar storage capability include Personal digital assistants (PDAs), memory cards, and video games. The focus of digital forensics is based on this data and usage of these devices. Digital forensics is the process of finding and reading electronic data. It can also be defined as the process involved in the collection, protection, documentation, validation, analysis, and presentation of digital evidence, obtained from computerized sources, and by the application of established scientific methods, which are beneficial in the reconstruction of events or criminology. Marcella and Menendez state that cyber forensics, e-discovery, digital, forensics, computer and computer forensics relatively mean the same thing yet none has emerged as a de facto standard (2008). They further presented an operational definition of computer forensics as "the science of locating, extracting, and analyzing types of data from different devices, which specialists then interpret to server as legal evidence." They also reiterated that computer forensics can be seen as an integration of law and computer science discipline because it involves the collection and analysis of data from computer systems, storage devices, grids, and wireless infrastructures in such a way that is acceptable as evidence in a court of law. Another definition identifies digital forensics as "the practice of scientifically derived and proven technical methods and tools toward the preservation, collection, validation, identification, analysis, interpretation, documentation, and presentation of subsequent digital information derived from digital sources for the purpose of facilitating or furthering the reconstruction of events as forensic evidence" (Willassen & Mjølsnes, 2005). This definition focuses on the reconstruction of events suggestively rather than criminality. Digital forensics utilizes comprehensive techniques in ascertaining viable information, from electronic gadgets, that may be accepted in court. This includes a chain of custody and documentation. The process of collecting digital forensic evidence can be divided into two distinct areas. The first area involves the collection of evidence without changing any of its contents and making sure that it is admissible in the court of law. The second area is the real usage of law enforcement grade and standard forensic policies that may allow the acceptability of the evidence in court. The objective of this document is to provide a succinct overview of the process involved in collection and appraisal of forensic evidence. Digital forensics is a constantly evolving scientific field with many subdisciplines. Some of these subdisciplines are;

(1) Computer forensics involves the identification, conservation, assemblage, documentation, and analysis of evidence obtained from electronic gadgets such as laptops, desktop computers, and other storage media to be used in technical examinations and legal proceedings.

(2) Network forensics involves the real-time tracking, capture, storing and scrutiny of network operations in order to detect the cause of cybercrimes, irregular network traffic, security infringement, and malware or virus attacks.

(3) Mobile devices forensics which involves the retrieval of electronic evidence from diverse gadgets such as smartphones, subscriber identity module (SIM) cards, PDAs, Global Positioning System (GPS) devices, tablets, and game consoles. (4) Digital image forensics involves the abstraction and examination of photographic images to confirm their originality by retrieving the metadata of the image file in order to discover its source.

(5) Digital video/audio forensics involves the assemblage, study, and assessment of audio and video recordings. This aspect of forensics is used to determine whether a recording is original,

altered, or mutilated. (6) Memory forensics involves the retrieval of digital evidence from the random access memory (RAM) of a running computer, otherwise known as live acquisition.

1.2 THE ORIGIN OF THE DIGITAL FORENSICS AND EVIDENCE

The origin of digital forensics can be traced back to the 1970s when investigators in the military began to delve into cybercrimes and needed detailed technical approaches to solve these issues. Many institutions now include computer forensics course in their programs to efficiently lecture students on its development and influence on individuals and the society in general. The adoption of this recently introduced professional innovation began in the United States when government agencies realized they need to employ investigative measures in solving criminal operations related to high-tech gadgets. The launch of Federal Bureau Investigation (FBI) Magnetic Media in 1984 was what prompted the introduction of computer forensics into the system. This program was later renamed as Computer Analysis and Response Team (CART).

Subsequently, the International Organization on Computer Evidence (IOCE) was created in 1995. From the mid-1990s to this time, the field of computer forensics has developed beyond imagination; hence, law enforcement agencies have taken as point of duty to train their workforce in the field of cybercrime in order to detect Internet criminals. 1984 FBI Magnetic Media Program created… this later becomes the CART 1993 First International Conference on Computer Evidence 1995 International Organization on Computer Evidence (IOCE) formed 1997 The G8 countries declared that "Law enforcement personnel must be trained and equipped to address high-tech crimes" in the Moscow Communiqué of December. 1998 In March G8 appointed IICE to create international principles for the processes relating to digital evidence 1998 INTERPOL Forensic Science Symposium 1999 FBI CART case load exceeds 2000 cases, examining 17 terabytes of data 2000 First FBI Regional Computer Forensic Laboratory established 2003 FBI CART case load exceeds 6500 cases, examining 782 terabytes of data

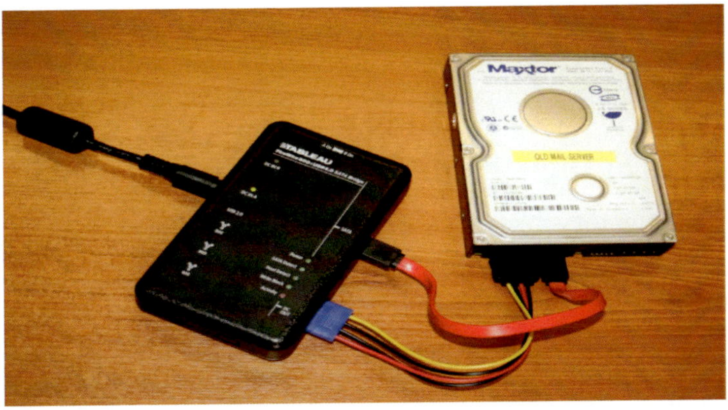

Figure 1.1: Digital evidence tools. *Source: https://www.tcea.org/blog/when-people-fail-technology/.*

Digital or electronic evidence is any probative information stored or conveyed in digital form that may be used at trial by a court. A court will prove if digital evidence is acceptable or relevant for the purpose for which it is meant. In the United States, many courts have applied Federal Rules of Evidence to digital evidence in a conventional manner although major differences such as the absence of customary standards and guidelines have been observed. Furthermore, digital evidence seems to be bulky, easily altered or copied and readily obtainable. As a result, some courts have occasionally used digital evidence in a different way for the purposes of validation, hearsay, the best evidence rule, and privilege. In December 2006, the Federal Rules of Civil Procedure legislated for new rules that required the protection and disclosure of digitally stored evidence. Digital evidence is often condemned for its genuineness because of its tendency to be altered, although courts are now prevailing over this argument without proof of tampering.

1.2.1 Types of Digital Evidence

There are two basic types of data in digital forensics, namely persistent data and volatile data. Persistent data is the form of data stored on local hard drive and it is retained when the computer is turned off while volatile data is the form of data that is stored in registries, cache, and RAM. There is tendency to lose volatile data when the computer is switched off or loses power because it is transient and an investigator needs to know the best way to recover data that may be vital for the identification and analysis of a security incident. However, Bates (2002) classified information sources into four types, namely temporary, volatile, semipermanent, and permanent.

1.2.2 Sources of Digital Evidence

Forensic investigators must identify the appropriate source of evidence to seize at a crime scene. Desktop computers now have enough disk storage space that is even too large to print. If too much of data is acquired, they muddle up the whole analysis and may also exceed the status of their search warrant. The U.S. Department of Justice described this situation in a journal.

...computer hardware, software, and electronic files may be important to a criminal investigation in two distinct ways: (1) the objects themselves may be contraband, evidence, instrumentalities, or fruits of crime and/or (2) the objects may be used as storage devices that contain contraband, evidence, instrumentalities, or fruits of crime in the form of electronic data. Rule 41 of the Federal Rules of Criminal Procedure permits the government to search for and seize computer hardware, software, and electronic files that are evidence of crime, contraband, instrumentalities of crime, and/or fruits of crime.

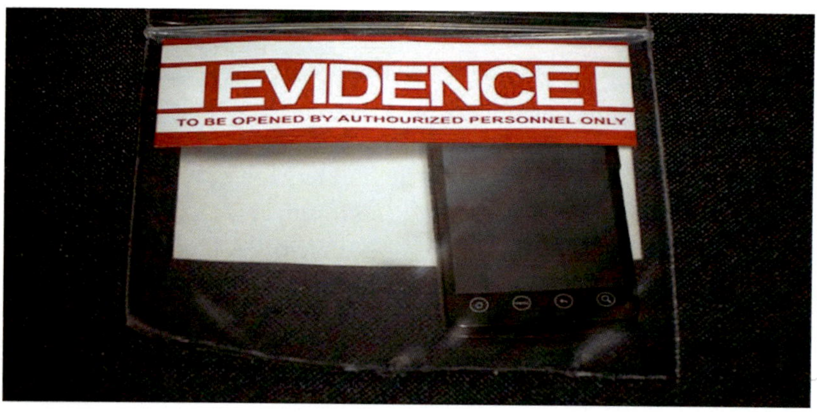

Figure 1.2: Evidence Bag. *Source: https://www.linkedin.com/pulse/holistic-mobile-cellular-investigations-patrick.*

This implies that software, hardware, or any other evidence can be seized if they are contraband such as illegally manufactured gadget, fruits of crime such as stolen copyright material, an instrumentality such as password cracking program and any digital evidence of a crime. Some apparent sources at a crime scene include fixed or removable hard disks, deleted file fragments, operating system temporary files, emails, and printed records. It is evident that conclusive cases cannot be built from single digital evidence while enormous quantities of data can crash operations; hence, there is a need for forensic specialists to perform information filtering at the crime scene.

1.3 PHASES OF FORENSICS INVESTIGATIONS

The high rate of criminal activities that involves the use of high-level technology can be better tackled by employing a well-planned investigation through forensic analysis. Digital forensic analysis is a careful process of revealing data and evidence that is important to the successful resolution of a case. However, the application of digital forensics in investigation requires a group of skilled forensic analysts, sophisticated forensics tools and a well-structured laboratory where retrieved evidence can be developed into organized reports thus facilitating the representation of defendants in a court. Here is a detailed view of the processes necessitated in carrying out an effective forensic investigation.

1.3.1 Selecting a Process of Investigation

Since 1984 till date, digital forensics has been an investigative method that has evolved with the pace of latest technologies. However, a digital forensic analyst has the sole responsibility of choosing an investigative method. A muddled process can lead to the buildup of random data and messy process of analysis can lead to the accumulation of random data and questionable evidence that may affect the outcome of a trial negatively. It is important to formulate a design plan and to select suitable tools and software to conduct the investigation and every stage is executed.

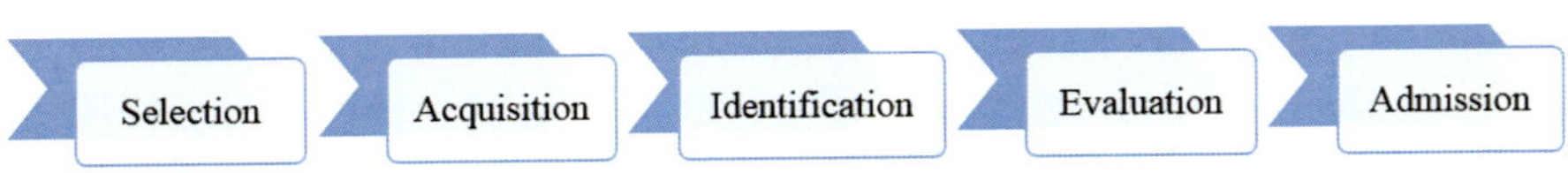

Figure 1.3: Phases of Digital Forensic Investigation.

1.3.2 Acquisition

Immediately the case study is finalized and there is a definite strategic plan, the first fundamental step involves the acquisition of data in form of electronic copies of files, videos, images, browser history, social media archives, emails, financial records, and other forms of data. Computer forensic analysts are professionals in the field of forensics and their job is to discover evidence by retrieving deleted files, emails, tracking real-time transactions, and extracting data from servers to support an investigation. Also, a major part of computer forensics entails retrieving information from mobile phones in form of appointment details, phonebook details, text messages, schedules, videos, and image files. In this stage, the experts make sure that evidence has been recovered using legal methods and appropriate approval of authorized personnel.

1.3.3 Identification

In this phase, analysts separate important discovery digitally and convert them into a file that can be easily deciphered by laymen and judges. The retrieved data can be stored in its raw form. The raw data may then be discarded and processed. The final result can then be arranged to produce a well-structured data using forensic tools. Forensic tools such as Forensic Toolkit (FTK), Mobile Phone Examiner (MPE+), and dtSearch are efficient search tools and are also used in the arrangement of recovered data. The vital data may be hosted on an evidence-based platform which is accessible through the Internet.

1.3.4 Evaluation

This phase is the most important of digital forensic investigation as it decides whether original and certain evidence has been found and consequently controls the outcome of the lawsuit. The forensic analysts attempt to inquire whether the information given is genuine evidence and whether it can be used during a trial. The mechanisms in the previous phases are identified, preserved, and connected so that a timeline of procedures is established and an extrapolation that is relevant to the case is drawn out to provide concrete support in favor of the defendant. This phase can be seen as a significant element of effective representation of the client because it determines the positive resolution of a case.

1.3.5 Admission

A court of law may disregard carefully prepared reports and factual evidence if they are useless and may be discarded as "inadmissible evidence." Therefore, it is mandatory that the pieces of evidence are obtained using legal methods with permission from the relevant authority. This factor will support the evidence by making it trustworthy especially if it has been retrieved by a Certified Computer Forensic Examiner and ensuring that it is admissible during a trial.

1.4 PRINCIPLES OF DIGITAL FORENSICS

Digital Forensics provides a large organization of proven exploratory techniques and methods for achieving the ends that are referenced extensively in this text. By forensic, we mean a feature of evidence that meets the acceptability standard for facts and its ability to convince based upon proof. In essence, forensic science is the application of science to law and is ultimately tested by use in court. For example, the scientific study of insects has many analytical applications including the study of insects on a decaying corpse—forensic entomology. Evidence related to the science of the science of entomology has been acknowledged by courts to help figure out the duration of an exposed body to fauna in a particular area. Another example of forensic science involves the study, preservation, and identification of shoe imprints left at a crime scene. Forensic examiners use the physical attributes of these shoe imprints to ascertain the type of shoe and eventually connect the shoes that left the imprints through careful analysis. Similarly, the methodical approach towards digital data becomes a forensic science when it relates to the investigation and prosecution of a crime. When hackers gain access to an organization's computer systems and steal personally identifiable information (PII), the organization must be ready to present evidence that will fulfill the guidelines of the regulatory bodies so as to be able to arrest and prosecute the criminals. Therefore, it is a necessity to handle digital evidence in a sensitive manner. Even when an agreement is handled completely within an organization, it is desirable to base vital decisions on concrete evidence. Eventually, any investigation can benefit from the influence of forensic science. Furthermore, forensic science can help in the reconstruction of criminal events through the application of scientific methods and testing of hypotheses and generation of theories which can help in the processing of discrete pieces of digital evidence. In essence, processing digital evidence in a proper way is important for resolving incidents and disputes in a business environment as well as criminal and civil matters. To encourage corporate digital investigators to apply the principles of forensic science presented in this book, forensic science can be better defined as the application of science to investigation and prosecution of crime.

1.4.1 Evidence Exchange

The main objective of any investigation is to follow the traces that criminals leave behind when committing the crime and to link the culprits to the crime scenes. Although witnesses may recognize a suspect, the participation of the individual in the crime is more compelling to identify a suspect; tangible evidence of an individual's involvement is usually more compelling and dependable. Forensic analysts are employed to expose the convincing relationship between the culprit, victim, and crime scene.

Figure 1.4: Forensic Digital Exchange (FDX). *Source: http://www.forensic-pathways.com/forensic-digital-exchange/.*

Locard's exchange principle states that the contact between two items will result in an exchange. This principle applies to any contact at a crime scene, including between an offender and victim, between a person with a weapon, and between people and the crime scene itself. This exchange occurs in digital and physical forms and can provide a direct link between them in the physical form; an offender might carelessly leave fingerprints or hair at the crime scene and take a fiber from the scene. For example, in a homicide case, the offender may plan to mislead investigators by typing a suicide note on the victim's computer, thereby leaving fingerprints on the keyboard unknowingly. The investigators can establish a likelihood of an offender's connection with a crime with this single evidence. However, with two pieces of evidence, the connection of the offender with the crime becomes stronger and more provable. Digital evidence can divulge information through a channel of communication between offenders and the victim, online operations and other information that provides a digital perspective to the investigation. In computer intrusions, the invaders will leave traces of their presence within the vicinity especially in the registry, network-level logs, file systems, and system logs. Furthermore, the invaders could carry along components of the crime scene back with them such as stolen passwords or PII in a file or database. This kind of evidence can be employed in the inquiry of an intrusion. The processes of sending messages that are rather destructive through a web-based e-mail service can also give a clue to the identification of the criminals. The web browser can be used to preserve files and data on the sender's hard drive coupled with the time reference. Therefore, forensic analysts may discover enough information pertaining to the sent message on the offender's hard drive including the exact content. In the same vein, investigators may likely acquire connected information such as Internet Protocol (IP) addresses, web server access logs, history, and bookmarks.

1.4.2 Evidence Characteristics

The exchanges that occur between individual and crime scene produce trace evidence belonging to one of the two general categories: (a) evidence with attributes that fit in the group called class characteristics and (b) evidence with attributes that fall in the category called individual characteristics. Consider the real world, for example, if a shoe imprint is left at a crime scene. Forensic analysis of those impressions might only show the brand and model of the shoe and categorize it under a class of all shoes of same brand and model. Therefore, if a suspect was discovered to be in custody of a pair of the same brand and model, a weak contingent connection can be made between the suspect and the offense. If forensic analysis discovers comprehensive patterns in the shoe imprints and also finds a similar pattern in the suspect shoes, a stronger connection can be established. The error margin can be reduced considerably by the discovery of an individual characteristic, making the connection less direct and difficult to disprove. In the digital world, we move into a simulated environment which is less real. Exchange of digital evidence often involves transferring a copy of the data without changing the original file. Furthermore, an individual's identity is unlikely to be disclosed because of the issue of anonymity which exists as a means of security or privacy on the Internet. Despite these issues, trace evidence is still left behind in the digital world with reference to class and individual characteristics that can be eventually used to answer important questions or unravel the mystery behind a case. For example, class characteristics in a questioned Microsoft Word document may help forensic analysts to determine if it is a fake document because it could have been produced using a version of Microsoft Word that was released several years after the alleged date of creation for the document. When there is concern that digital evidence has been obscured or mutilated, class characteristics may reveal that a particular mechanism for encryption or data destruction was used on the computer in which evidence was stored. It is scarcer to get more decisive individual characteristics but it is easier to identify through comprehensive forensic analysis. Certain printers mark every page with a pattern that is unique to the device. To ascertain the involvement of a suspect who used a scanner or digital camera, unique marks are placed on a digital photograph. Similarly, a precise floppy drive may make unique magnetic impressions on a floppy disk, helping to establish a connection between the floppy disk and the suspect's device. These are instances of the preferable category of evidence because of the strong linkage with an individual source. Generally, however, the amount of work required to ascertain this level of information is weighty and may be useless, especially, if a verified method for its recovery has not been examined and accepted in the digital forensic community and used to establish a model in the courts. This risk, coupled with the fact that the objects of analysis change in design and complexity at such a rapid pace, makes it difficult for applied research in digital forensics to keep pace with changes in technology. Classification of characteristics from various types of digital components has yet to be approached in any formal way but the value of this type of information cannot be taken too lightly. Class characteristics can be used together to determine a probability of involvement and the majority of this type of evidence can be a factor in deducing an individual's guilt or innocence. The significance of physical evidence depends on its ability to provide validation of events with data that are most likely free of human errors and prejudice. It is the thread that binds together other investigations that are more dependent on the human verdict and, therefore, more prone to human shortcomings. The more supporting evidence that crime investigators can acquire, the more attention will be given to the evidence in court and there is more decisiveness that will lead to their deductions. The classification of digital evidence as described can be of advantage to investigators by allowing them to present the comparative values of the evidence and help them sustain the fairness called for by the investigative process.

Figure 1.5: A photograph of an impression evidence.

Source: https://www.forensicmag.com/article/2011/06/step-toward-better-track-evidence-photos

1.4.3 Forensic Soundness

Digital evidence must be preserved and scrutinized in a sound manner that will make it useful in an investigative process. Some experts in digital forensics think that a method of preserving or examining digital evidence is only sound if it does not change the original evidence source in any way. This is not factual. Conventional forensic disciplines such as deoxyribonucleic acid (DNA) analysis show that the degree of forensic soundness does not require the actual evidence to be left unaltered. When samples of organic material are collected, the process generally smudges the actual evidence. Forensic analysis of the evidential sample further alters the sample because DNA tests are deleterious. Despite the variations that occur during the preservation and processing, these methods are considered forensically sound and DNA evidence is regularly admitted as evidence. In digital forensics, the monotonous task of acquiring data from a hard drive, even when using a hardware write-blocker, alters the unique state of the hard drive. Such alterations can include making a concealed area of the hard drive available or updating information sustained by self-monitoring, analysis, and reporting technology (S. M. A. R. T) on modern hard drives. Furthermore, most methods of acquiring the contents of memory on live computer systems and mobile devices change or overwrite portions of memory, but this is widely accepted in digital forensics. In fact, courts are starting to compel preservation of volatile computer data in some cases, which requires digital investigators to preserve data on live systems. In Columbia Pictures Industries V. Bunnell, for example, the court held that RAM on a web server could contain important log data and was, therefore, within the scope of discoverable information in this case. It may be impossible to comply with such standard and, therefore, conforming to such a standard may be impossible in some circumstances and, therefore, proposing this standard as the "best practice" will subject digital evidence to criticisms that have no link with the investigative issues. One of the keys to forensic soundness is documentation. A case is built on supporting documentation that reports on where the evidence originated and how it was handled. From a forensic point of view, the acquisition process should change the original evidence as little as possible and any variations should be documented and evaluated in the context of the final logical results. A forensically sound digital evidence can be validated based on a complete and accurate acquisition process of the actual data which an absolute representation of the actual data. When preserving volatile data, digital investigators must record the date and time that data were preserved. MD5 hash value of all outputs as discussed later in this book. When dealing with computers, it is important to note the date and time of the computer and compare it to a dependable time source.

1.4.4 Authentication

Some texts relating to digital forensics assert that authentication is the process of ensuring that the recovered evidence is the same as the initially seized data but the concept is understated. From a technical point of view, it is not always possible to compare the obtained data with the actual one. The contents of RAM on a running computer are constantly fluctuating. In a way, both memory contents and network traffic are transient and must be captured while it is in transit. Once network traffic is captured, only copies remain and the actual data are not available. Inadvertent errors and omissions in processing digital evidence may not annul the evidence. Concerns about how an item of evidence was managed may be addressed through documentation, forensic analysis, or testimony. Therefore, the best way to deal with any problems that occur is to record them thoroughly and seek ways to alleviate the impact on the evidence. The worst thing you can do is attempt to conceal a mistake because this could muddle up the whole process and may call your credibility into question. From a legal point of view, authentication is the process of determining whether the evidence is worthy. Authentication means satisfying the court that; (a) the contents of the record have remained unchanged, (b) that the information in the record does in fact originate from its purported source, whether human or machine, and (c) that unnecessary information such as the apparent date of the record is accurate. The necessary degree of authentication may be proved through oral and circumstantial evidence, if available or via technological features in the system or the record. Authentication is actually a two-step process, with an initial examination of the evidence to determine that it is what its proponent claims and, later, a closer analysis to determine its probative value. In the initial stage, it may be sufficient for an individual who is conversant with the digital evidence to testify to its authenticity. For example, the individual who obtained the evidence can verify that the evidence presented in court is the same as when it was collected. Similarly, a system administrator can testify that log files presented in court originated from her/his system.

1.4.5 Chain of Custody

One of the most important aspects of authentication is maintaining and documenting the chain of custody of evidence. This is otherwise known as continuity of possession. Each person who held evidence may be required to testify that the evidence presented in court is the same as when it was processed during the investigation. Although it may not be necessary to produce at trial every individual who handled the evidence, it is best to keep the number to a minimum and maintain documentation to demonstrate that digital evidence has not been altered since it was collected. Without a solid chain of custody, it could be argued that the evidence was handled improperly and may have been altered or exchanged with implicating evidence or contaminated in some other fashion. Potential costs of breaking the chain of custody include misidentification of evidence, adulteration of evidence, and loss of evidence or pertinent elements.

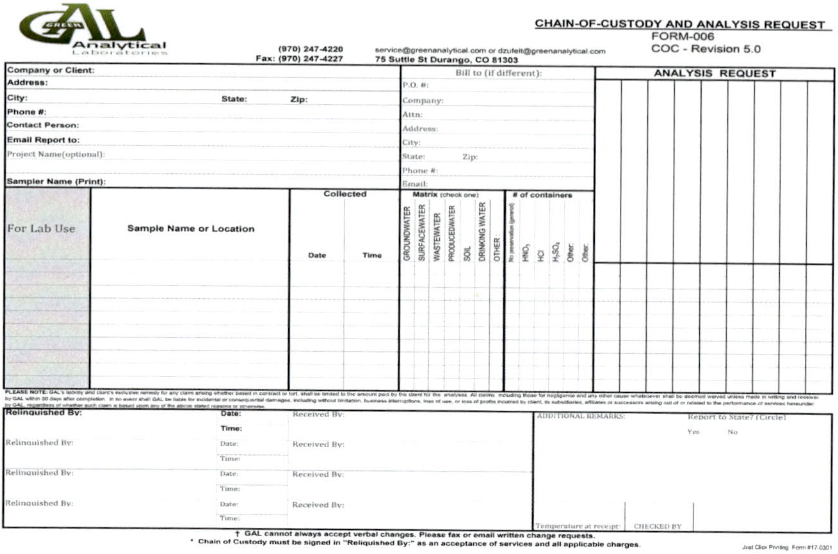
GAL Analytical Laboratories

(970) 247-4220
Fax: (970) 247-4227

service@greenanalytical.com or dzufelt@greenanalytical.com
75 Suttle St Durango, CO 81303

CHAIN-OF-CUSTODY AND ANALYSIS REQUEST
FORM-006
COC - Revision 5.0

Company or Client:
Address:
City: State: Zip:
Phone #:
Contact Person:
Email Report to:
Project Name(optional):
Sampler Name (Print):

Bill to (if different):
P.O. #:
Company:
Attn:
Address:
City:
State: Zip:
Phone #:
Email:

ANALYSIS REQUEST

For Lab Use	Sample Name or Location	Collected: Date	Collected: Time	Matrix (check one): GROUNDWATER	SURFACEWATER	WASTEWATER	PRODUCEDWATER	SOIL	DRINKING WATER	OTHER	# of containers: No preservation (general)	HNO_3	HCl	H_2SO_4	Other:	Other:

Relinquished By: Date: Time: Received By:
Relinquished By: Date: Time: Received By:
Relinquished By: Date: Time: Received By:
Relinquished By: Date: Time: Received By:

ADDITIONAL REMARKS:
Report to State? (Circle) Yes No
Temperature at receipt: CHECKED BY

† GAL cannot always accept verbal changes. Please fax or email written change requests.
* Chain of Custody must be signed in "Reliquished By:" as an acceptance of services and all applicable charges.

Figure 1.6: Chain of Custody form. *Source: http://greenanalytical.com/forms/.*

1.4.6 Evidence of Integrity

The purpose of integrity checks is to show that evidence has not been altered from the time it was collected, thus backing up the authentication process. In digital forensics, the process of verifying the integrity of evidence generally involves a comparison of the digital fingerprint for that evidence taken at the time of collection with that of the evidence in its present state. To understand how this verification process works, it is necessary to have a basic knowledge of message digests and cryptographic hash values. For the purpose of this book, a message digest algorithm can be referred to as a black box that accepts a digital object (e.g., a file, program, or disk) and produces a number. Message digest algorithm always generates the same number for a given input. Also, a good message digest algorithm will generate a different number for different inputs. Therefore, an exact copy will have the same message digest as the original but if a file is changed even slightly, it will have a different message digest from the real one. Authentication software is used to confirm that the evidence has not been altered. Currently, the frequently used algorithms for calculating message digests in digital forensics are MD5 and Secure Hash Algorithm 1 (SHA-1). SHA is very similar to MD5 and is currently the U. S. government's message digest algorithm of choice. MD5 generates hash code that is encrypted. MD5 adopts an implied mathematical calculation method to save the data to the drive or document. This is used to confirm that the duplicate data and the original data are the same. Decryption tools are required to gain access to password-protected computers, files, or both. If data retrieved from a suspect's computer is encrypted, then certain procedures must be followed. The MD5 algorithm receives a message of arbitrary length as input and generates a 128-bit "fingerprint" or "message digest" as output. It is estimated that it is impractically to generate two messages having similar message digest or to generate any message having a particular prestated message digest. Note the use of the word fingerprint. The purpose of this analogy is to emphasize the proximate uniqueness of a message digest calculated using the MD5 algorithm. Basically, the MD5 algorithm uses the statistical data in a digital object to compute a combination of 32 numbers and letters. This is essentially a 16-character hexadecimal value, with each byte denoted by a pair of letters and numbers. It is very unlikely that two items will have similar message digest unless they are duplicates. This is very similar to human fingerprints and DNA. It is also estimated that the probability of generating two messages having similar message digest is on the order of 264 operations and the probability of generating a particular message digest is on the order of 2128 operations. This feature of proximate uniqueness is what distinguishes message digest algorithms like MD5 as a powerful tool for recording digital evidence. For example, by calculating the MD5 value of a disk prior to collection and then again after collection, it can be established that the collection process did not modify the data since it was collected. Bear in mind that MD5 and SHA-1 values alone do not specify that the linked evidence is trustworthy; as someone could have modified the evidence before the hash value was computed. *For example*, if the person who collected the evidence altered it prior to calculating a digital fingerprint, then the alteration will not be detected by a later evaluation of the digital fingerprint. Eventually, the credibility of digital evidence comes down to the credibility of individuals handling it and the strength of supporting documentation.

1.4.7 Objectivity

The basis of a forensic analysis is objectivity. The interpretation and presentation of evidence should be free from prejudice to provide decision makers with a good understanding of facts. It can be difficult given preconceived notions and the external pressures to reach specific conclusions. The most effective approach to remain neutral is to let the evidence finish the process on its own. Every conclusion should be presented along with all of the supporting factual evidence. Another effective approach to ensuring objectivity is to have a peer review process that assesses a forensic analyst's results for bias or any other weakness.

1.4.8 Repeatability

A significant aspect of the scientific method is that any experiments or observations must be repeatable in order to be autonomously verifiable. This is essentially important to be able to autonomously verify discoveries in a forensic context, when a person's liberty and source of income may be affected. Therefore, it may become necessary for one forensic analyst to repeat the technical analysis performed by another forensic analyst wholly or partially. To enable such a verification of forensic discoveries, it is important to record the steps taken to find and analyze digital evidence in sufficient detail to enable others to verify the results on their own. This documentation may include the location and other characteristics of the digital evidence, as well as the tools used to analyze the data.

1.5 ANTI-FORENSICS

With the vast development of the computer technologies in the last decade, usage of technology has had both positive and negative impact. While some folks use technology to invent useful things that will benefit the society, others use it to the detriment of the society. One key problem of technology is that as soon as a technology is discovered for the purpose of identification and investigation of criminals, criminals will likewise dig out another technique that will help them to hide their identity. A good example is virtual private network (VPN) that helps in concealing the identity and location of an individual but criminals have been using this to perpetrate their illegal acts. This is a massive challenge forensics agents face today. Unlike many other sources of physical evidence, digital evidence is easily modified, removed or hidden without leaving a trace or clue that will help in identifying the criminal. So, anti-forensics has become a major challenge for digital forensics. According to Rekhis and Boudriga (2010), anti-forensic techniques can be classified into categories as listed below:

1. Encryption
2. Steganography

3. Covert channel
4. Data hiding in storage space
5. Residual data wiping
6. Tail obfuscation

1.5.1 Encryption

Encryption is process of scrambling information that can only be decoded and read by someone who has the correct decoding key. Encryption is used to hide or make the evidence unreadable on the compromised system. In 2007, an incident happened when the US Customs found child pornography on Canadian citizen and legal US resident Sebastian Boucher's laptop (Balogh & Pondelic, 2011). The laptop was seized as evidence and he was charged with transporting the pornography across borders. The problem appeared when examiners tried to open the incriminating drive Z and found out that it was a pretty good privacy encrypted container. Although a forensic duplicate of hard drive was created after shutdown of the notebook, the examiner could not open the encrypted container. Attackers use various encryption methods and in order to make the data usable, investigators have to decrypt the encrypted data. This process is tedious and time-wasting and sometimes the encrypted data cannot be decrypted.

1.5.2 Steganography

Steganography is data that is concealed in plain sight. Steganography is a complementary technique that can be used with cryptography to encrypt data. Steganography techniques can be applied to images, a video file or an audio file. Typically, however, steganography is written in characters including hash marking, but its usage within images is also common. At any rate, steganography protects from pirating copyrighted materials as well as aiding in unauthorized viewing. Steganography also has an additional branch known as watermarking, which is a means of hiding data within a text document or any other type of copyright materials in order to mark that cover and prevent illegal duplication of the files.

Figure 1.7: Image Stenography. *Source: https://prateekvjoshi.com/2013/03/20/image-steganography/.*

1.5.3 Covert Channel

"Covert channel in communication protocols allows attackers to hide data over the network and possibly bypass intrusion detection techniques. Typically, a network protocol is chosen and its header is modified to leak messages between attackers, exploiting the fact that few fields of the header are modified during transmission." (Rekhis & Boudriga, 2010). A covert channel can be used to extract information from or implant information into an organization. An Internet covert channel is the digital equivalent of a briefcase with a secret compartment that a spy might use to slip sensitive documents past security guards into or out of a secure facility. An attacker can use Internet covert channels to transmit sensitive documents unobserved—in this case, bypassing network security measures rather than bypassing security guards. And just as a spy can use that same secret compartment to conceal a weapon from security guards when entering a secure facility, an attacker can use an Internet covert channel to conceal a cyberweapon, for example, a download of malware from an external server onto a host within an organization's private network.

1.5.4 Data Hiding in Storage Space

Attackers hide some data inside storage areas and make them obscure to the usual system commands and programs. It makes the investigation more complicated and more time consuming and sometimes data can be corrupted too. Rootkit is one of the most popular techniques used to hide data in storage space. According to Microsoft (2014), malware designers use rootkits to hide malware inside victims' computers. It is very hard to identify rootkits and most computer users do not know how to remove these rootkits. User mode rootkits are capable of hiding processes, files, system drivers, network ports, and even system services (Kassner, 2008).

1.5.5 Residual data wiping

When the attacker uses a computer for his objective, a few hidden processes (e.g., temporary files, history of commands) are running without the knowledge of the attacker. But an intelligent attacker can avoid this risk by covering his tracks and wiping off every trace that will make the system work as if it has not been used before.

1.5.6 Tail Obfuscation

The most common technique is the obfuscation of the source of the attack (Rekhis & Boudriga, 2010). Here, the attacker uses some false information in order to mislead the investigator (e.g., false email headers, and changing file extensions). Therefore, sometimes the investigator might lose some data that have forensic value. There are a few nuances to hard drives that enable a crafty individual to conceal the presence of voluminous data on them. The first cylinder on a disk which is also known as the maintenance track is used to store information about the drive such as its geometry and the location of bad sectors. By deliberately marking portions of the disk as bad, an individual can hide data in these areas from the operating system.

REFERENCES

1. Andrew J., & Craig V. (2008). *Building a digital forensic laboratory: Establishing and managing a successful facility.* Burlington, MA: Elsevier Academic Press.
2. Casey, E. (2000). *Digital evidence and computer crime: Forensic science, computers and the internet*. London: Academic Press.
3. Casey, E. (ed.). (2010). *Handbook of digital forensics and investigation*. London: Elsevier Academic Press.
4. National Institute of Justice. (2015). *Digital evidence and forensics.* Retrieved November 23, 2017, from http://www.nij.gov/topics/forensics/evidence/digital/Pages/welcome.aspx
5. Rekhis, S., & Boudriga, N. (2010). Formal digital investigation of anti-forensic attacks. *Proceedings of the Fifth International Workshop on Systematic Approaches to Digital Forensic Engineering*. Oakland, CA: IEEE Press.
6. Searching and seizing computers and obtaining electronic evidence in criminal investigations. (2002). Retrieved November 23, 2017, from http://www.usdoj.gov/criminal/cybercrime/searching.html
7. US-CERT. Computer Forensics. (2008). Retrieved November 23, 2017, from http://www.us-cert.gov/sites/default/files/publications/forensics.pdf
8. Willassen, S., & Mjølsnes, S. (2005). Digital forensics research. *Telektronikk*, *1* 92-97.

CHAPTER 2

DIGITAL FORENSIC MODELS

"Digital Forensic is an exact science—not the procedures but the results."
—Edewede Oriwoh

CONTENTS

Law enforcement is in a perpetual race with criminals in the application of digital technologies and requires the development of tools to systematically search digital devices for pertinent evidence. Digital forensic science provides tools, techniques, and scientifically proven methods that can be used to acquire and analyze digital evidence. The digital forensic investigation must be retrieved to obtain the evidence that will be accepted in the court. This research focuses on a structured and consistent approach to digital forensic investigation. The chapter reviews some of the existing digital forensic models and highlights new paradigms and techniques being considered. It also analyzes their capabilities and weakness in order to help the investigators choose the appropriate forensic investigation model(s).

2.1 THE FORENSICS PROCESS MODEL

The U.S. Department of Justice published a process model in the *Electronic Crime Scene Investigation: A Guide to First Responders* that consists of four phases:

(a) Collection: Involves the evidence search, evidence recognition, evidence collection, and documentation. (b) Examination: This is designed to facilitate the visibility of evidence, while explaining its origin and significance. It involves revealing hidden and obscured information and the relevant documentation.

(c) Analysis: This looks at the product of the examination for its significance and probative value to the case.

(d) Reporting: This entails writing a report outlining the examination process and pertinent data recovered from the overall investigation.

The analysis phase of this model is improperly defined and ambiguous. For example, it emerges as an interpretation of the results from the examination phase, and in the process confuses analysis with interpretation despite these being two distinct processes.

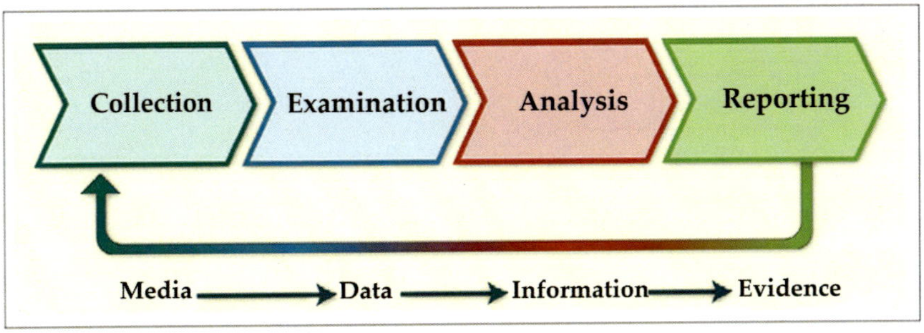

Figure 2.1: The Forensics Process Model. *Source: http://itlaw.wikia.com/wiki/Forensic_process.*

2.2 DFRWS INVESTIGATIVE MODEL

The analysis roadmap from Digital Research Workshops proposed in 2001 a common function digital forensic framework composed of six primary phases. This model was the basis of additional enhancement because it was very stable and homogeneous, the phases particularly: identification, preservation, collection, examination, analysis, and presentation (then a pseudo extra step: decision). Each section consists of some sub-strategies or strategies. The first is identification and includes occasion or crime detection, resolving signature, anomalous detection, system monitoring, audit evaluation, and many others. Followed by preservation step through which an accurate case administration is ready, imaging applied sciences are used, and all measurements are taken to make sure an correct and acceptable chain of custody, preservation is a guarded precept throughout all forensic phases. Collection comes immediately after through which allied knowledge is gathered based mostly on acceptable strategies, software program, and; on this step, we make use of various restoration strategies and compression free of loss additionally. Following this step are two attention-seeking and really important phases—examination and analysis, whereby proof traceability, sample matching are guaranteed, then concealed knowledge have to be found and extracted. At this level, "mining" of knowledge and timeline are carried out. The most recent section of this model is presentation. Processes associated with this step which are documentation, clarification, and mission affect affirmation, advice and countermeasures are taken and consultants testimony.

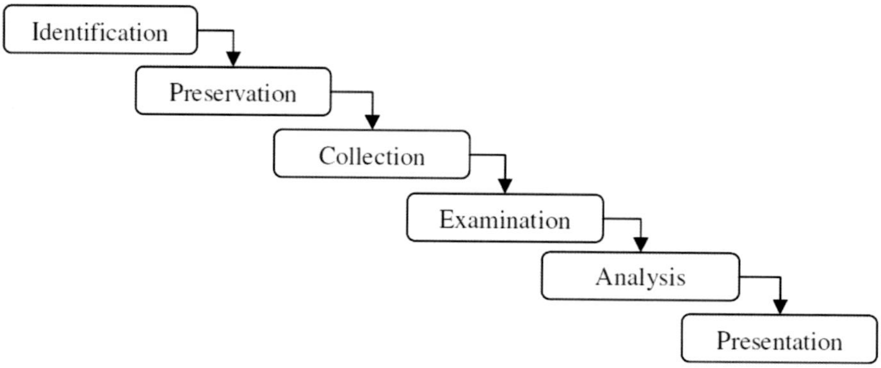

Figure 2.2: DFRWS Model. *Source: http://lmsaidi.blogspot.com.ng/2015/08/masalah-dan-solusi-dari-rangkuman-paper.html.*

2.3 ABSTRACT DIGITAL FORENSICS MODEL

According to the abstract digital forensics model (ADFM), the identification section assumes that the incident sort is efficiently recognized and decided. This is a vital step since all upcoming steps depend on it. Followed by the preparation step, that is, the basic launched phase where the instruments, strategies, search warrants, checking authorization, and administration assistance are ready. This step is adopted by the second launched step—approach strategy. This step is supposed to maximize the collection of the proof whereas minimizing the effect on the victim by formulating entirely different approaches and procedures to comply with. In the next section which is preservation, all acquired knowledge has to be isolated and secured to preserve them in their exact state. All acquired digital evidence is reproduced, and the bodily scene is recorded, based mostly on standardized procedures; these duties are carried out below the collection section.

The ADFM proposes a standardized digital forensics process that consists of nine components:

(a) Identification; which recognizes an incident from indicators and determines its type.

(b) Preparation; which entails the preparation of tools, techniques, search warrants, and monitoring authorizations and management support.

(c) Approach strategy; that develops a procedure to use in order to maximize the collection of untainted evidence while minimizing the impact on the victim.

(d) Preservation; which involves the isolation, securing and preservation of the state of physical and digital evidence.

(e) Collection; that entails the recording of the physical scene and duplicates digital evidence using standardized and accepted procedures.

(f) Examination; which involves an in-depth systematic search of evidence relating to the suspected crime.

(g) Analysis; which involves determination of the significance, reconstructing fragments of data, and drawing conclusions based on evidence found.

(h) Presentation; that involves the summary and explanation of conclusions.

(i) Returning evidence; that ensures that physical and digital property is returned to proper owner.

Although this model is generally a good reflection of the forensic process, it is open to at least one criticism. Its third phase (the approach strategy) is to an extent a duplication of its second phase (the preparation phase).

Advantages

(a) Diverse methodology suitable for array of digital devices

(b) This methodology can easily be appreciated by non-technical observers

(c) Potential for incorporating non-digital, electronic technologies within the abstraction.

Disadvantages

(a) The generality of the model may pose some practical challenge.

(b) There is no easy or obvious methodology for testing the model.

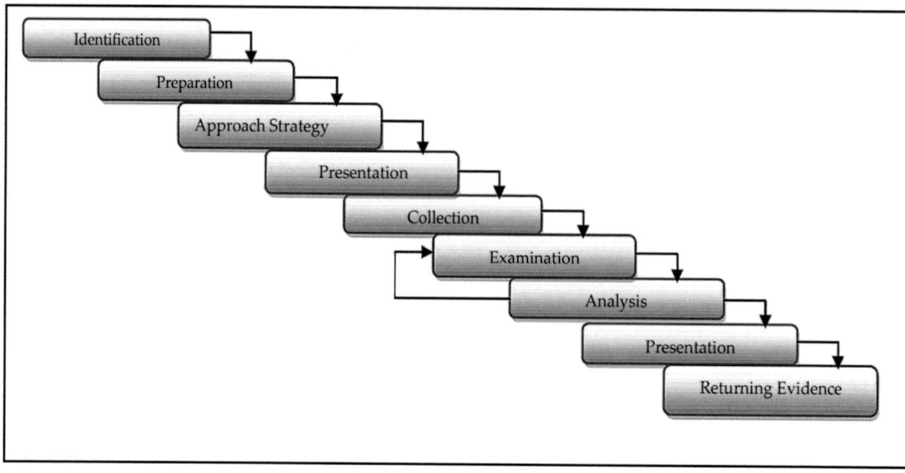

Figure 2.3: Abstract Digital Forensics Model. *Source: http://resources.infosecinstitute.com/digital-forensics-models/.*

2.4 THE INTEGRATED DIGITAL INVESTIGATION MODEL

Brian Carrier and Eugene Spafford proposed yet another model—the Integrated Digital Investigation Process (IDIP) which is organized into 5 groups consisting of 17 phases in all. It is an out and out model which considers the dual investigative nature of the digital forensic investigation by including the digital and the physical crime scene investigation phases. The model envisaged that although the crime was perpetrated using a digital device as a means or target, the forensic investigation encompasses both physical and digital crime scenes and hence the need to include them in the investigations. Replication in digital environment is relatively easier, making it easier to create a complete forensically sound image backup for analysis in the lab. Unlike many process models that focus primarily on the digital evidence, the interaction existing between the digital and physical environment is vividly highlighted in this model.

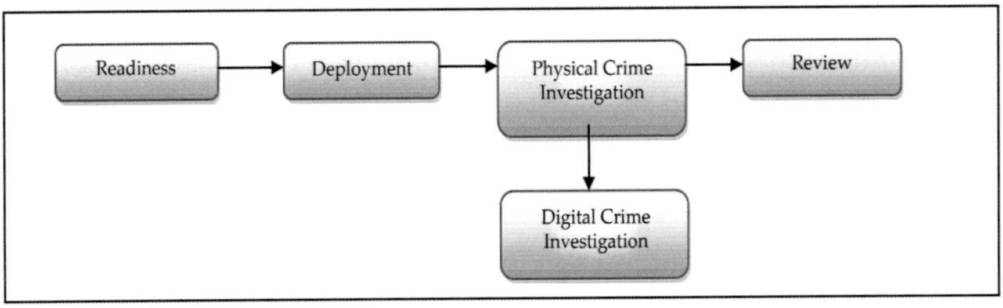

Figure 2.4: Integrated Digital Investigation Process.

Source: http://www.rroij.com/open-access/survey-on-different-phases-of-digi-talforensics-investigation-models.php? aid=53809

2.4.1 Readiness Phases

The goal of this phase is to ensure that the operations and infrastructure are able to fully support an investigation. It includes two phases:

(a) Operations readiness phase; which ensures that human capacity is fully trained and equipped to deal with an incident when it occurs.

(b) Infrastructure readiness phase; that ensures that the underlying infrastructure is sufficient enough to deal with incidents that come. For example, equipment such as video cameras and card readers being there and in good working condition.

2.4.2 Deployment Phases

The purpose is to provide a mechanism for an incident to be detected and confirmed. It includes two phases:

(a) Detection and notification phase; where the incident is detected and then appropriate people are notified.

(b) Confirmation and authorization phase; which confirms the incident and obtains authorization for legal approval to carry out a search warrant.

2.4.3 Physical Crime Scene Investigation phases

The goal of these phases is to collect and analyze the physical evidence and reconstruct the actions that took place during the incident. It includes six phases:

(a) Preservation phase which seeks to preserve the crime scene so that evidence can be later identified and collected by personnel trained in digital evidence identification.

(b) Survey phase that requires an investigator to walk through the physical crime scene and identify pieces of physical evidence.

(c) Documentation phase which involves taking photographs, sketches, and videos of the crime scene and the physical evidence. The goal is to capture as much information as possible so that the layout and important details of the crime scene are preserved and recorded.

(d) Search and collection phase that entails a thorough search and collection of the scene is performed so that additional physical evidence is identified and hence paving way for a digital crime investigation to begin.

(e) Reconstruction phase which involves organizing the results from the analysis done and using them to develop a theory for the incident.

(f) Presentation phase that presents the physical and digital evidence to a court or corporate management.

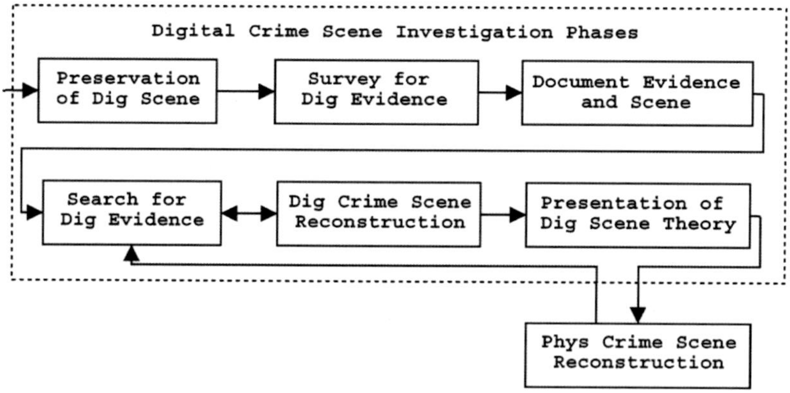

Figure 2.5: Physical Crime Scene Investigation phases.

Source: https://www.researchgate.net/publication/220542528_Getting_Physical_with_the_Digital_Investigation_Process/figures? lo=1

2.4.4 Digital Crime Scene Investigation Phases

The goal is to collect and analyze the digital evidence that was obtained from the physical investigation phase and through any other future means. It includes similar phases as the physical investigation phases, although the primary focus is on the digital evidence. The six phases are:

(a) Preservation phase; which preserves the digital crime scene so that evidence can later be synchronized and analyzed for further evidence.

(b) Survey phase: whereby the investigator transfers the relevant data from a venue out of physical or administrative control of the investigator to a controlled location.

(c) Documentation phase; which involves properly documenting the digital evidence when it is found. This information is helpful in the presentation phase.

(d) Search and collection phase; whereby an in-depth analysis of the digital evidence is performed. Software tools are used to reveal hidden, deleted, swapped, and corrupted files that were used including the dates, duration, log file, etc. Low-level timelining is performed to trace a user's activities and identity.

(e) Reconstruction phase; which includes putting the pieces of a digital puzzle together and developing investigative hypotheses.

(f) Presentation phase; that involves presenting the digital evidence that was found to the physical investigative team.

2.4.5 Review Phase

This entails a review of the whole investigation and identifies areas of improvement. The IDIP model does well at illustrating the forensic process, and also conforms to the cyber terrorism capabilities which require a digital investigation to address issues of data protection, data acquisition, imaging, extraction, interrogation, ingestion/normalization, analysis, and reporting. It also highlights the reconstruction of the events that led to the incident and emphasizes reviewing the whole task, hence ultimately building a mechanism for quicker forensic examinations.

However, the IDIP model is open to some criticisms. First, despite incorporating all the earlier models, there is reason to question the IDIP model's practicality. It, for instance, depicts the deployment phase which consists of confirmation of the incident as being independent of the physical and digital investigation phase. In practice, however, it seems impossible to confirm a digital or computer crime unless and until some preliminary physical and digital investigation is carried out. Second, it does not offer sufficient specificity and does not, for instance, draw a clear distinction between investigations at the victim's (secondary crime) scene and those at the suspect's (primary crime) scene. Neither does it reflect the process of arriving at the latter. Since a computer can be used both as a tool and as a victim, it is common for investigations to be carried out at both ends so that accurate reflections are made. Henry Lee defines the primary crime scene as the place where the first criminal act occurred. The process of tracing back to it can be challenging when dealing with larger networks and in particular, the Internet.

2.5 COMPUTER FORENSICS FIELD TRIAGE PROCESS MODEL

The computer forensics field triage process model (CFFTPM) is defined as those investigative processes that are conducted within the first few hours of an investigation, that provide information used during the suspect interview and search execution phase. Due to the need for information to be obtained in a relatively short time frame, the model usually involves an onsite/field analysis of the computer system(s) in question. The emphases of the model are to: find working evidence instantly; ascertain victims at critical risk; monitor the current investigation; ascertain possible charges; and precisely evaluate the offender's threat to the society.

Being able to conduct an examination and analysis on scene, in a short period of time, and provide investigators with time-sensitive leads and information provides a powerful psychological advantage to the investigative team. Suspects are emotionally more susceptible within the first few hours of their initial contact with police, especially when this contact occurs in their place of business or home. This cooperation can be critical in certain cases such as abductions, sexual predatory offenses, etc. What is crucial to the investigator during this initial time period is the knowledge of the full extent of the crime and/or involvement of the suspect and "triggers" that further increase the suspect's willingness to talk and cooperate. These triggers may be found in the digital evidence located on the suspect's system(s). Examples are email correspondence, digital maps, pictures, and chat logs. The CFFTPM uses phases derived from the Carrier and Spafford (2002) IDIP and the digital crime scene analysis (DCSA) model as developed by Rogers (2006). The phases include: planning, triage, usage and user profiles, chronology, Internet activity, and case-specific evidence. These six phases constitute a high level of categorization and each phase has several sub-tasks and considerations that vary according to the specifics of the case, file system and operating system under investigation, etc. The use of higher order categories allows the process model to be generalized across various types of investigations that deal with digital evidence. The need for a general model has been identified in several studies as a core component of a pragmatic approach for law enforcement investigations. Before discussing each of the model's phases, it is important that qualifications be placed around the use of the CFFTPM, as the model is not appropriate for all investigative situation.

Due to length constraints, this section will only provide a brief description of the six phases and key sub-tasks. The primary investigative considerations that are relevant for each of the phases will be presented.

The CFFTPM begins with the planning phase, which is critical to improve the chances of successful investigation. The investigator is concerned about capabilities of the suspect, their activities, location, time, and types of machines. Second is the triage phase under which examiner identifies evidence and things are arranged according to importance and probably priorities. Of concern, here are potential places in the systems where evidence could be located like volatile memory, temporary files among others. Information from the suspect is very critical in supporting the above revelations. Next is the usage profile phase where the examiner focuses on the user's profile and activities and information found in home directory, system registries, and file properties. After usage profile analysis, the investigator needs to build the case in a chronological order. Under the chronology phase which deals with issues to do with when a file was accessed, modified, or created. In Internet phase, examinations of relevant artifacts like instant message logs, web browsers, and emails are done. It should be noted that emails require a lot of time to analyze but can yield very substantial evidence. The last phase in this model is case-specific evidence phase. It is required that the investigator adjusts and focuses his attention to the case at hand depending on the type of crime.

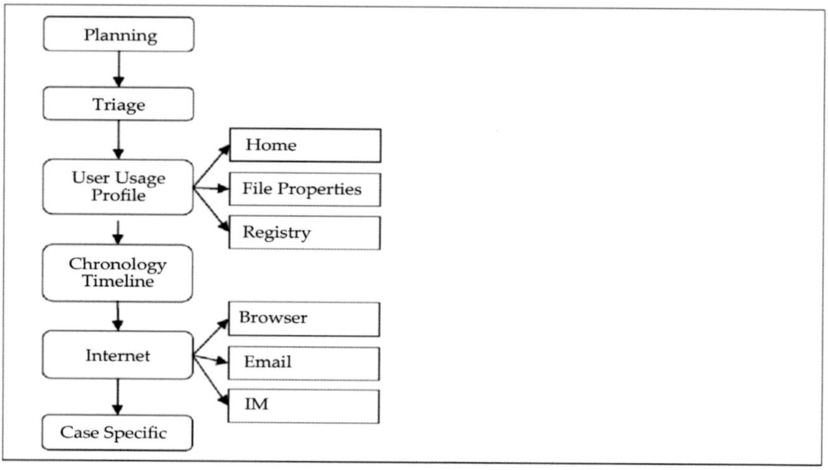

Figure 2.6: Computer Forensics Field Triage Process Model.

Source: https://www.researchgate.net/publication/279270088_An_Introduction_to_Digital_Crimes/figures? lo=1

2.5.1 Planning

The first phase in the CFFTPM is proper prior planning. Ideally, a lead investigator will have a matrix that quantifies the various possibilities of the crime scene, the suspect, and the digital evidence and qualifies the expertise of the various investigators on the investigation team. For the lead investigator, this matrix is used to define what is known and what is not known thus aiding in determining what is wanted to be known. Similar to a situation paragraph of a military operations order (OpOrd), this matrix identifies the "enemy" and "friendly" situations providing preemptive case intelligence. In the OpOrd, the enemy is defined characteristically by collecting intelligence through the acronym SALUTE: strength, activity, location, uniform, time, and equipment. This same acronym can be used in gathering case intelligence about the enemy/suspect prior to arriving at the crime scene. Strength initially determines the suspect count and any other involved cohorts (specific numbers can be helpful), but could also include known or possible capabilities of the suspect. Activity defines the specific actions of the suspect (even small details could later be important). Location is not only the physical location of the scene but also the virtual possibilities of cyberspace. Uniform relates more to the military, but in terms of cyberspace, it can include email addresses, uniform resource locators (URLs), usernames, passwords, network domains, and other related deterministic markings, symbols, or corporate or agency identifiers. Time obviously builds upon other previously gathered case intelligence providing the chronological scope for investigative searches. Finally, equipment covers the various types of wired and wireless hardware devices and software applications that can be expected when approaching the digital crime scene. Dependent upon the case intelligence determined by the SALUTE, the lead investigator will have many specific decisions to make prior to arriving at the crime scene. Once the enemy/suspect elements of the SALUTE matrix are determined, the lead investigator can then identify friendly information for attacking this crime scene. From the OpOrd, this section of the matrix includes the mission of the investigation, the identification of the necessary personnel to provide the expertise for the investigation, and the knowledge of how to handle the unexpected. The mission of the investigation is normally determined by the type of crime committed in turn determining the level of investigation and the level of expertise necessary for the investigation. If the crime warrants expertise in multiple physical and virtual locations, multiple wired and wireless networks, multiple OS, personal digital technologies, or other specific technical needs, the investigator can plan accordingly. However, if there are unknowns in the investigation, it is imperative that the lead investigator determines who else can be contacted to aid in the investigation. With this compiled situational case intelligence, both about the suspect and the investigative team, the lead investigator can then formulate a plan of attack for determining what evidence is to be sought after and used to further the investigation.

2.5.2 Usage/User Profiles

Once a system or storage media has been identified and prioritized during the triage phase, the actual examination and analysis are conducted. When convincing evidence is found on digital media, it is essential to show a link between that evidence and a specific, identifiable suspect. In some cases, this is almost a fait accompli; for example, when it can be clearly shown that only one person had physical access to a PC. In many cases, multiple persons have access to a PC, making it necessary to find and examine digital artifacts and their properties to ascertain which individual or individuals are responsible for, or even had knowledge of, incriminating data found on the storage media. Often it is necessary to place artifacts in context with verifiable real-world events. The payoff can be significant. A suspect presented with clear evidence indicating that he or she and no other person responsible for evidence recovered during an interview may feel compelled to admit their guilt. This challenge has always existed and is an essential element of most "traditional" examinations of digital evidence. In the context of the CFFTPM, the challenge is not only to do this quickly but also to expeditiously determine if it can even be done within the time constraints. (In some cases, the specifics of the evidence can obviate the need for this evaluation, for example, when contraband files are found only in a specific user's home directory). A thorough knowledge of user profiles and artifacts relating to usage are essential to accomplishing this goal.

2.5.3 Home Directory

In Microsoft Windows operating systems, the most obvious user-related artifact is the "Home Directory." By default, the home directory is only accessible by the associated user account. Also by default, the location of stored files associated with various applications is set to a subfolder inside the home directory. The presence of incriminating files in the suspect's home directory or one of its subfolders (including such notables as "desktop" "my documents" and "favorites") is a reliable indicator that only the suspect (or anyone who could log onto that account) had access to those files. Additionally, the creation of a subdirectory structure with unique subfolder names can go a long way towards showing knowledge of and culpability for evidentiary objects found in the subdirectory structure

2.5.4 Security Properties of Files

It may be useful and time-efficient to check ownership and security properties of objects with known evidentiary value. The ability to set and read security permissions is not available in FAT, and is off by default in Windows XP, even when the NTFS file system is used. When NTFS is used, and the feature turned on, a file's security properties, most notably "owner" and "permissions," may be useful in establishing which account had access to or even created that particular file (National White Collar Crime Center, 2003). When a file is created, the user account logged on is recorded as the "owner" as part of the file's security descriptor. (This can be changed only if an Administrator "takes ownership" of the file, in which case the Administrator is recorded as the owner).

Permissions may also be of limited usefulness in establishing culpability. Only those accounts with the permission to do so may access an object; however, this can be one or more user accounts and the accounts that have permission to the object may change over time. An account that had "read" access on the 25th of February might not have had that same access on the 24th.

2.5.5 Registry

The registry can be a trap, causing the needless expenditure of valuable time, if the examiner does not have a precise idea of what they are looking for and exactly where to go to find it. On the other hand, a knowledgeable examiner with a clear vision of what information they want to recover can find several highly valuable items in less than a few minutes. For example, the HKEY_USERS\suspect's SID\Software\Microsoft\Windows

2.5.6 Chronology

The chronological scope of the investigation can be defined by the case intelligence. In an investigation, digital evidence is defined by its temporal value, known as MAC times (Casey, 2004). Without going into a detailed narrative of the specifics of MAC times specifically to each OS, the following are some general guidelines for Windows MAC Times. Windows MAC times are defined in the FAT32 and NTFS file systems as:

(a) Modification is defined by when a file contents have been changed.

(b) Access time is defined by when a file was viewed.

(c) Created time is defined by when a file was created.

Although MAC times appear simple, it is well-documented that there are many inconsistencies with MAC times and there are many other weaknesses when describing other vendor specific operating systems, such as those used on personal digital technologies devices (e.g., PDAs, Cellphones, MP3 players). Once an investigator gains access to the files in question and their individual MAC times, they can start to qualify their searches, thus quantifying their evidence (Casey, 2004). For the CFFTPM, several quantifications should be examined by sorting the files on their various MAC times within the chronological scope of the investigation. The first such quantification includes the time periods of normal use by the suspect and other known users of the computer or device (Casey, 2004; Farmer &

Venema, 2005). This can be obtained by correlating known users accessing the computer with files that have been modified, accessed, or created during those times. Organization by user or by time period helps to quantify who was doing what during what time periods. Such organization may also provide time periods that stand out or look unique. These types of unique time periods could be studied outward in an attempt to find other significant relationships or value.

Another quantification includes the identification and analysis of software applications and data files used or accessed during qualified times of interest. Again, this can be obtained by correlating known users with MAC times possibly providing unique time periods that could be of significant value. Organization of applications or files within a certain time period quantifies activities that occurred during these time periods. An application or file that is accessed prior to, during, or after a criminal incident can be a major indication of involvement or intent.

Finally, the third quantification includes the identification and analysis of recent shortcuts and stored information. These could include, but are not limited to items on the desktop, commonly used software applications, and the various locations of Internet browser cookies, cache, and the index.dat file. Note that various Internet structures (cookies, cache, and the index. dat file) can be very useful in determining chronological intelligence in that these provide much more time-based evidence than just MAC times. Specifically, each index.dat file provides date-time stamps for each Internet server request.

2.5.7 Internet

Almost every case will require an examination of artifacts associated with Internet activity, such as instant messaging (IM), email, and web browsing (see Chapter 3, Network and Internet). The value, time cost, and time criticality will vary widely, depending on circumstances including the specific applications involved, type of activity being examined, and whether the PC being examined belongs to a suspect or a victim (e.g., in a missing person case). An effective practice is for the computer forensic examiner to evaluate what type of Internet activities they believe the suspect (or victim) was involved in, and to evaluate if and how each of those activities relates to the case. Types of activities may include web browsing, email, instant messaging, reading or posting to USENET newsgroups, trading files.

(1) Browser Artifacts

While the specifics vary, most web browsing applications store some method for storing "cookies," either as a file or as separate files, some means of storing temporary Internet files, and some means of storing user information and preferences, such as typed URLs and "favorites."

The specific content of individual cookies is determined by each individual website and is rarely of evidentiary value. In most cases, the evidentiary value of a cookie is limited to its name. Typically, the name of a cookie will match the URL of the site that deposited the cookie, indicating that the PC had visited that site at some point in the past. This does not go to show intent as the cookie will be created whether the browser was redirected from another site, or intentionally pointed to the site with a typed URL. Dates and times associated with cookies may help to determine when a site was visited and can be useful in creating investigative timelines.

Temporary Internet files are essentially cached copies of web page components (often graphics) stored on the local PC. The investigative value is that these files are stored locally without the intent or intervention of the user, and that some files, for example, contraband images, have inherent evidentiary value. An investigator must keep in mind that these files are easily cleared out by most browsing applications or with third-party tools. Most importantly, investigators must weigh the potential value against the time; it will take to search through even a moderately populated cache. Examiners should expect a search of temporary Internet files to take hours or days. In many cases, that requires more time than the examiner has.

(2) Email Artifacts

Email artifacts may be of enormous evidentiary value but can require a very expensive investment in time. Procedures for examining email and extracting useful data are usually specific to the particular email client and can be time-consuming to implement. If extraction of email is successful, even a cursory screening of all the email in a suspect's mailbox could take many hours. If web-based email is used, there is often no local storage of email artifacts.

(3) Instant Messaging Artifacts

Most instant messaging clients maintain some type of contact information and have the capability to record and store logs of the conversations that take place between the user and his or her online contacts. In most cases, this logging capability is off by default but can, and often is, turned on by the user. Contact information for most IM applications is maintained at the server, and may not be found on the local PC. Chat logs can contain a wealth of data, including the conversation itself as well as the screen names of other parties. A single chat log may contain hours of conversation. A thorough examination of multiple logs may bear a prohibitive cost in time. If it is necessary to examine chat logs, it is important for the examiner to have a clear idea of what he or she is looking for. String search tools should be implemented as much as possible. An "old-fashioned" examination would likely involve a thorough examination of all of these and many other artifacts. The mandates of the CFFTPM require that the examiner judiciously evaluate the potential benefit of examining each of these artifacts with the time cost of doing so.

2.5.8 Case-Specific Evidence

It is important for the computer forensic examiner to be able to adjust the focus of every examination to the specifics of that case. This is a skill set that requires the ability to reconcile a number of conflicting requirements in the manner most appropriate not just to a type of case but to each specific set of circumstances. There are several practices that can facilitate an effective optimization of resources. A computer forensic examiner should be able to evaluate time resources, utilize pre-raid intelligence, customize search goals, and prioritize search goals. Of all the resources available to the examiner, time is usually in shortest supply. One consideration when taking stock is whether the time requirement is "bounded" or "unbounded." Is there a defined deadline ("bounded") beyond which the search is halted, or the evidence loses all value? Is the mandate to find evidence as soon as possible, but even if it takes days ("unbounded")? For example, a permissive search might only be allowed until the end of an interview, whereas the search of a missing person's PC might be conducted as rapidly as possible, but still go on for hours. Time is clearly of the essence in both cases, but the lack of a time limit in the unbounded case can justify some avenues of investigation that would not be feasible in a bounded situation. In all cases, time is an expensive commodity. The time cost of any examination activity must be weighed against the potential for fruitful results of that activity. As a general rule, it is usually best to perform those tasks which can be accomplished most quickly first. The value of planning and pre-raid intelligence cannot be overemphasized. Reliable information on search terms, contacts, types of activities, applications used, etc. in advance of the search can allow the examiner to develop at least some search strategies before arrival on scene. Every minute saved in this manner is potentially another minute available to conduct the search itself.

Advantages

(a) This model is much concerned about time and hence helps to undertake quick information and investigation in a time-critical situations.

(b) This model is used to conduct investigation on scene which provides additional benefit of having feedback loop with the investigator(s).

(c) It also affords computer forensics analyst to modify their searches right on the scene based on input from the primary investigator(s) as well as those in direct contact with the suspect.

Disadvantages

(a) This model is only appropriate for investigation conducted at the scene.

(b) It may be seen as an incomplete investigative model and the case under investigation may require additional work to be done off the scene.

(c) There is a likelihood of compromising evidence in the usage of this model, due to its time-critical nature.

2.6 DIGITAL FORENSIC MODEL BASED ON MALAYSIAN INVESTIGATION PROCESS

Perumal proposes a digital forensic investigation model from the Malaysian investigation process flow (2009). The model consists of seven phases as shown in the figure below. As shown in the diagram, the first two phases, that is, planning and identification are common in most digital forensic models. The Reconnaissance phase is concerned with collection of evidence from running systems commonly called live forensics. According to the author, acquiring live data which focuses on volatile evidence improves the probability of successful investigation. In the next two steps, data is securely moved and stored safely waiting for analysis. Next, the data is then examined with the right methods and tools. In presentation, just like in the other previous models, the investigator has to prove his or her findings. The last step deals with proper keeping of evidence for future.

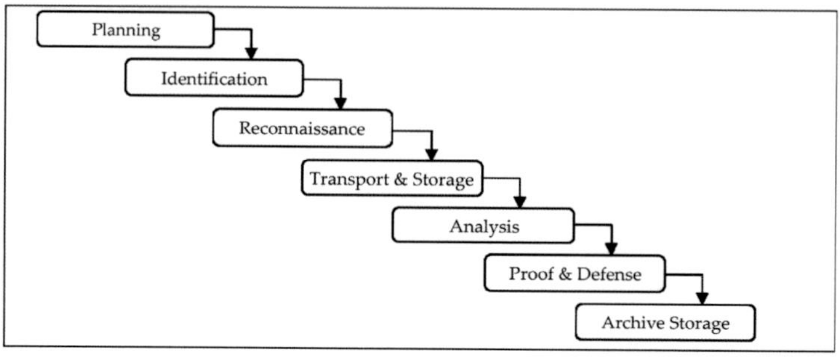

Figure 2.7: Digital Forensic Model Based on Malaysian Investigation Process.

Source: https://www.semanticscholar.org/paper/Common-Phases-of-Computer-Forensics-Investigation-Yusoff-Ismail/10488dd8d6a9cb665f10909b1632d996f3217d02

2.7 THE ENHANCED DIGITAL INVESTIGATION PROCESS MODEL (EDIP)

EDIP, developed by Venansius et al. (2004), is an investigative model hinged on the expansion of the deployment phase in the Brian et al. (2003) IDIP model. The EDIP model has two categories of crime scenes, which is the suspect's or the primary crime scene and the victim's or the secondary crime scene.

This model has five major phases namely, readiness, deployment, traceback, dynamite, and review. The model starts with the readiness phase which deals with operations and infrastructure readiness, and the needed human capacity is properly trained and equipped to deal with the situation. The deployment phase provides mechanism for the detection and confirmation of an incident. This phase has five sub-phases which include detection and notification, physical crime scene, digital crime scene, confirmation, and the submission sub-phases. The traceback phase tracks down the operations of the suspect's physical crime scene and has two sub-phases: digital crime scene investigation and authorization phase. Succeeding the traceback phase is the deployment phase. The entire investigative process is reviewed and possible areas of improvement are identified in the review phase.

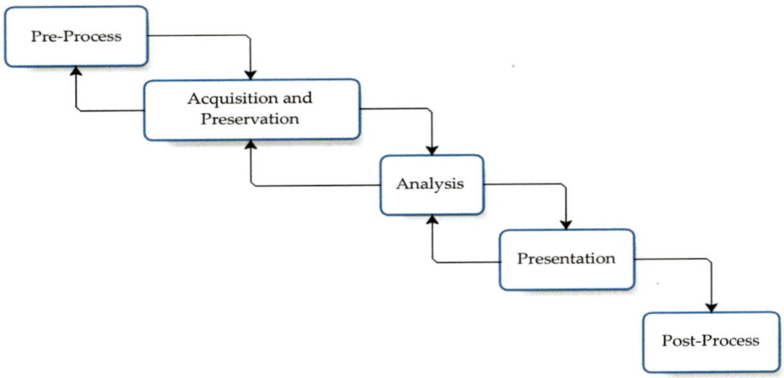

Figure 2.8: Enhanced Digital Investigation Process Model.

Source: http://lmsaidi.blogspot.com.ng/2015/08/masalah-dan-solusi-dari-rang-kuman-paper.html

2.7.1 Readiness Phases

(1) Deployment phases

The deployment phases provide a mechanism for an incident to be detected and confirmed. They take place at the place where the crime was detected and consist of five phases:-

(a) Detection and notification phase; when an incident is detected and the appropriate people notified.

(b) Physical crime scene investigation; when a physical examination of the scene is performed and potential digital evidence identified.

(c) Digital crime scene investigation phase; when an electronic examination of the scene is performed and digital evidence obtained with possibly an estimation of the extent of the impact or damage.

(d) Confirmation phase; when the incident is confirmed and authorization is given to obtain legal approval to carry out a search warrant and further investigations at suspect premises.

(e) Submission phase; which involves presenting the physical and digital evidence to legal entities or corporate management.

(2) Traceback phases

Within these phases, the perpetrator's physical crime scene of operation is tracked down leading to identification of the devices that were used to perform the act. They consist of:

(a) Digital crime scene investigation; whereby primary crime scene is traced from the clues obtained from the previous phases. For example, acquiring public and private IP addresses and mapping them to the country and institution will eventually lead to the host computer. IP addresses can be easily obtained by using the following commands: ping, nslookup, dig, tracert from a DNS server. Locating the country and institution is simplified by various tools and websites like ip-to-location.com and whatismyipaddress.net.

(b) Authorization phase; when authorization from local legal entities is obtained to permit further investigations and access to more information.

(3) Dynamite phases

Dynamite phases investigate the primary crime scene with the aim of collecting and analyzing items that were discovered at the scene to enhance the apprehension of potential criminals. They would consist of:

(a) Physical crime scene investigation phase; when a physical examination of the scene is carried out to identify potential digital evidence.

(b) Digital crime scene investigation phase; when an electronic examination of the scene is performed to obtain digital evidence of the incident and possibly an estimation of the time and dates when the incident was launched.

(c) Reconstruction phase; that includes putting the pieces of a digital puzzle together and identifying the most likely investigative hypotheses.

(d) Communication phase; which involves presenting the final interpretations and conclusions about the physical and digital evidence that has been investigated by a court or corporate management.

Advantages

(a) The model provides a wide spectrum to include electronic and non-digital technologies.

(b) Create consistent and standardized framework for digital forensic development.

(c) This investigative model framework is suitably applicable to future digital technologies.

Disadvantages

(a) Additional sub-phases introduce some ambiguity with respect to the activities performed.

(b) There seems to be duplication of activities, for example, digital crime scene investigation activity appears under the deployment phase, traceback phase, as well as dynamite phase.

2.8 GENERIC COMPUTER FORENSICS INVESTIGATION PROCESS MODEL

Yusoff et al. proposed a five generic grouped phase forensic investigation model known as the Generic Computer Forensics Investigation Process Model (GCFIP) after reviewing existing forensics investigation models (2011).

The pre-process phase deals with activities that are carried out prior to the actual investigation and official collection of data such as getting the necessary approval from relevant authority, etc. Under the acquisition and preservation phase, tasks related to identifying, collecting, transporting, storing, and preservation are performed. Next is the analysis phase which is considered as the core of the forensic investigation processes and various types of analysis are performed on the acquired data to identify the crime source and possibly the perpetrator of the crime. The presentation phase is where various outcomes of the analysis phase are documented and presented to authority in a format which is easily understood and mostly backed by sufficient and acceptable evidence.

Finally is the post-process phase where proper closing of the investigation exercise is done, rightfully owners are given the needed digital and physical evidence, and review of the investigation process is done for lessons to learnt and improvement is done for future investigation.

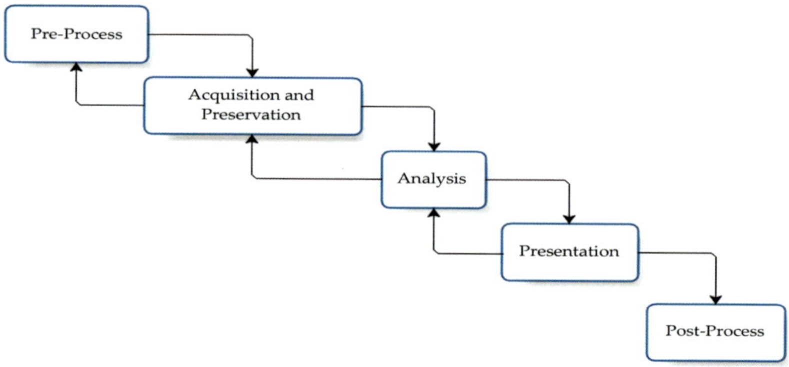

Figure 2.9: Generic Computer Forensics Investigation Process Model. *Source: http://intruderit.blogspot.com.ng/2012/12/gcfim-model.html.*

2.9 COMMON DIGITAL FORENSICS TOOLS

Digital forensics is one of the many fields that have offered the investigators with flexible tools to solve the criminal cases. However, the ability of a single tool to have general functionality is still unusual. The analysis of vast amount of information like that in terms of petabytes in real time and the usage of mobile phones are some of the unexpected circumstances that are yet to be adapted by digital forensics. It would seem expedient if one tool could be useful to any situation; however, it could not be applied to these types of sudden developments. Also, the multitasking tools may deliver some tools which are not even required by the investigator and may be a burden to them. The classification of the forensic tools is done on the basis of the user embracing them. On one hand, law enforcement agencies might need tools which can generate reliable results without compromising the integrity of the evidence, whereas, on the other hand, network administrators may require tools that would support them in the detection of any kind of compromise on their networks. This leads one to deduce two credible truths about digital forensic tools. The first deduction is that no single tool can act as a general functional tool and the second deduction is that all professionals (investigators, attorneys, and so on) require solutions that provide illegal data consistently. On the basis of these two conclusions, FTK would be offering a wide variety of tools which the investigators can use according to their corresponding fields. The following gives a brief overview of three of the commonly used tools used by the digital forensic investigators:

2.9.1 EnCase

EnCase is a forensic software that is established by the Guidance Software. It is a 1-megabyte program written in C++. It has a number of products in its collection which includes EnCase cybersecurity, Encase portable, EnCase forensics, and EnCase eDiscovery. Over 2000 law enforcement agencies use the tool globally. It can be used for range of purposes including analysis, reporting, and acquisition of evidence. The software also has EnScript which is a scripting facility that is used in conjunction with the evidence. Encase enables the examiners to identify, search, and scrutinize the evidence in order to decide whether there is a need for additional investigation is required or not; this saves a lot of time and decreases backlog. The tool collects evidence from the file systems, mobile devices, and operating systems as well and this ensures that there is no absence of evidence in any case.

The investigators place the hard disk drive of the person in question on the forensic computer; it can be from any operating system like Windows, Linux, or DOS machine. EnCase makes bit stream mirror image of the drive, which is mounted as *read only* so that it cannot be altered by any individual. To confirm that it is same as original, Encase computes MD5 hash values and redundancy checksums. The tool restructures the file assembly/system of the drive and then inspects the drive through a Windows GUI. Encase goes deep into the operating system while doing so, in unassigned space or in windows swap files, where deleted files can be preserved.

2.9.2 Forensic Toolkit

FTK is a digital forensic software made by AccessData. It scans and examines the hard drive for any data that the examiner needs such as deleted emails or scan the disk for text string to use them as potential passwords to crack any encryption. The toolkit has a simple but concise disk imaging program known as the FTP Imager. The FTP Imager keeps the image of the hard disk in a file or in segments which can be reassembled whenever needed. The FTK is simple to use and is driven by database, that is, all the data is stacked in one case database which amplifies the reusability and lowers the cost and intricacy. Any failure that is related to memory-based tools is not encountered in FTK. It is a high-speed tool that is invented to give precise, fast, and consistent processing with multithreaded support and distributed processing. The FTK estimates the hash value which is given by the MD5 hash algorithm to confirm the integrity of the achieved data before discarding any file. It gives the product in the form of an image file(s) which can be saved in several formats.

2.9.3 Network Mapper

NMAP is an acronym for Network Mapper and it is a free and open source forensic tool written by Gordon Lyon. It is used for security auditing and for discovering services and hosts on a network thus giving us a "map" of the network; also many network administrators and systems use it for routine tasks like monitoring service or host uptime and managing service upgrades as well. Although it was originally created for large networks, it works effectively against a single host as well. NMAP started as Linux-only utility but it works on almost all operating systems like Linux, Windows, Solaris, AmigaOS, and Mac and has official binary packages for them. It can adjust to any network condition like latency and congestion while doing the scan and is portable, simple, powerful, flexible, and well documented. The tool uses specially crafted IP packets and directs it to the targeted host(s) to know what host and services are available on the network, reverse DNS names, what type of firewall is in use, operating system detection, MAC address, and much more. Additionally, NMAP offers a debugging tool (Ncat), a GUI version (Zenmap), and more. The NMAP generated a result which includes "interesting port table," including information like the service name, port number, protocol, etc. The state can be open, closed, filtered, or unfiltered. Open means that the target machine has an application that is listening for packets on that port. Closed means "that no application is listening on them." Filtered means that NMAP cannot convey the right message as to whether a port is open or closed because it is being blocked by any network obstacle or firewall. Unfiltered is a state when the NMAP is indeterminate about the state. NMAP conceals itself from the source workstation so that the system is not notified by thinking that it is a malware attack.

REFERENCES

1. Carrier, B. (2005). *File System Forensic Analysis*. Upper Saddle River, NJ: Addison Wesley Professional.
2. Carrier, B., & Spafford, E. (2003). Getting physical with the digital investigation process. *International Journal of Digital Evidence*, *2*(2), 20.
3. Casey, E. (2004). *Digital evidence and computer crime: forensic science, computers and the internet*. San Diego: Academic Press.
4. Computer forensics field triage process model. Retrieved March 15, 2018, from https://www.researchgate.net/publication/288761713_Computer_Forensics_Field_Triage_Process_Model
5. Farmer, D., & Venema, W. (2005). *Forensic discovery*. Upper Saddle River, NJ: Pearson Education, Inc.
6. Palmer, G. (2001). *A road map for digital forensic research*. Technical Report DTR-T001-01 for Digital Forensics Workshop (DFRWS), Utica, New York.

CHAPTER 3

NETWORK AND INTERNET

"Given the widespread use of computers and the wide use of networks, it would be a grave error to overlook them as a source of evidence in any crime."

—Casey et al., 2011

CONTENTS

The creation of the Internet was to serve the communication needs of the defense establishments. However, it has evolved into a system utilized by hackers to steal users' identity and launch malicious attacks on servers. The issue of security and the rise in intricacy of cyberattacks are the major factors of network forensics. Most attackers now cover their tracks in such a way that they would not be detectable. This chapter discusses the various tools and techniques required to conduct network forensics and highlight the various IP traceback mechanisms. The last page of this chapter describes the frameworks such as Honeynet Architecture and Honeypots, and their application in detecting cyberattacks, traffic, and shielding the production systems. Each of the phases in the framework is interpreted.–

3.1 TECHNICAL OVERVIEW OF NETWORK AND INTERNET

The Internet is the most powerful means of communication presently because it conveys wide range of data and helps to promote businesses, services, economic growth, and sustenance. It is a safe haven for many users; however, it has become a platform for all types of cyber warfare. The eCommerce industry is a major target for cybercriminals because all transactions are being carried out online and directly. The Internet needs to be protected from these attacks and a proper measure must be adopted in order to reduce its negative impact. Network forensics is defined as "the use of scientifically proven techniques to collect, fuse, identify, examine, correlate, analyze, and document digital evidence from multiple, actively processing and transmitting digital sources for the purpose of uncovering facts related to the planned intent, or measured success of unauthorized activities meant to disrupt, corrupt, and or compromise system components as well as providing information to assist in response to or recovery from these activities" (Palmer, 2001). In a simple term, network forensics is the capture and examination of network traffic with footage in response to the events that occurred in order to ascertain the source of security breaches. It involves checking network traffic to see if there is an anomaly. If there is, the nature of cyberattack is determined and an incident response can be obtained. The goal of network forensics is to examine traffic data logged through firewalls or wireless network devices such as routers or intrusion detection methods, thereby, tracing the source of the attacks so that the criminals are indicted. Network forensics is being researched for several years but it still seems a very young science as many issues are still not very clear. Network forensics is not another term for network security. Network security is an essential part in network forensics as data for forensic analysis can be collected from security products placed to detect and prevent intrusions. Network forensics involves certain crimes which are legally prosecutable but they may not breach the network security policies. Network security protects the system against attack while network forensics does not.

Network security products look for possible harmful behaviors related with various attacks and monitor the network 24 hours a day. Network forensics is postmortem investigation of the attack in many cases. It is case restricted and is started after crime notification specifically addressing a particular attack. Network forensics ensures that the attacker spends more time and energy to cover his tracks making the attack costly. Network criminals are also cautious to avoid prosecution for their illegal actions. This acts as a deterrent and reduces network crime rate, thus improving security. Network forensics also can initiate investigation in real time provided resources are available to handle the traffic and analyze it.

3.2 CONNECTION OF FORENSIC NETWORK USING TCP/IP

Network devices, such as routers and servers, are good sources for collecting Internet-related evidence. According to Wikipedia, a router is a networking device that forwards data packets between computer networks. Servers are computers designed to accept and respond to requests made by another computer program or device known as "clients." It is essential for companies that utilize these network devices to keep logs of the data packets that pass through them. This allows static monitoring and duplication of activity across the network. Transmission Control Protocol/IP (TCP/IP) packets have an exceptional role to play in forensic investigations and are a good example of why corporate organizations should preserve network traffic logs. When a message is sent through the Internet, it is created and transmitted in TCP/IP packets, then rearranged on the other end. Each packet comprises a header which includes information about the source and target computer. The addresses are of major interest during a forensic investigation. The origin address may provide information about the attacker's identity, the destination address may provide information about a precise target within a system, and the data may recognize the source of the attack on its own. Each packet also comprises several additional fields that can be beneficial during an investigation. For example, error checking information can be used to confirm that data complies with addresses. Furthermore, the header contains six extra bits that are left empty when the packet is sent. Most firewalls are designed to check these six bits and throw away packets that have information in these bits. However, the information in these bits may be important if an attack occurs. So, if a system discovers one of these packets, it should redirect it to a safe place and keep a log of it.

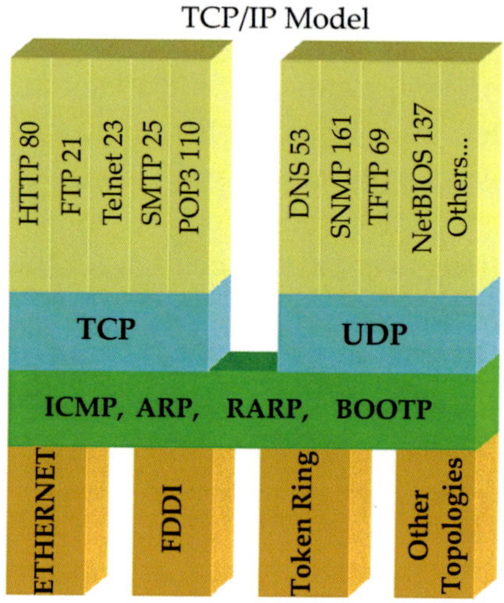

Figure 3.1: TCP/IP Protocol Models. *Source: https://www.pinterest.com/pin/315252042638657528/.*

3.3 TYPES OF NETWORK FORENSIC SYSTEMS

Garfinkel divided the network forensic systems into two types: Catch-it-as-you-can systems and Stop-look-and-listen systems (2002).

3.3.1 Catch-it-as-you-can Systems

This system captures network traffic and has the capability of storing voluminous data and analyzing the data in batch mode. This approach requires large amounts of storage.

3.3.2 Stop-look-and-listen Systems

Every packet is analyzed in an elementary way in memory and only certain information is saved for future analysis. This requires a faster processor to match the pace of incoming traffic. This system does not have the storage capacity of the former.

3.4 NETWORK FORENSIC ANALYSIS TOOLS

Network forensic analysis tools (NFATs) enable administrators to track the networks, accumulate all information about anomalous traffic, contribute to the investigation of network-induced crime, and help in generating a proper output in form of incident response. NFATs also help in examining in-house theft cases and abuse of resources, predict future attacks, perform risk assessment, appraise network performance, and defend intellectual property. NFATs capture the entire network traffic, allow the users to study, and discover important features about the traffic. NFATs synergize with intrusion detection system (IDSs) and Firewalls and make possible the long-term preservation of network traffic records for quick analysis (Corey et al, 2002). The attack traffic can be replayed and attackers' actions can be scrutinized for malicious intention. NFATs promote organization of the captured network traffic packets in such a way that it can be viewed as individual transport layer and connections between machines, which in effect allow the user to analyze packet content and protocol layers, execute transmission of data, and extract traffic configurations between various machines. There are many proprietary and open source tools used for network forensic analysis. SilentRunner is the major player in the NFAT market. It provides the administrators with a three-dimensional view of their network. It also gives them the opportunity to analyze packet layer and know the current happenings on the network. Its core function is to monitor the network and provide analysis if an anomaly is detected in the traffic. With its ability to aid administrators in acquiring evidence about a particular event, SilentRunner is able to truncate the time allotted for investigations. There are various tools now that allow administrators to get notifications of changes in the network. However, traffic not recognized by the IDS or log files that seem too much for one or few people can be a serious issue at stake and a security hole. SilentRunner has three major parts: collector, analyzer, and visualizer.

The collector executes the function of capturing the packets without interrupting network performance and reassembles the sessions based on Hypertext Transfer Protocol (HTTP), Post Office Protocol (POP), Internet Message Access Protocol (IMAP), Simple Mail Transfer Protocol (SMTP), Telnet (Teletype Network), and Network News Transfer Protocol (NNTP) content. The analyzer is the basic reporter and the component that draws the collector data together. After carrying out this operation, the analyzer uses n-gram analysis to define patterns for the administrator. The analyzer is also able to do more work than just a Sniffer or IDS because it can analyze firewall logs and IDS data. The last component which is the visualizer is able to create a three-dimensional picture of the whole network. Many commands in the popular operating systems also support the role of NFAT: nslookup, traceroute, netstat, nbtstat, whois, ping, and wget. There are two additional tools which are known for network forensic analysis: Python Forensic Log Analysis GUI (pyFLAG) and System Internet-Level Knowledge (SiLK), which analyze pcap files and netflow records, respectively.

Table 2.1: Network Forensic Analysis Tools

Proprietary	Open Source
NetIntercept	Wireshark tcptrace
NetDetector	Snort tcpstat
NetWitness	Bro nmap
SilentRunner	Tcpdump p0f

Source: A Generic Framework for Network Forensic (2010) International Journal of Computer Applications (0975–8887)

3.4.1 Python Forensic Log Analysis graphical user interface

The PyFlag, where GUI stands for graphical user interface, is an advanced forensic tool for the analysis of large bulks of log files like hard disk images and network captures. The PyFlag is utilized in log analysis, file carving, disk forensics, memory forensics, and network forensics. The PyFlag is also able to analyze network captures in tcpdump format (.pcap files) while acting as backup for a number of network protocols.

Network forensics tools must be able to process very large capture files, extract high-level information, and be able to authenticate each deduction. The network forensic module of PyFlag integrates all the above aspects as it delivers higher level information, while locating accurately where each piece of data was derived from. Its architecture has the ability to recursively examine data at multiple levels and this is ideally suited for network protocols which are usually layered, with higher level protocols being executed before level protocols. The major functional components of the network forensic module are stream reassembler, packet handler, and stream dissectors. The PyFlag parses the pcap files, extracts the packets, and breaks them down them at low-level protocols (IP, TCP, or User Datagram Protocol). Associated packets are collected into streams using reassembler. Higher level protocol dissectors such as HTTP and Internet Relay Chat (IRC) are then used to dissect these streams. The PyFlag does not only have the capability of Hypertext Markup Language (HTML) rendering but it is also able to dissect explicit data in a higher level application. It manages each case autonomously and uses a unique identity for input and output sources while loading. It identifies the type, populates the virtual file system, and displays in tree structure. The outgoing and incoming traffic between various sources and destinations is displayed. The contents of each packet and protocol information can be viewed. The connections established, chat conversations, and Domain Name System (DNS) requests are also displayed for analysis.

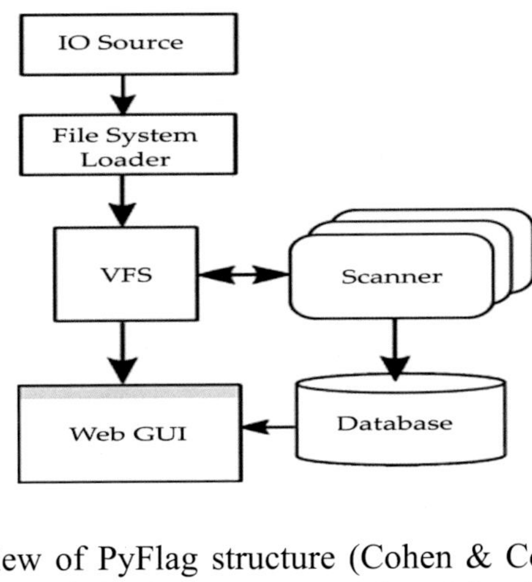

Figure 3.2: Overview of PyFlag structure (Cohen & Collett, 2005). *Source: https://commons.erau.edu/cgi/viewcontent.cgi? article=1071&context=jdfsl*

3.4.2 System Internet-Level Knowledge

The SiLK supports efficient capture, storage, and analysis of network flow data based on Cisco NetFlow. The SiLK tool suite was developed by the CERT Network Situational Awareness (NetSA) group. The tool suite provides analysts with the means to understand, query, and summarize both new and past traffic data in network flow records. This tool supports network forensics in recognizing relics of intrusions, exploitation of weakness, worm behavior, etc. The suite comprises two primary components, the collection system, and the analysis tool set. The collection system converts Cisco NetFlow V5 protocol data units (PDUs) into a compressed binary format. A range of analysis tools work on these records, and control and summarize the data. Collection system minimizes the storage space by storing the required fields, reduces the number of bits used to store some information, and saves space by avoiding storage of irrelevant information.

There are six fundamental tools in SiLK. rwfilter retrieves data and partitions it to isolate flow records of interest. Rwstats offers an assemblage of statistical analysis and counting facilities that enables organizing and ranking traffic by different elements. rwcount provides a time-binned count of the number of bytes, packets, and flow records. rwcut tool reads filter files and produces a readable version of the output to the user in a pipe-delimited tabular format. rwsort is a high-speed sorting tool for SiLK flow records. Rwuniq counts records per combination of multiple-field keys.

There are many analytical tools in SiLK that control flow record files. rwcat and rwappend tools are used for merging flow record files. rwdedupe is designed to allow analysts to remove duplicate flow records efficiently. rwsplit divides a bulky flow record file into pieces and simultaneously analyzes each piece separately. rwptoflow tool generates a single packet flow record for every IP packet in a tcpdump file. rwpmatch takes a tcpdump file and filters it based on flow records from a SiLK record file. SiLK is a key tool with high-level performance because it manages massive traffic by storing information that deals with security, divides files into predefined categories to minimize lookup time, and reads zipped file easily. It also helps in analysis of worm detection, scanning operation, and SYN flooding.

3.5 DIGITAL EVIDENCE ON INTERNET

In 2000, email and AOL instant messages provided the compelling evidence to convict Sharee Miller of conspiring to kill her husband and abetting the suicide of the admitted killer (Jerry Cassaday) who she had seduced via the Internet. Miller meticulously influenced the killer's perception of her husband, going so far as to disguise as her husband to send the killer offensive messages. In this (scenario), the authenticity of the AOL instant messages was questioned in light of the possibility that such an online conversation could be staged (Bean, 2003). This scenario defines the importance of digital evidence extracted from the Internet and its application in fishing out crime perpetrators.

3.5.1 Instant Messengers

Instant messengers (IM) became an important means of communication. The global Internet community regardless of age, nationality, and level of computer literacy uses IM daily. This is the reason why digital evidence can be discovered in IM chat histories. To name a few, Live Messenger, ICQ, Yahoo! Messenger, Viber, Trillian, Skype, and WhatsApp are among the most commonly used. In China, QQ Messenger is very popular with over a billion registered accounts.

3.5.2 Social Networking

Social networks are gradually becoming the new face of conventional IM. More and more communication is migrating from public chat rooms and private messengers into online social networks. Communications extracted from social networks can be extremely valuable to forensic investigators.

3.5.3 Web Browsers

Web forensics has to do with the acquiring critical information related to a crime by exploring the browsing history of a suspect, the number of web page or site visits, the duration of each visit, the cookies setup during web page download, and all uploaded and downloaded files on different websites. Web browsing is also known as surfing. The importance of web browsers is critically seen here as it carefully helps investigators to expose suspicious activities. Web cache may store prohibited content as well as JavaScript-based malware. Significant digital evidence can be obtained by examining web browsing history, cached pages and images, and stored passwords. Less noticeable crimes can be analyzed with Google search. There are many web browsers in use today. Some prominent ones are Microsoft's Internet Explorer (IE), Mozilla Firefox, and Google Chrome. Each of these browsers has its own unique way of saving activities done on the web. This is otherwise known as web browsing history. IE stores the browsing history of a user in the index.dat file and the Firefox/Mozilla/Netscape family browsers save the web activity in a file named history.dat. These two files are normally hidden and cannot be viewed without first setting up the browser to show both system files and hidden files. Another issue is that these two files cannot be deleted normally. Also, there is no confirmed proof that deleting the files can optimize users' experience during browsing. Mandiant web historian assists users in reviewing website URLs that are stored in the history archives of the frequently used web browsers. The tool allows the forensic examiner to determine the action, time, location, and means by which the intruders looked into the different sites.

Web historian can be used to parse a specific history file or iteratively search through a given folder or drive and find all the browser history files that the tool knows how to analyze. Web historian produces a single report, which can be saved in diverse formats, as an output. It locates the online activities from all of the web browser history. The index.dat analyzer is a forensic tool to view, examine, and delete the contents of index.dat files. The tool can be used to view the browsing history, the cache, and the cookies at the same time or independently. The tool can give essential information about a cookie, the time and date reference associated with the cookie, the website URL associated with it, etc. It also provides support to directly visit the website listed in the output of the analyzer and also to open the file uploaded to or downloaded from the website. A supplementary tool to these two tools is known as Total Recall. It can be used to extract the list of favorite websites stored in the browser history.

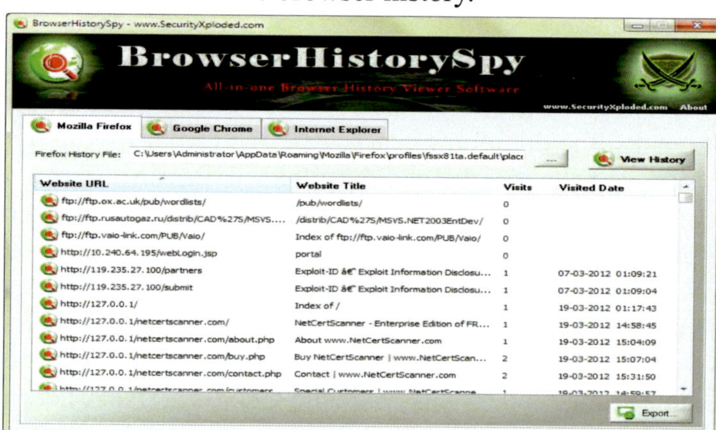

Figure 3.3: Browser History Software. *Source: http://securityxploded.com/browser-history-spy.php.*

3.5.4 Email

Email forensics involves studying the source and content of electronic mail as evidence, identifying the real sender and recipient of a message, the date, time, and the location if possible. Despite the increase in the use of instant messaging service and social networks, email is still a major means of conveying information which is especially true for corporate organizations. Email is one of the powerful means of communication, ranging from internal meeting requests to distribution of documents and general conversation. Emails are now being used for various kinds of communication including providing privacy, verification, non-repudiation, and data integrity. Microsoft Outlook, Outlook Express, Windows Mail, Live Mail, Thunderbird, TheBat, and many other email applications are available on the market. With many online and offline email clients, it is too easy to ignore important evidence without checking it properly. As email usage increases, attackers and hackers began to use emails for illegal activities. Spam emails became a major issue within the Internet community. Emails are more vulnerable to being captured and might be used by hackers to get secret information. Emails often contain malwares, threats, and scams that can result in the forfeiture of data, confidential information, and even identity theft. The tools described in this section provide a flexible browser format, automated reporting, and easy toolbar access features. The tools help to identify the source of the message, trace the path navigated by spam messages in, and also to locate the phishing emails that try to obtain confidential information from the receiver.

eMailTrackerPro analyzes the header of an email to detect the IP address of the machine that sent the message so that the sender can be tracked down. All email messages contain a header, located at the top of the email. In the "From" line and the "Received" lines, the header lists out every point where the email was intercepted during transmission along with the date and time. The message header provides an inventory path of every machine the email has passed through. eMailTrackerPro has an inbuilt location database which helps to track emails to a country or region of the world, showing information on a global map. To use this tool, one will just copy and paste the header of the email in eMailTrackerPro. A basic trace will be shown on the main GUI and a diagnostic report is obtained. This diagnostic report provides an alternative way of resolving this issue. One can report the misuse of the particular email address to the administrators of the sender or victim networks and also contains some vital information that can be useful for forensic analysis and investigation. The report includes the geographic location of the sender's IP address, and if this cannot be established, the report at least includes the location of the target's Internet Service Provider (ISP). The report also includes the domain contact information of the network owner or the ISP, depending on the sender email address. The domain registration gives information with regards to the website address, time, number of emails sent, and so on.

SmartWhoIs is a freeware network utility used to find information about an IP address, domain name, country, state or province, city, name of ISP, administrator, and the contact details of technical support service. Sometimes, one has to use SmartWhoIs along with eMailTrackerPro in order to get complete information. Once installed on a machine, a SmartWhoIs button will be added to the Internet Explorer (IE) toolbar as an extension. Using this simple tool button, one can use SmartWhoIs anytime to get additional information about recently or currently visited sites. Using SmartWhoIs, one can also probe multiple IP addresses, hostnames, or domains at a time.

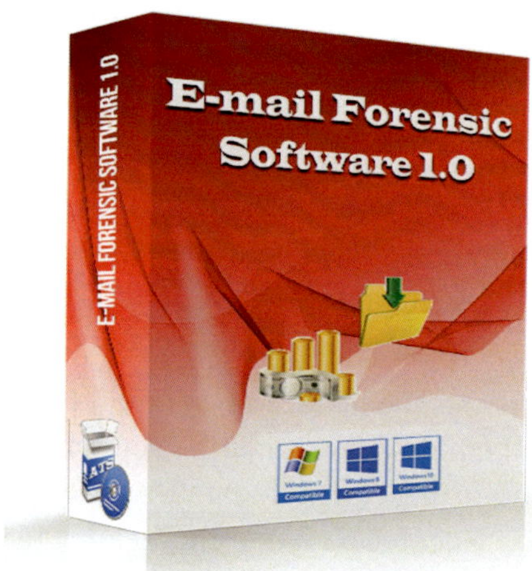

Figure 3.4: Email Forensic Software. *Source: http://www.bulkecommerce.com/store/e-mail-forensics-software-136.html.*

3.5.5 Peer-to-Peer and File Exchange Software

Peer-to-peer, also known as P2P, is distributed system that is created by a set of interconnected nodes where each node has similar capability. Formation and maintenance of these networks are based on clearly defined communication protocols used by nodes to combine networks and exchange information.

P2P and file exchange clients such as the popular Torrent exchange software may contain crucial evidence including illegal images or videos, stolen intellectual property, and copyright infringement. Information about files being downloaded, shared, and uploaded can be a good addition to collected evidence base. Peers promote exchange of information at the application layer which helps in the maintenance of networks and has various applications. Generally, a P2P system for performing network forensics has the following requirements:

(a) It must allow peers to act both as producers and consumers of data.

(b) It must allow the dynamic addition and subtraction of peers to the system.

(c) It must communicate with a range of platforms.

(d) It must reduce network traffic overhead.

(e) It must promote the exchange of data in a common format.

(f) It must ensure privacy.

(g) It must make sure that integrity is not compromised.

(h) It must ensure availability.

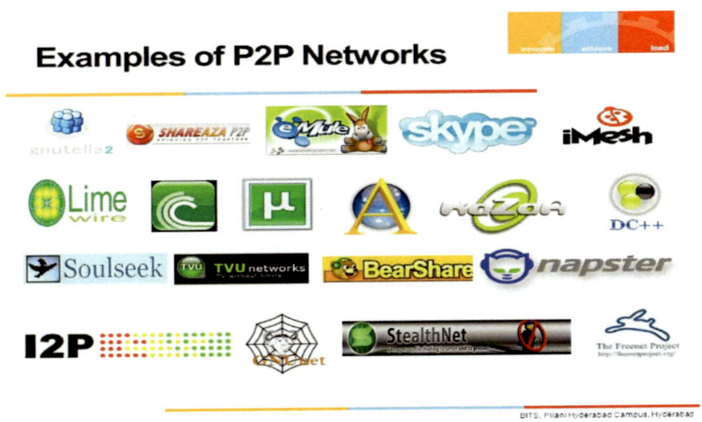

Figure 3.5: Examples of P2P Networks. *Source: http://slideplayer.com/slide/4615691/.*

P2P networks can be classified into three categories namely centralized, completely decentralized, and semi-centralized networks. (1) Centralized networks: A central index server maintains a list of active nodes on the networks. Nodes that want to join the network must send identity information to the central index server periodically. An example is the Napster protocol. Napster is the first P2P sharing tool that allows users to share audio files directly with one another. When Napster was seen as illegal, the Gnutella protocol was introduced with fully decentralized P2P services. (2) Completely decentralized networks: Here, all the nodes are very similar in terms of information and functionality. No node contains more information than any of its peers. Also, none of the nodes performs more function than any of its peers. There is no central index server in this type of network. Gnutella protocol Gnutella (v0.4) is an example of a decentralized P2P protocol. However, when Gnutella protocol depended on flooding each node on the network to detect files, recently introduced protocols such as Chord and Kademlia use as distributed hash table (key, value pairs) to locate files on the network. (3) Semi-centralized networks: There are multiple nodes on the network which contains index information. Kazaa is an example of a hybrid P2P model, combining the benefits of both the centralized and fully decentralized approaches. This semi-centralized network essentially takes a decentralized model and creates smaller sub-networks, each with as central server known as a super peer. Each super peer maintains a list of files hosted within its sub-network and shares that information with other super peers (Pavel & Marcus, 2011).

3.6 PAGE FILE AND HIBERNATION FILE ANALYSIS

With the launch of Windows 2000, Microsoft introduced a hibernation feature that enables a system to be powered down, while still maintaining its volatile state. This is established by saving the contents of RAM and the processor context to disk in a file called hiberfil.sys before shutting down. When the computer again powered on, the volatile state is restored and the system resumes from the saved state. Hibernation files are a good source of information for digital forensic practitioners, because they store data that are only short-lived from the contents of RAM to non-volatile storage without the need to run specific tools on the target device. Memory analysis frameworks like Volatility and Rekall make it easy to analyze hibernation files in a way similar to memory dump; however, these tools do not share common conventions or are rather not compatible with hibernation files from the most recent versions of Windows. This development is due to the release of Windows 8 by Microsoft which also included a modification of the hibernation format. Hibernation file, also known as suspend to disk hibernation, is a feature of many desktop operating systems which allows for the current state of the system to be serialized to non-volatile media. This state takes the form of a hibernation file and can be used to resume the system at a future date. Apart from this, the hibernation file contains a fragment of the physical memory used by the system. By examining this file, it is possible to restructure parts of the system's address space. To increase the hibernation process, operating system vendors usually only include the bare minimum necessary to restore the condition of the system. This means that parts of the address space not currently in use by the system are omitted. However, these regions can contain expedient information such as the remnants of terminated processes. Hence, hibernation files do not provide a whole image. Hibernation is often considered as a safer, more reliable alternative to sleep mode (commonly referred to as suspend to RAM or S3). When a system, usually a notebook, is put to sleep, all components other than the memory modules are shut down. As the memory is still receiving power, its contents are preserved, allowing for a system to revive rapidly from suspension. While significantly faster than hibernation, suspension to RAM does require that the memory modules remain active for the period. This is a challenge to both desktop and notebook systems. In an attempt to improve, these versions of Windows since Vista and Mac OS X since Leopard have integrated a feature, called safe sleep, into the system whereby a hibernation file is produced before putting the system to sleep. In the case of power failure, this file is used to resume the system. Forensic point of view is that hibernation files are also available on users who suspend their computer systems to memory. This also provides a convenient means for an investigator to produce a hibernation file as an output. Many systems are designed to go to sleep when either the power button is pressed or in the case of notebooks, when the lid is closed. Different operating systems have different internal configuration of hibernation files and is rarely recorded. The file is usually compressed and occasionally encrypted for security purposes. For this purpose, special programs are required in order to examine them.

In the case of an encrypted hibernation file, often the encryption key is created from the user's login password. If the hibernation file was produced when the system was put to sleep, as is the case with safe sleep technologies, the key can sometimes be recovered. This is because it is highly possible that the key is present in the memory of the system and can be obtained some imaging techniques. The main benefit of hibernation files is that they are exceptionally consistent. As a matter of fact, such consistency is necessary in order to restore the state of a system. However, the reliability of hibernation files is debatable. Most operating systems have hooks that enable an application to be notified when the system hibernates itself, making it possible for a malicious software to terminate itself upon hibernation. A drawback to this feature is for a piece of software, whether original or malicious, to remain on a system, it must be able to survive a hibernation process. Any piece of software that does not have the ability to do this will definitely have a short half-life. This places restriction on how an application can respond to hibernation. Another issue is that the file must be located on disk that it can be modified ex post facto by any application with adequate privileges. This can be resolved by ensuring that no application on the system has the opportunity to change the hibernation file after it has been written. This usually means acquiring the file before it is used to resume the system. It is noteworthy that hibernation files cannot be used to execute live analysis of a system due to their very nature.

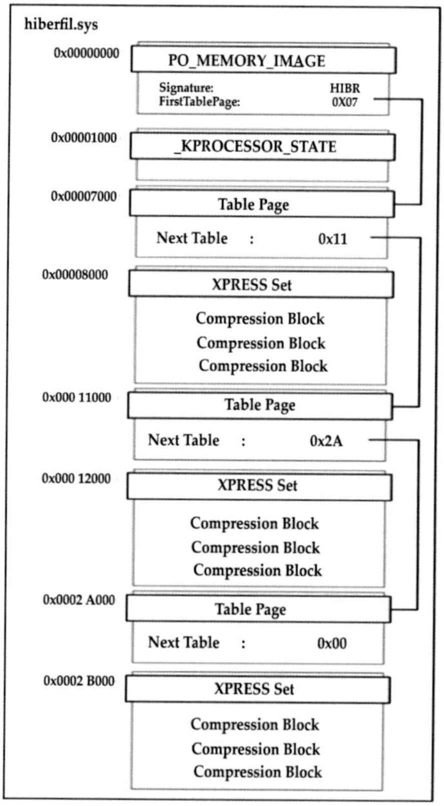

Figure 3.6: Windows 7 hiberfil.sys layout. *Source: www.elsevier.com/locate/diin.*

3.7 LIVE SOFTWARE ACQUISITION

Usually, operating systems have provided a special device file for gaining access to the physical address space of the system. By reading from this file, an application can generate a memory dump; in Microsoft Windows, the files are specified as \Device\PhysicalMemory, while Unix-like systems, including Mac OS X and GNU/Linux, provide /dev/mem for that purpose. Recently, however, there has been a tendency towards limiting access to such files. With the release of Windows Server 2003, Service Pack 1 Microsoft removed the ability for user mode applications to access the Physical Memory device and Apple opted to disable /dev/mem by default with the Intel port of Mac OS X Tiger. Although /dev/mem is still present in many GNU/Linux distributions, it is often limited to the first 1 MiB of memory. Developers of imaging applications have responded to this by including kernel modules to emulate the missing functionality. Therefore, most tools available on the market today are two-part, consisting of a kernel module to provide an appropriate devices file and a user mode application to read from this file. Many imaging tools are available, both open source and proprietary. Tools for Microsoft Windows include the GPL-licensed MDD (ManTech International, 2009) and the proprietary MoonSols Windows Memory Toolkit (MoonSols, 2010). For GNU/Linux, the crash module can be used to emulate the functionality of/dev/mem. All of these tools require administrator privileges to run, whereas Windows and Mac OS X generally maintain binary compatibility for modules between releases the Linux kernel does not. It is usually not possible to load a module compiled against one release of the Linux kernel on a system running a different release. Investigators wishing to use software acquisition in the field may therefore be required to keep several versions of a particular module or driver. The speed of software tools depends heavily on the bandwidth of the device being used to store/send the image. Using a 1 Gbit/s Ethernet connection or S-ATA, hard disk transfer rates upwards of 80 MiB/s can be obtained. Live software acquisition is plagued by reliability concerns. Imaging tools rely on system calls provided by the operating system in order to function. These calls are required for, among other things, launching processes, loading modules/drivers into the kernel, and accessing the file system. Any piece of software that can interfere with these calls has the potential to tamper with the resulting image. Detection of such software, which may often take the form of a rootkit, is difficult. In some instances, it may even be impossible without the aid of hardware acquisition. This makes live software acquisition unsuitable for imaging potentially hostile systems. The use of any software tool will leave behind tool marks. The degree of these marks depends on several variables, including the memory footprint of the imaging application, the size of any kernel modules loaded, and the method used to save the output image. Sending an image to a networked device is likely to leave fewer marks than writing to a removable mass storage device (which must itself be inserted into the system). The two-part design of modern imaging tools is not so ideal as far as consistency is concerned. The consistency of an image depends heavily on the number of active processes running on the system at the time of acquisition. Processes that are inactive are not modifying memory and so are unlikely to be the source of inconsistencies. It is therefore desirable to phase out userspace applications running on the system while a memory snapshot is taken. An approach similar to this is used in order to put a system in a state of hibernation. However, this is only practical if the imaging tool does not depend on userspace in order to function. The problem here lies with existing part tools since they all utilize a userspace component. By moving this code into the kernel, it becomes possible to exert a significant degree of control over the acquisition process.

3.8 HONEYPOTS AND HONEYNETS

A Honeynet is a network specifically designed for the purpose of being compromised. A compromised Honeynet can be used to observe the activities and behavior of the intruder. A Honeynet allows to conduct a thorough analysis of the tools used by the intruders and to identify the weaknesses exploited by the intruders to compromise the Honeypots. In general, a Honeypot could range from a simple port-listening socket program to a full production system that can be emulated under various operating systems. Sometimes, a Honeypot would pull traffic by acting as a decoy system by presenting itself to the Internet as a legal system offering services. The essential idea is that any traffic referred to Honeypot is known to be an attack or intrusion. Any connection initiated inbound to Honeypot is possible to be a scan, probe, or attack. Any outgoing connection from a Honeypot implies that someone has compromised the Honeypot and has commenced outbound operation. Hence, forensic analysis of the operations of a Honeypot is less expected to result in false negatives and false positives when compared to the more elusive and signature-dependent network intrusion detection systems. Honeypots can help us to identify vulnerabilities that are vague or unseen before. Honeypots can be classified into two types depending on the configured services available for an attacker to compromise or probe the system: low-interaction and high-interaction Honeypots. A high-interaction Honeypot can be compromised completely. It gives an attacker the access to all facets of the operating system and privilege to launch more network attacks. The larger the number of Honeypots installed, the more likely that one can efficiently get information about network attacks. For instance, most of the TCP connection requests are generated and sent to erratically selected IP addresses. One can recognize that prior to a connection request, a TCP handshake is over and the load containing malicious contents is received. The more likely this happens, the more the number of Honeypots increases.

A Honeynet normally utilizes a Honeywall, which acts as a firewall to protect the external world from attacks stemming from within the Honeynet. In order to secure systems that are not Honeypots from attacks stemming from a compromised Honeypot, a Honeywall with numerous data control and data capture features could be established. A Honeywall could restrict the number of bound connections allowed per hour. It could also restrict the bandwidth range available to the attacker's traffic. A Honeywall can also limit on-the-fly change malicious data packets that precisely target weaknesses on other systems and make them benign. A Honeywall can capture and monitor all incoming, outgoing, and resident data traffic in the Honeynet. The captured data can be used to investigate the steps an attacker took to compromise a Honeypot and how a compromised Honeypot is being used further. In order to prevent a Honeywall from blocking the communications, an attacker may sometimes install encryption software to encrypt all technical and intelligence information between the attacker's machine and the Honeypot. In such situations, a Honeywall may not be able to decrypt the communications. To address this issue, logging software called Sebek has been recently developed. Sebek is a software tool integrated into each Honeypot and is part of the machine's operating system. Sebek merely blocks the data after the attacker's encryption software decrypts it. The decrypted information is directed to a remote server for further investigation.

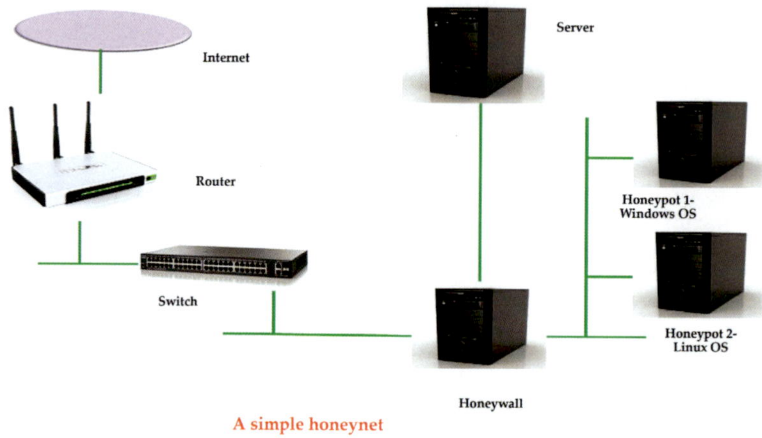

Figure 3.7: Schematic representation of Honeynet.

Source: http://adityaabeysinghepresentationsit.blogspot.com.ng/2014/06/honeypots-and-honeynets.html

3.8.1 Virtual Honeypots

A physical Honeypot is a real machine with its unique IP address. A virtual Honeypot is a simulated machine that can be modeled to perform as required. Multiple virtual Honeypots, each running similar or different operating systems, can be simulated on a single system. Each of these virtual Honeypots can be configured with specific services that will be exploited by the attackers to gain access to a Honeypot. As attackers attempt to connect to machines with randomly selected IP addresses, the higher the number of virtual Honeypots set up with the same kind of services, the more it helps to capture the connection requests and payload traffic created by the attackers. Honeyd is a framework for virtual Honeypots to simulate computer systems at the network level. It forms virtual networks that comprise arbitrary routing topologies with configurable link features like delay, bandwidth, packet loss, etc. Honeyd is used as a deception tool for TCP/IP stack fingerprinting tools like Xprobe or Nmap and to make the attackers believe that a virtual Honeypot is running a specific operating system. This is done by simulating the TCP/IP of the target OS. A virtual Honeypot responds to network requests based on the services that are installed on it.

3.8.2 Serial and Parallel Architecture

A Honeynet could be set up based on either a serial architecture or a parallel architecture. With a serial architecture, the Honeywall filters all traffic dispatched to the firewall of the production system (the network of machines that provide important services) and all incoming and outgoing traffic in production system passes through the Honeynet. If a Honeynet is compromised, the firewall of the production system is notified. Even if the attack is in progress in the Honeynet, the firewall will make sure the attack does not encroach on the production system. When sufficient evidence is collected in the Honeynet, one can stop running the Honeynet and start analyzing the anomalous traffic sent to it. The advantage of a Honeynet with a serial architecture is that it shields the production system from direct malicious attacks. However, the disadvantage would be the delay suffered for every incoming and outgoing packet, including the genuine benign ones, at the Honeynet or firewall.

With a parallel architecture, both the Honeynet and the production system are exposed directly to the Internet so that the delay incurred for every packet at the Honeynet or firewall could be avoided. On the other hand, a blackhat could attack the production system directly and hence the firewall at the production system should be configured with tough packet filtering policies to reduce the odds of troublesome attacks. If the Honeynet gets some traffic, it analyzes that traffic and informs the firewall depending on the nature of the traffic received. The firewall will then become tougher in protecting the production system.

3.9 DATA CARVING

Carving is a generic term for extracting organized data out of raw data based on format specific characteristics present in the organized data, for example, recover deleted file from unallocated disk space. Data carving is a basic approach that allows for the retrieval of files or data generally whenever files system information has been corrupted or lost. To use this method of extraction, a file should have a standard file signature called a file header (start of the file). A search is performed to locate the file header and continued until the file footer (end of the file) is reached. The data between these two points will be extracted and analyzed to validate the file. The extraction algorithm uses different methods of carving depending on the file formats. However, many file carving implementations struggle to recover fragmented files accurately or do not scale well enough to be practical given the enormous data volumes common today. Of primary concern in both traditional criminal investigations and computer emergency response is the accuracy of a given forensic method and its speed of execution. Inaccurate or untimely evidence has little to no value in these pursuits. The two common general file carving techniques are structure-based carving and content-based carving. However, there are other strategies which are discussed thereafter.

3.9.1 Structure-based Carving

This technique uses the internal layout of a file. Elements are header, footer, identifier strings, size information, etc. Structure-based carving was one of the first file carving strategies proposed and was implemented in tools such as Foremost, PhotoRec, and Scalpel. During structure-based carving, the data volume is searched for known values or data structures associated with specific file types. A common example, also used later in this project, is the header and footer search. Some file types have a specific byte sequence which acts as the effective beginning and end of the file, the supposed header and footer. A simple carver using this strategy finds the memory cluster containing a header, finds the memory cluster containing an associated footer, and assumes that the clusters in between the two (inclusive) belong to the file to be recovered. Note that this assumption is only true if the file was stored as one contiguous memory segment, with no other allocated or empty clusters in between the header and footer, and that such a simple strategy will fail to recover fragmented files.

3.9.2 Content-based Carving

This is a system comprising loose structure (MBOX, HTML, XML). This technique has features like content characteristics, character count, white- and blacklisting of data, text/language recognition, information entropy, and statistical attributes (Chi^2). Advanced carving techniques include graph theoretic carving, smart carving, encrypted volume carving, and bifragment gap carving.

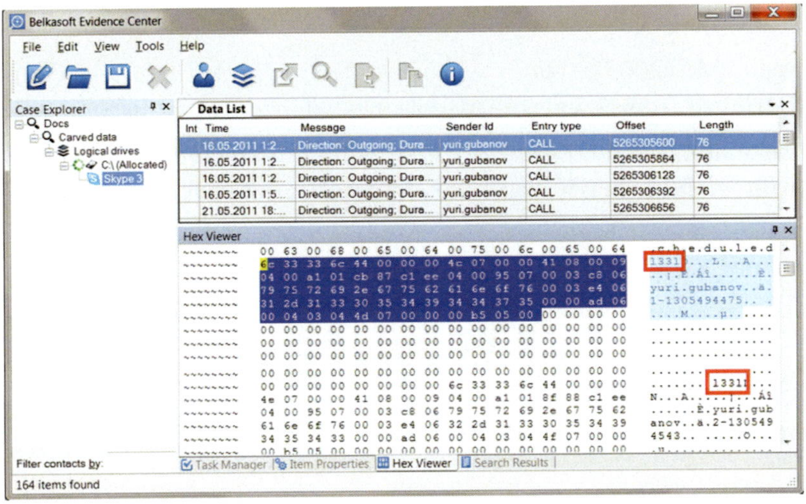

Figure 3.8: HexViewer window as shown by Belkasoft Evidence Center. *Source: http://ru.belkasoft.com/en/retrieving-digital-evidence-methods-techniques-and-issues.*

In the figure above, Belkasoft Evidence center carved out this data in 2012 and it shows that the characteristic signature 1331 precedes an actual Skype 3 call.

3.9.3 Other Carving Techniques

Another approach involves accumulating the fragments and attempting to open them in the proper application. If the file opens, it is presumed not to be a corrupted false-positive. Other research defines carving as a mapping function between the image data and the file data allowing the problem to become an optimization of function problem. The issue has also been described as an optimal path construction problem. Context-based carving is another suggested approach. The fragments are first put into categories representing the files in it. They could belong to such as text or executables. Then the fragments of similar type are reassembled based on possibilities that a certain fragment would follow the preceding fragment. SmartCarver is another solution to file carving. SmartCarver lessens the amount of data to be processed in the carving stage by removing any disk cluster which is identified as being allocated and only carving unallocated clusters. This is, to some extent, a different problem than conditions where there is no existing file system. However, it is remarkable to see that file carving is required even in cases where the file system is available.

REFERENCES

1. Bean, M. (2003). *Mich. v. Miller: Sex, lies and murder*. Court TV. Retrieved from www.courttv.com/trials/taped/miller/ background.html
2. Garfinkel, S. (2002). *Network forensics: Tapping the internet*. Retrieved from http://www.oreillynet.com/pub/a/network/2002/04/26/nettap.html
3. Palmer, G. (2001). *A road map for digital forensic research* (pp. 15–30). First Digital Forensic Research Workshop, Utica, New York.
4. PyFlag. Retrieved from http://www.pyflag.net
5. Sira, R. (2003). *Network forensics analysis tools: An overview of an emerging technology*. GSEC (1.4).

CHAPTER 4

OPERATING SYSTEMS IN FORENSIC INVESTIGATION

"I think Linux is a great thing, because Linux is an alternative to Windows, and because, of all the operating systems that are at all relevant today, Unix is the best of a bad lot."

—Jamie Zawinski

CONTENTS

Operating systems, and the file systems they support, could be intrinsically designed and implemented in a way that makes forensic investigation less time consuming and more reliable, and assists the use of the uncovered evidence in prosecution of perpetrators. Currently, there are many external software tools investigators use, and all of them rely on the interface the operating system provides. This chapter takes you through the critical components of investigation and operating system functionality, including file systems, data recovery, memory forensics, system configuration, Internet access, cloud computing, tracking artifacts, executable layouts, malware, and log files. Essentially, it covers key technical topics that focus on the relationship between computer forensics and operating systems design and implementation.

4.1 TERMINOLOGIES

4.1.1 Disk

A disk refers to a physical storage device—an SCSI or SATA hard drive, or a Secure Digital Card from a digital camera, for example. Analysis of items at this level is usually beyond the capabilities of most examiners—physical media analysis of conventional hard drives requires extensive specialized training and knowledge, access to a clean room, and expensive electron microscopy equipment. With the rise of flash media and Solid State Disks, however, analysis of media at this level may be in the realm of possibility for a larger pool of examiners.

4.1.2 Volume

A volume is created using all or part of one or more disks. A single disk may contain several volumes, or a volume may span several disks, depending on configuration. The term "partition" is often used interchangeably for a volume; carrier makes a distinction wherein a "partition" is limited to a single physical disk, and a volume is a collection of one or more partitions. Put simply, a volume describes a number of sectors on a disk(s) in a given system.

4.1.3 File System

A file system is laid down on a volume and describes the layout of files and their associated metadata. Items in the file system layer include metadata specific to and solely used for the file system's operation—the Ext2 superblock is a good example.

4.1.4 Data Unit

A data unit is the smallest available freestanding unit of data storage available in a given file system. On Unix-derived file systems, these are known as blocks. These are generally some power of 2 multiple of the physical sector size of the disk. Historically the sector size of every disk was 512 bytes—most modern file systems will use 4096 bytes (4K) or larger as the smallest addressable data unit. The information available at the data unit layer is simple: the content of that data unit. If that data unit is allocated to a JPEG image, the data unit will contain a portion of JPEG data. If the data unit was allocated to a text file, the data unit will contain text.

4.1.5 Metadata

Metadata refers to data about data. Given that the data unit layer holds data in a file system, the metadata layer then contains data about the data units. On Unix-derived file systems these metadata units are called inodes. The exact content of metadata units depends on the actual file system being discussed, but generally, this layer will at least consist of file time stamps, file ownership information, and data units allocated to this metadata unit.

4.1.6 File Name

The file name layer is where humans operate. Unsurprisingly, this layer consists of file and folder/directory names. Once again, artifacts available in this layer vary depending on the file system. At the very least, file names have a pointer to their corresponding metadata structure.

4.2 WINDOWS XP

Windows XP has been a standard Microsoft OS for workstations for years. Since it hit the scene in 2001, millions of Windows users have grown comfortable with its user-friendly interface, comparatively efficient operation, and improvements over previous versions such as Windows 2000 and Windows ME. Windows XP comes in three primary editions (i.e., Home, Media Center, and Professional), which were targeted at different parts of Microsoft's workstation computing customers. From a file system standpoint, XP continues to run on top of the File Allocation Table (FAT) and

New Technology File System (NTFS) structures with which examiners have grown familiar. There are many features in Windows XP that can be very useful for forensic examiners. Evidence of user actions is often recorded in areas (such as Internet history, Event logs, Prefetch files, thumbs.db files, and link files) that are easy to view for the trained digital investigator with the right tool. However, other challenges (such as analyzing restore points, analysis of data in the Windows registry, collection, and analysis of memory, dealing with RAIDs and dynamic disks, overcoming Windows encryption, and documenting data destruction) can present a much greater challenge, even for more experienced digital investigators. Regardless of its utility, Microsoft stopped selling XP in 2008 but plans to continue support for this beloved Windows version until 2014, which means it will most likely be a big part of examiners' lives for many years to come. Throughout this chapter, unless otherwise stated, discussions of Windows XP operation and artifacts also generally apply to Windows Server 2003 systems.

4.3 WINDOWS FILE SYSTEMS

The simplest Windows file systems to understand are the FAT (file allocation table) file systems: FAT12, FAT16, and FAT32. Although relatively old, FAT file systems are still used on many storage systems such as removable storage media in digital cameras and mobile devices. Given their widespread use and simple structure, FAT file systems are a good starting point for forensic analysts to understand file systems and recovery of deleted data. It is also important to understand the fundamentals of NTFS, which is more complex than FAT and has substantially different structures. This section provides an overview of both Windows file systems, concentrating on aspects that are important from a forensic analysis viewpoint.

4.3.1 File Allocation Table

The FAT file system is perhaps one of the simplest file systems available and has been widely available on Microsoft operating systems, starting with MS-DOS. FAT was the primary file system on MS-DOS systems and floppy diskettes and was also used extensively on Windows 3.x and Window 95 and 98. This file system is still used on removable storage devices such as thumb drives, as well as compact flash cards used in digital cameras. The FAT file system is supported by other operating systems, so it makes a good medium for moving from one system (Linux, MacOSX) to another (Windows); if you are conducting analysis via a Linux system, you can save extracted files and data and easily access it later from a Windows system. However, keep in mind that the FAT file system does not have the same security mechanisms as other file systems, including NTFS. The FAT file system comes in a number of different flavors; FAT12, FAT16, FAT32, and exFAT. FAT is also considered to be a rather simple file system in that it possesses relatively few data structures. With the FAT file system, the disk or volume is broken up into clusters of a specific size, based on the version of FAT used. For example, for FAT12, the cluster size ranged from 512 bytes to 8 kilobytes (KB). For FAT16, the cluster size ranges from 512 bytes to 64 KB. Microsoft provides a Knowledge Base article that describes the FAT32 file system from a high level. As part of this description, Microsoft states that the FAT32 file system can support disks up to 2 terabytes (TB), but that Windows 2000 only supports partitions up to 32 gigabytes (GB) in size. Using 4-KB clusters, FAT32 uses space more efficiently; cluster sizes can range from 512 bytes to 32 KB. The primary difference between FAT16 and FAT32 is the logical partition size. On disk, the FAT file system begins with the boot sector (Microsoft Knowledge Base article 140418 provides a detailed description of the FAT boot sector) and is followed by FAT areas 1 and 2 (the second FAT area is a copy of the first), the root folder, files, and other folders. The FAT maps to each cluster within the volume and tells the operating system how each cluster is used; whether it's used, in use as part of a file, or the end of the file. Files are laid out within the FAT volume in clusters and are referenced by 32-byte entries that contain the address of the starting cluster number for the file. If a file consumes more than one cluster, then the starting cluster ends with the number of the next cluster and so on until the last cluster is reached. This final cluster is marked with an end-of-file indicator (0xffff). A FAT-formatted volume uses directories and a file allocation table to organize files and folders. The root folder (e.g., C:\) is at a pre-specified location on the volume so that the operating system knows where to find it. The folder contains a list of files and subdirectories on a floppy diskette with their associated properties as shown in through X-Ways Forensics.

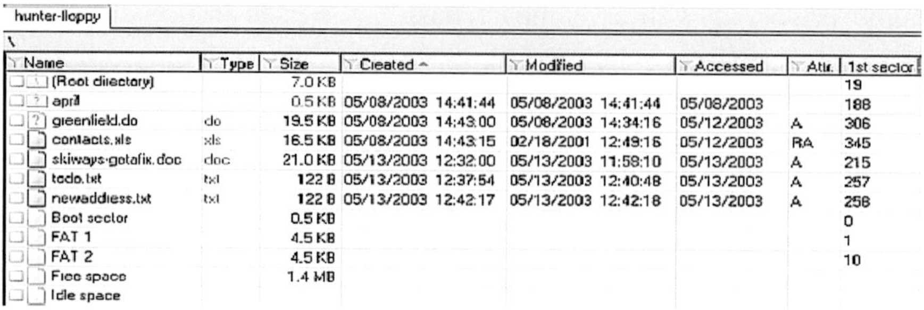

hunter-floppy

\

Name	Type	Size	Created	Modified	Accessed	Attr.	1st sector
(Root directory)		7.0 KB					19
april		0.5 KB	05/08/2003 14:41:44	05/08/2003 14:41:44	05/08/2003		188
greenfield.do	do	19.5 KB	05/08/2003 14:43:00	05/08/2003 14:34:16	05/12/2003	A	306
contacts.xls	xls	16.5 KB	05/08/2003 14:43:15	02/18/2001 12:49:16	05/12/2003	RA	345
skiways-getafix.doc	doc	21.0 KB	05/13/2003 12:32:00	05/13/2003 11:58:10	05/13/2003	A	215
todo.txt	txt	122 B	05/13/2003 12:37:54	05/13/2003 12:40:48	05/13/2003	A	257
newaddress.txt	txt	122 B	05/13/2003 12:42:17	05/13/2003 12:42:18	05/13/2003	A	258
Boot sector		0.5 KB					0
FAT 1		4.5 KB					1
FAT 2		4.5 KB					10
Free space		1.4 MB					
Idle space							

Root directory of floppy diskette viewed using X-Ways Forensics.

Figure 4.1: Root directory of floppy diskette viewed using X-Ways Forensics. *Adapted from Source: http://codes.pratikkataria.com/file-systems/.*

This view of the folder shows the starting cluster and date-time stamps associated with each file. Notably, FAT file systems do not record the last accessed time, but only the last accessed date. Listing the contents of a volume using the dir command displays some of this information but does not show the starting cluster—a critical component from the file system perspective. In addition to indicating where the file begins, the starting cluster directs the operating system to the appropriate entry in the FAT. The FAT can be thought of as a list with one entry for each cluster in a volume. Each entry in the FAT indicates what the associated cluster is being used for. The following output from Norton Disk Editor shows a file allocation table from the same floppy diskette. Clusters containing a zero are those free for allocation (e.g., when a file is deleted, the corresponding entry in the FAT is set to zero). If a FAT entry is greater than zero, this is the number of the next cluster for a given file or folder.

For instance, the root folder indicates that file "skyways-getafix.doc" begins at cluster 184. The associated FAT entry for cluster 184, shown in bold, indicates that the file is continued in cluster 185. The FAT entry for cluster 185 indicates that the file is continued in cluster 186, and so on (like links in a chain) until the end-of-file (EOF) marker in cluster 225 is reached. In this example, Cluster 226 relates to a different file ("todo.txt") that occupies only one cluster and therefore does not need to reference any other clusters and simply contains an EOF.

[] Disk Editor

object Edit Link View Info Tools Help

0	0	0	0	0	0	0	0
185	186	187	188	189	190	191	192
193	194	195	196	197	198	199	200
201	202	203	204	205	206	207	208
209	210	211	212	213	214	215	216
217	218	219	220	221	222	223	224
225	<EOF>	<EOF>	<EOF>	0	0	0	0
0	0	0	0	0	0	0	0
0	0	0	0	0	0	0	0
0	0	0	0	0	0	0	0
0	0	0	0	0	0	0	0
0	0	0	0	0	0	0	0
0	0	0	0	0	0	0	0
0	0	0	0	0	0	0	0
0	0	0	0	0	0	0	0
0	0	0	0	0	0	0	0
0	0	0	0	0	0	0	0
0	0	315	316	317	318	319	320
321	322	323	324	325	326	327	328
329	330	331	332	333	334	335	336
337	338	339	340	341			

FAT (1 st Copy) Sector 1
Drive A: Cluster 184, hex B8

Figure 4.2: Output from Norton Disk Editor showing a FAT from the same floppy diskette.

Source: http://codes.pratikkataria.com/file-systems/

4.3.2 New Technology File System

The NTFS is perhaps the most widely used file system on Windows systems, as it offers a number of advantages over the FAT file system, including the ability to set access control lists (ACLs, or permissions) on file objects, journaling, compression, and a host of other capabilities not offered on the FAT file system.

Directories are treated much like any other file in NTFS but are called index entries and store folder entries in a B-Tree to accelerate access and facilitate resorting when entries are deleted. Instead of using ASCII to represent data such as file and folder names, NTFS uses an encoding scheme called Unicode. This difference must be taken into account when performing text searches. NTFS has a more formal file initialization process than FAT file systems, but the same issues can arise, such as storage space reserved for a new file not being used in its entirety, or at all, which can be misinterpreted as backdating. When only a portion of the disk space that was reserved for a new file is used to store data associated with that file, this leaves a discrepancy between the logical file size and the actual amount of data stored in the file. As a result, you can have a file that appears to have a logical size larger than the actual amount of data stored for that file. The space between the end of valid data and the end of file is called uninitialized space. (Eoghan Casey, 2001)

(1) MFT

The most notable source of valuable information for an analyst from the NTFS file system is the Master File Table (MFT). NTFS creates MFT entries as they are needed and, when a file is deleted, NTFS simply marks the associated MFT entry as deleted and available for a new file. It is possible to recover all of the information about a deleted file from the MFT entry, including the data for resident files and the location of data on disk for non-resident files. However, recovering deleted files in NTFS can be complicated by the fact that unused entries in the MFT are reused before new ones are created. Therefore, when a file is deleted, the next file that is created may overwrite the MFT entry for the deleted file. However, if many files are created and then deleted, causing the MFT to grow, those entries will remain indefinitely as new files will reuse earlier entries in the MFT. Another feature of NTFS that makes it more difficult to recover a deleted file is that it keeps folder entries sorted by name. When a file is deleted, a resorting process occurs that may overwrite the deleted folder entry with entries lower down in the folder, breaking a crucial link between the file name and the data on disk. The location of the starting sector of the MFT can be found in the boot sector of the disk, and every file and directory in the volume has an entry in the MFT. Each MFT entry is 1024 bytes in size, making the MFT very simple to parse. Each MFT record, or entry, begins with ASCII string “FILE” (if there is an error in the entry, it will begin with “BAAD”) and consists of one or more (most often, more) attributes, each with their own identifier and structure.

The first 42 bytes of each MFT entry comprise a header structure with 12 elements, and the remaining 982 bytes depend largely on the values within the header and the various attributes contained within the entry. Not all of the elements within the header of the MFT entry are immediately useful to a forensic analyst; however, the figure below illustrates five of the elements that are immediately useful. As illustrated below, we see the

"FILE" signature visible at the beginning of the record. Then we see the sequence number or value, which is incremented when the entry is allocated or unallocated. Because this particular MFT entry is actually the first record within the MFT and refers to the file "$MFT," it stands to reason that the sequence number is 1. Next is the link count, which refers to the number of directories that have entries for this record (hard links cause this value to incremented). Next is the offset with the record to the first attribute; if you look at offset 0×38 within the record, you'll see that the first attribute has an identifier of 0×10, or 16. Finally, we see the flags value, which tells us if the entry is allocated (if the 0×01 bit is set) and if the entry is a directory (if the 0×02 bit is set). In short, from these two values, we can determine if the entry is allocated or deleted, and if it is for a file or directory. The figure below illustrates a portion of an MFT entry.

MFT Entry Header

0x0	0 – 3	Signature ("FILE") if good otherwise ("BAAD")	No
0x4	4 – 5	Offset to fixup array	Yes
0x6	6 – 7	Number of entries in fixup array	Yes
0x8	8 – 15	$LogFile LSN	No
0x10	16 – 17	Sequence value	No
0x12	18 – 19	Link Count	No
0x14	20 – 21	Offset to first attribute	Yes
0x16	22 – 23	Flags (in-use and directory)	Yes
0x18	24 – 27	Used size of MFT entry	Yes
0x1A	28 – 31	Allocated size of MFT entry	Yes
0x20	32 – 39	File reference to base record	No
0x28	40 – 41	Next attribute ID	No
0x2A	42 – 1023	Attributes and fixup areas	Yes

Figure 4.3: MFT Entry Header.

Source: http://slideplayer.com/slide/7914625/

(2) NTFS Alternate Data Streams

Another interesting feature of the NTFS file system is alternate data streams (ADS), or "ADSs." ADSs have been part of the NTFS file system since the first version of Windows NT 3.1 and were included for compatibility with the Macintosh Hierarchal File System (HFS). HFS utilized resource forks for maintaining file metadata, and ADSs provided interoperability when moving files from one file system (HFS) to another (NTFS). ADSs are actually an additional stream associated with a file, and while all versions of Windows include a means for creating arbitrary ADSs (some versions of Windows actually create and use specific ADSs), it wasn't until Windows Vista that native functionality became available for viewing arbitrary ADSs. As of Windows Vista, the 'dir/r' command would allow an analyst to search for arbitrary ADSs on a live system. However, Windows systems running the NTFS file system have long had the native ability to create and use arbitrary ADSs.

In order to demonstrate how to create an arbitrary ADS, create a new directory called "ads" (via the DOS md or mkdir command, if you like), open a command prompt to or cd to that directory, and type the following command:

C:\ads>echo "this is an ADS" > myfile.txt: ads.txt

If you type the *dir* command, you'll see that the file "myfile.txt" exists and is zero bytes in size. We just echo'd a string that is 14 bytes in length into a file (apparently), so where did it go? If we use the 'type' command to attempt to view the string we just entered into the ADS, on Windows XP we'll get an error message about the syntax of the command. Type the following command:

C:\ads>notepad.\myfile.txt: ads.txt

When the Notepad window opens, we can see the string we typed in … where did it come from? The string was stored in the alternate data stream, which is a file but is denoted by the colon in the name. ADSs can be added or attached to files or to directory listings (using a command such as "C:\ads>: ads.txt").

Some Windows applications will actually employ specific ADSs. With Windows XP Service Pack 2, the Attachment Manager would add an ADS called "Zone. Identifier" to files downloaded via Internet Explorer or as OutLook attachments. These ADSs were usually no more than 26 or 28 bytes in length and simply identified the files as having been downloaded via zone 3. Whenever a user would attempt to open or execute a downloaded file, they would be presented with a warning, asking if they were sure that they wanted to launch the file in question. ADSs can also be used to "hide" executable content. On many versions of Windows, executable image files (.exe files) can be hidden in and run from ADSs. Not only will Perl run scripts that are "hidden" in ADSs, but Windows Scripting Host files can also be "hidden" in and run from ADSs.

Again, ADSs are artifacts specific to the NTFS file system. Many commercial forensic applications will display ADSs in red within the GUI of the application. Dave Roth [6] has published a Perl script named "listdatastreams. pl" that can be used on a live system to locate ADSs. This script uses Dave's Win32: API: Prototype module and relies on native Windows application programming interface (API) functions.

4.4 LINUX SYSTEM

Linux systems will be increasingly encountered at crime scenes as Linux increases in popularity, particularly as the OS of choice for servers. The skills and expertise required to recover evidence from a Microsoft Windows-based system, however, do not necessarily translate to the same tasks on a Linux system. For instance, the Microsoft NTFS, FAT, and Linux EXT2/3 file systems work differently enough that understanding one tells httle about how the other functions. In this chapter, we demonstrate digital forensics procedures for Linux systems using Linux command line utilities. The ability to gather evidence from a running system is particularly important as evidence in RAM may be lost if a forensics first responder does not prioritize the collection of live evidence. The forensic procedures discussed include methods for identifying and recovering deleted files from RAM and magnetic media, identifying notables files and Trojans, and finding hidden files and renamed files (files with renamed extensions.

We begin by describing recovering deleted files from RAM on a live (running) Linux system. Because Linux systems are commonly employed as servers, most of the demonstrations are directed toward activities and techniques that intruders are known to use after breaking into a system.

4.4.1 Linux File Systems Architecture

At the time of this writing, most current Linux systems use the Ext3 file system. Ext3 is the successor of Ext2, which added journaling but retained Ext2's underlying structure otherwise. In fact, an Ext3 volume will happily mount as Ext2 if the user issues the mount command appropriately. Many other file systems are available via the Linux kernel, including ReiserFS, XFS, and JFS. Because these file systems are not generally used in a default Linux installation, their presence may indicate a purpose-built system (as opposed to a general-use desktop system).

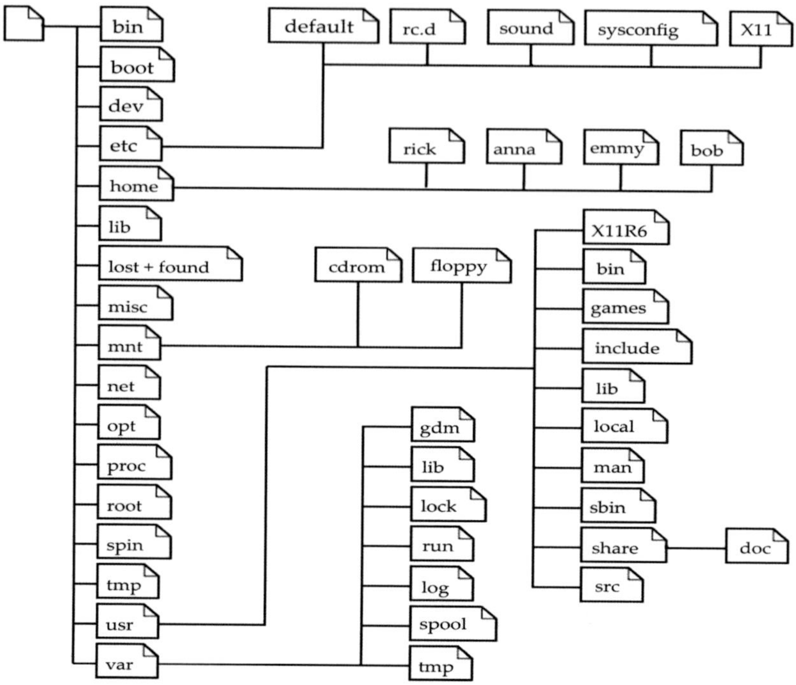

Figure 4.4: A Typical Linux file structure.

Source: https://www.everything-linux-101.com/blog/linux-file-system-structure-explained/

4.4.2 File System Layer

Ext file systems have two major components that make up their file system layer structures: the *superblock* and the *group descriptor tables*. The superblock is a data structure found 1024 bytes from the start of an Ext file system. It contains information about the layout of the file system and includes block and inode allocation information, and metadata indicating the last time the file system was mounted or read. The group descriptor table is found in the block immediately following the superblock. This table contains allocation status information for each block group found on the file system. The fsstat tool in the Sleuth Kit can be used to parse the content of these data structures and display information about the file system.

4.4.3 File System in Linux

Linux treats its devices as files, stored in/dev. Most Linux distributions share a basic directory structure, with files organized in the following directories:

/bin: Common commands

/boot: Files needed at boot time, including the kernel images that are pointed to by LILO or GRUB

/usr: Local software, libraries, games, etc.

/var: Logs and other variable files

/dev: Interface files that allow the kernel to interact with hardware and the file system

/home: Directories for each user on the system, containing user-specific personal and configuration files/mnt: Mount points for external, remote, and removable file systems/etc: Administrative configuration files and scripts

/root: The root-user home directory

/sbin: Administrative commands and process-control daemons

/lib: Basic system libraries

/opt: Optional and third-party software

In order to find system information, the following commands can be used:

(a) uname -a: returns the computer name and Linux version

(b) ls -l: returns the list of files in the current directory

(c) ls -ul [filename]: returns the access time of the file

(d) netstat -s: returns protocol information

UNIX and Linux use a tree or hierarchical, structure for storing files and directories. In a UNIX disk structure, the topmost directory is the root directory and is denoted by a forward slash (/). A root directory has a number of directories, and these directories have subdirectories. A subdirectory is known as a child of the parent directory from which it is branched. For example, in the directory/usr/game,/game is the child of/usr, and in turn,/usr is the parent of/game.

When a file system is created, a superblock is also created that keeps track of metadata including the type of file system, device block size, maximum file volume, name, and other information related to the file system.

After the superblock, another important structure is the inode. An inode acts as an index of the file. Each node represents a file stored on the disk. Using the -I option with the ls command, a user can see the inode number of the file.

The second extended (ext2) file system is perhaps the most convenient Linux file system. It has improved algorithms and extra date stamps for last access, last inode modification, and last data modification. It can also track the state of the file system.

4.4.4 Types of Linux Distributions

Linux is a free, UNIX-based, open source operating system originally created by Linus Torvalds with the assistance of developers around the world. It comes in several different versions, called distributions, including Red Hat, SUSE, Debian, and Ubuntu. Each edition is unique, with its own particular strengths and weaknesses.

There are three basic types of Linux distributions:

(a) Desktop distributions, which include a graphical interface and common applications, suitable for home use.

(b) Server or enterprise distributions that are used primarily for business applications, but can also be used as a home server.

(c) Live-CD distributions that are stored on bootable storage devices. A Live CD is a bootable version of an operating system that is loaded directly into RAM and functions outside and independently of the target computer's operating system

4.4.5 Linux Boot Sequence

(1) The first step in the bootup sequence for Linux is loading the kernel. The kernel image is usually contained in the/boot directory.

(2) The soft link to the current kernel image is available in the/boot directory and is referenced by the Linux Loader (LILO) or, as has become more common, with GRUB. Details of the bootloader can be gained from LILO or GRUB using more/etc/lilo.conf or more/etc/grub.conf.

(3) The third step is initialization. The file that controls initialization is/etc/inittab. The file that begins the process is/sbin/init. The run level and startup scripts are initialized, and the terminal process is controlled.

4.4.6 Recovering Files from RAM

A deleted file whose contents have been overwritten on disk may still be recovered. To illustrate the forensic technique, say an intruder may execute a program and then delete it from disk to hide its existence.

This happens, for example, when an intruder installs a backdoor on the victim system by executing the net cat utility, then deleting the utility from the disk. As long as the program remains as a running process in memory, the original executable can be recovered. The file is recoverable because the Linux kernel uses a pseudo file system to track the general state of the system, including running processes, mounted file systems, kernel information, and several hundred other pieces of critical system information. This information is kept in virtual memory and is accessible through the/proc directory. The (partial) listing below shows the contents of the/proc directory on a running Linux system.

Each of the numbers below corresponds to a processor ID and is a directory that contains information on the running process.

Is/proc

1 4 4513 4703 4777 execdomains mdstat swaps

1693 40 4592 4705 acpi fb meminfo sys

2 4045 4593 4706 asound filesystems misc

2375 41 4594 4708 buddyinfo fs mm sysvipc

2429 4163 4595 4709 bus ide modules tty

2497 4166 4596 4712 cmdline interrupts mounts uptime

2764 4186 4597 4713 config.gz iomem mtrr version

29 42 4620 4715 cpufreq ioports net vmstat

To illustrate the recovery of a deleted file, say that an intruder has downloaded a password cracker and is attempting to crack system passwords, which is a very common goal for an intruder. The intruder runs the john (www.openwall.com) password cracker with a list of passwords in a file called pass. The intruder subsequently deletes both the executable and the text file containing the passwords, the executable remains running in memory until the process is killed. The ps command displays running processes. The listing below shows the executable "John" has been called with the "pass" file at 10:10 am, has been running for 22 seconds, and is owned by root.

4.4.7 Use of Linux as a Forensic Tool

Linux is often used in computer forensics for the following reasons;

(a) Greater control;
(b) Treats every device as a file;
(c) Does not need a separate write blocker;
(d) Power;
(e) Can be booted from a CD;
(f) Can recognize several file systems;
(g) Flexibility;
(h) Distributions such as The Farmer's Boot CD and Sleuth make Linux a forensic tool in and of itself.

Advantages of Linux in Forensics

There are several advantages of using Linux in forensic investigations, including the following;

(a) Software availability and accessibility;
(b) Freely available software and source code;
(c) Tools can be closely analyzed;
(d) Efficiency; (e) Allows for a good deal of automation and scripting;
(f) Optimization and customization;
(g) Software can be modified to fit special requirements;
(h) Support;
(i) Supports ad-hoc community;
(j) Uses open, published standards;
(k) Compatible across technologies and organizations.

Disadvantages of Linux in Forensics

There are, of course, disadvantages to using Linux in forensics. Since the Linux operating system is very different from Windows or Mac OS, the investigator may need to be specially trained to use Linux. Also, because Linux is an open-source operating system, it is frequently updated. It takes time to implement these changes, which are never to be considered permanent or final.

4.5 MACOS X SYSTEM

Apple Macintosh systems receive less attention than other systems as a source of digital evidence, probably because there are fewer of them and people are less familiar with them. However, these systems cannot be ignored as criminals use them and the user-friendly graphical user interface does not translate into a user-friendly digital examination. If anything, digital evidence examiners need to dedicate more attention to these systems. More of the newer, colorful, compact Macintosh desktop and laptop systems are being sold worldwide and the emergence of UNIX-based Mac OS X has attracted more technical users who appreciate the power of UNIX and the convenience of the Macintosh interface. Although some forensic examination of Macintosh systems can be performed using digital forensic tools, it is most effective to examine these systems using a specially configured Macintosh system with Macintosh native tools.

In order to set an application to start at system startup, a user needs to perform the following basic steps:

(a) Create a subdirectory under/Library/StartupItems. For example, if the user is setting up a startup item for MySQL, he or she might create the directory/Library/StartupItems/MySQL.

(b) Put a startup file in that subdirectory. It should have the same name as its parent folder, as in/Library/

StartupItems/MySQL/MySQL. For example, the user can look at the Mac OS X's startup item for

Apache,/System/Library/StartupItems/Apache/Apache.

(c) At a minimum, add a StartupParameters.plist file to that subdirectory. Again, see an existing startup item for a template.

(d) If the user used a control variable to determine whether the daemon starts at boot (Apache uses

WEBSERVER), the user must set that variable to -YES- or -NO- in/etc/hostconfig

4.5.1 OS X File System

As with other systems, Macintosh stores its partition table in the first sector on disk. The first sector of each volume contains the boot sector and additional details about the volume are stored in the third sector. The file system used by OS X is called *HFS Plus* or *Mac OS Extended*. HFS+ is the successor to the Hierarchical File System (HFS) used on pre-OS X Mac operating systems. There are currently two variant HFS+ formats used to support journaling (*HFSJ*) and case-sensitive file names (*HFSX*). Like FAT16 and FAT32, the Macintosh HFS and HFS Plus (HFS+) file systems use 16 and 32 bits, respectively, to address clusters on a disk. HFS supports a maximum of 216 (65536) clusters and HFS Plus has a maximum of 232 clusters. The main files comprising HFS are the Catalog and Extents Overflow files. The Catalog file is comparable to a master file table, containing records for each file and folder on the system with attributes such as date-time stamps. HFS represents time as the number of seconds since midnight, January 1, 1904, GMT. Records in the Catalog file are stored in a balanced tree (B-tree), which is a simple database that enables efficient searching. Each record in the Catalog file has a unique number called a catalog node ID (CNID). The Catalog file has four types of records: folders, files, folder threads, and file threads. Although the format of folder and file records varies between HFS and HFS Plus, they contain similar information. Folder records contain the following fields, in addition to some details used by the system.

Beyond these extended capabilities, because these variants do not change the function or artifacts available to the examiner, we will treat them all as "HFS+" throughout this chapter.

4.5.2 File Attributes

Macintosh operating systems can support file identification by both extension and type and creator codes. Forensic tools may not always display the type and creator codes, but they can be found in the Catalog tree alongside the other details about a file system object of interest.

4.5.3 Data versus Resource Forks

Macintosh file systems natively contain multiple "forks" for a file. By default, a data and resource fork are maintained. Since this is somewhat of a foreign concept to other file systems, the two forks are often displayed as two files by forensic examination tools. The forensic tools often provide some form of notation along with a resource fork to differentiate it and this fork often contains information that is much more difficult to understand on non-Macintosh systems.

4.5.4 File Deletion

Because of the nature of HFS, HFS+, and HFSX volumes, recovery of deleted file system details is particularly difficult. Unlike many Windows and Unix systems, recovery of deleted file system information on Macintosh systems is nearly impossible because nodes in the Catalog file are so frequently overwritten. This is largely due to the B-tree balancing process in the Catalog file, which obliterates previous file system details. Standard data carving techniques can be used to recover some file contents from Macintosh volumes, but only the data fork. This fork will retain what is a "typical" structure of media, document, application files with well-defined file formats, and header signatures that tools like Foremost rely on for carving. The real difficulty comes in further correlation; pairing the carved data for each fork would be very difficult, especially since a lot of the data in resource forks is undocumented. Additionally, tying specific files to a user can be very difficult when file system details are no longer available in a Catalog file record. Therefore, attributing a file to a particular user is often possible only through forensic examination of data contents.

4.5.5 HFS+ Structures

Hierarchical File System Plus (HFS+) was developed by Apple to substitute the HFS as a default Macintosh file system in 2000. HFS+ added some improvement over HFS supporting 32-bit length for block address and allocation mapping table, encoding the file and directory names using Unicode (UTF-16) and adding the concept of nforked. Furthermore, In Mac OS X 10.4 Apple added the Access Control List (ACL) functionality to the HFS+ file system. HFS+ has different elements such as volume header, catalog file, extend overflow, allocation file, and startup file. Focusing on forensics purpose, the most important element is the Catalog File, a B-tree structure that contains the metadata of all files and folders: times, user and group (HFSPlusBSDInfo), permission, file id, etc. Regarding to the timestamp, it contains four different timestamp: the last time when the metadata of the file was modified (modified time of crime), the last time when the file was acceded (atime or access time), the last time when the data of the file was modified (mtime or modified time) and finally the time when the file was created (crtime or created time). All the timestamp fields are an unsigned 32-bit integers (UInt32) value with the seconds since midnight, January first from 1904 in GMT time. Then, as an unsigned 32-bit integer, it can store timestamps until February 6, 2040 at 06:28:15 GMT. Also, the developers must be aware to convert the GMT value into local time during the application implementation. Each file and directory in the Catalog File contains attributes called DataFork and ResourceFork. Both of them are HFSPlusForkData type which contains two important attributes: logicalSize and totalBlocks. The logicalSize contains the bytes of the data assigned or reserved to the file (indeed the fork) whereas the totalBlocks contains the number of blocks allocated, used, by the file. Regarding to DataFork, it contains the location and the size of the reserve file to this file whereas ResourceFork contains relevant data and resource information. Moreover, each file in the catalog contains a HFSPlusExtentDescriptor structure that indicates the number of the first block (startBlock) and the number of blocks in that position (blockCount).

The volume header is one of the core structures of an HFS+ volume. It stores data about the file system, including the allocation blocks size, the volume creation time stamp, and the location of the special files required for HFS+ operation, discussed later in the chapter. The volume header is always located 1024 bytes from the start of the volume, with a backup copy located 1024 bytes before the end of the volume. HFS+ uses *allocation blocks* as data units. The size of a single allocation block is defined in the volume header, but 4K bytes is a common value. Allocation blocks can be further grouped into *clumps*, which are somewhat similar to the block allocation groups found in Ext file systems under Linux. A file's data are addressed in terms of *extents*. An HFS+ extent is simply a 4-byte pointer to a starting allocation block and a 4-byte value indicating the length of the extent. HFS+ files may have any number of data streams called *forks* associated with it. The two primary forks are the *data fork* and the *resource fork*. Generally, the data fork holds the actual file content, while the resource fork will be empty or contain nonessential supporting information about the file. Additional forks may be created for a file for application specific purposes. We can use the fsstat command from the Sleuth Kit to read information about the file system from the volume header. We will use the *nps-2009-hfsjtest1/img.gen1.dmg* file from the Digital Corpora as our test image while examining basic file system data.

```
FILE SYSTEM INFORMATION
--------------------------------------------
File System Type: HFS+
File System Version: HFS+
```

Volume Name: image
Volume Identifier: 9bee54da586b82f5
Last Mounted By: Mac OS X, Journaled
Volume Unmounted Properly
Mount Count: 11
Creation Date: Thu Jan 29 09:33:30 2009
Last Written Date: Thu Jan 29 09:33:42 2009
Last Backup Date: Wed Dec 31 16:00:00 1969
Last Checked Date: Thu Jan 29 09:33:30 2009
Journal Info Block: 2
METADATA INFORMATION

Range: 2–28
Bootable Folder ID: 0
Startup App ID: 0
Startup Open Folder ID: 0
Mac OS 8/9 Blessed System Folder ID: 0
Mac OS X Blessed System Folder ID: 0
Number of files: 7
Number of folders: 4
CONTENT INFORMATION

Block Range: 0–2559
Allocation Block Size: 4096
Number of Free Blocks: 443
Altheide & Carvey, 2011)

From this output, we can confirm the 4K allocation block size, some relevant time information associated with access to the volume, and a couple other pieces of OS X operating system-specific startup metadata that are not relevant on a nonsystem volume and are thus displayed as "0." These include the two Startup items and the "Blessed" System Folder lines. These would point to items in the/System/Library/

CoreServices directory on an OS X boot volume. Although the format of folder and file records varies between HFS and HFS Plus, they contain similar information. Folder records contain the following fields, in addition to some details used by the system.

Record type: 0x0100

Name: folder name

Valence: number of files and folders directly contained by this folder

CNID: unique catalog node ID

Creation date: when this folder was created

Modification date: when a file or folder was created or deleted inside this folder, or when a file or folder was moved in or out of this folder

Access date: when a file or folder was last accessed (not maintained by some version of Macintosh operating system)

Backup date: when this folder was last backed up

File records contain the following fields, in addition to some details used by the system.

Record type: 0x0200

Name: file name

CNID: unique catalog node ID

Creation date: when this file was created

Modification date: when a file modified by extending, truncating, or writing either of the forks

Access date: not maintained by HFS (always set to zero)

Backup date: when this file was last backed up

Data fork: information about the location and size of the data fork

Resource fork: information about the location and size of the resource fork

The attentive reader will notice that folder records do not contain lists of their contents, and files have two storage areas on disk also known as forks. HFS uses folder and file thread records in the Catalog file to link names with the associated file or folder records using the unique CNID. These file and folder thread records also contain references to parent folders that are used to construct the file system hierarchy and directory listings that most users are familiar with. Files on an HFS volume have two forks: a data fork that stores the contents of a file, and a resource fork with a special data structure for information such as icons and menu items. The first eight clusters of each fork (a.k.a. extents) are listed in each file's Catalog record. Any additional extents are stored in the Extents overflow file, which is also organized as a B-tree.

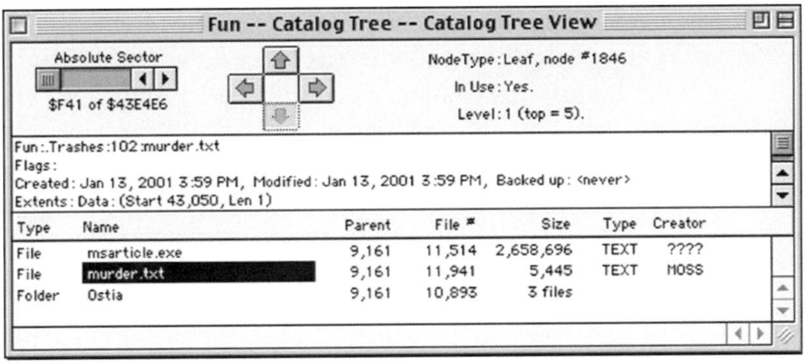

A

Figure 4.5: File record interpreted using Norton Disk Editor. *Source: Digital Evidence and Computer Crime (Casey, E.).*

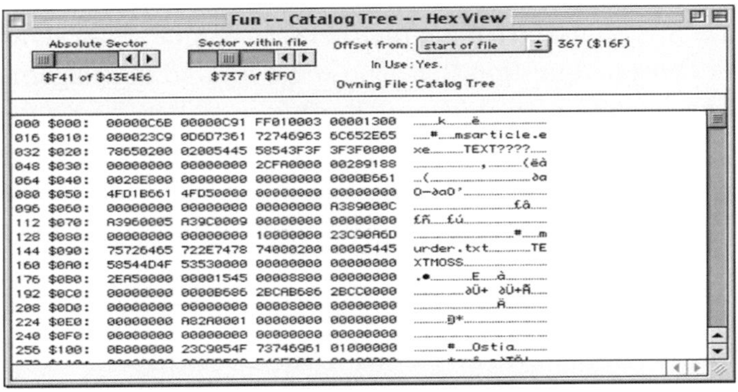

B

Figure 4.6: Same file record in hexadecimal form. *Source: Digital Evidence and Computer Crime (Casey, E.).*

4.5.6 Evidence Types

Mac OS X stores a group of important forensics evidence inside the file system. These evidences are stored using different types of formats. Some of them are well known such as ASCII plain text, XML or database files; whereas others are binary structures used only by Mac OS X. Binary files have a few or do not have the required documentation to understand how the information is stored. For this reason, a reversing engineering is required to try to understand how this information is saved. The first and easy approach to understand the format files is read the content of the file using a hexadecimal editor that can represent the information as a hexadecimal value, binary values or ASCII character representation. The approach done to analyze these evidences was applied in different steps. Some binary files have header and one or more entries, whereas other do not have header. The identification if the binary has header, when the header ends and when the entry starts must be done to identify which part of the file corresponds to the header and witch part the entry. Having this information, an analyze process must be done to try to recognize the information taking into account ASCII strings and the integer value from the hexadecimal combination between: nibble, byte, 2 bytes, 4 bytes and 8 bytes that can be saved in Little Endian or Big Endian that can represent values such as timestamp, length, UID, GID, PID, IP address, return values, etc.

4.6 DELETION AND DESTRUCTION OF DATA

Specific actions of users are often at the heart of a digital investigation. "When were they logged on? What Internet sites did they visit? Did they send any email?" But one question that is asked over and over again, it seems, is "did the user knowingly delete or destroy any data, particularly if that destruction was done to prevent investigators from obtaining benefit from it?" In many civil and criminal cases, users (and indeed, whole organizations) are placed under legal directives to make every effort to retain and protect from destruction the data deemed relevant to a current or future inquiry; when these types of directives are violated, it is called "spoliation" and can mean the difference between winning or losing a contested legal action. As such, digital investigators are often called upon to attempt to answer this important question, but (unfortunately) it is not always as easy a question to answer as it sounds.

4.6.1 Data Destruction

In the case of actual destruction of data (e.g., wiping), there are several techniques that can be used in attempts to verify that data was actually destroyed and (if so) who did the destroying. For example, data destruction tools sometimes leave behind distinguishable patterns; specific files and folders that have been wiped can have their names changed to something nonsensical and may show something a bit more obvious, such as aaaaaaaaaaaa.aaa or DELETED_DELETED_DELETED_DELETED. By locating non-deleted files of the same logical size, the digital investigator may even be able to find an unaltered copy of the wiped data. The same types of data patterns can be seen in large chunks in unallocated space as a result of some disk cleaning tools (although it can sometimes be difficult to distinguish massive\x00 patterns as wiping as opposed to pure unused disk space). Other tools, such as the Windows-native utility cipher.exe, wipe free space (by default) with seemingly random data. An investigator, first attempting to establish the presence of a data destruction utility and installed program locations, can perform keyword and hash searches against the evidence looking for hits on terms or files associated with known data destruction utilities, but this method can be a bit hit-or-miss.

4.6.2 Defragmentation

Another method of data destruction that can be encountered by investigators resulting from the execution of Windows (or third-party) cluster defragmentation tools. Defragmentation takes data structures that are spread across the disk (such as the $MFT or a 1.3 GB. AVI file with numerous file extents) and places them into contiguous clusters (if possible), thereby boosting system operation and enhancing the experience for the user. As the defragmentation process takes data from one location on the disk and writes it to another, the rewritten data often overwrites data in unallocated space that could have been identified by the digital investigator, thereby making it more difficult to recover deleted files and folders. Defragmentation on a Windows system generally occurs in one of three ways: (a) manual defragmentation by the user (b) user-scheduled defragmentation (c) Windows automatic (limited) defragmentation.

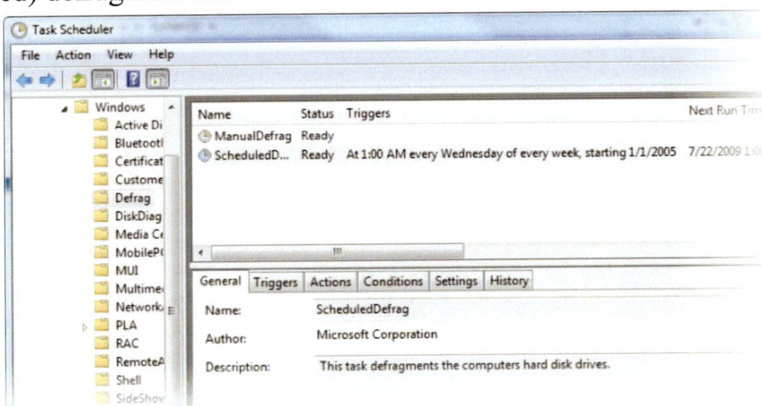

Figure 4.7: Task Scheduler.

Source: https://digital-forensics.sans.org/blog/2009/08/17/de-mystifying-defrag-identifying-when-the-windows-defragmenter-has-been-used-for-anti-forensics-part-2-vista

4.6.3 File Deletion

Evidence of file deletion (as opposed to destruction/wiping) by a particular user presents its own set of challenges, particularly since no specific program or utility is required to delete a file in Windows. Simply sending a file to the Recycle Bin (as covered in depth earlier in this chapter) is not (by the most common forensic definition) actual deletion of the file; however, a user sending a file to the Recycle Bin is often viewed as legally significant in a case where the user was supposed to be preserving or protecting data. Further, a file in the Recycle Bin is usually easy to identify and data provided by INFO2 records or $I files (Vista/7 Recycle Bin operation) can help the investigator pinpoint where the file was when it was deleted, as well as when the data was sent to the Bin and by which user account. Even if the Recycle Bin is empty, looking at the Last Written date-time stamp on the associated INFO2 record can provide the investigator with valuable data about the approximate time the Recycle Bin was cleared. Forensic examiners can often recover data and associated metadata for deleted files, even when Recycle Bin information is not available. In particular, when dealing with NTFS, a recovered MFT entry can provide all the information a forensic examiner needs about deleted data. In any case, it is paramount for an investigator to correlate and weigh each piece of evidence carefully before opening on the source of a file's deletion.

REFERENCES

1. Carvey. H. (2014). *Windows forensic analysis toolkit*. Burlington, MA: Syngress.
2. Carvey, H, & Altheide, C. (2011). *Digital forensics with open source tools*. Burlington, MA: Syngress, 2011.
3. Casey, E., Daywalt, C., Johnston, A., & Maguire, T. (2009). *Network investigations. Digital forensics and investigation*. Boston: Elsevier.
4. The role of operating systems in computer forensics. Retrieved March 17, 2018, from https://www.researchgate.net/publication/228748574_The_role_of_operating_systems_in_computer_forensics

CHAPTER 5

CLOUD COMPUTING AND DIGITAL FORENSICS

"The cloud services companies of all sizes...The cloud is for everyone. The cloud is a democracy."

—Marc Benioff, Founder, CEO and Chairman of Salesforce

CONTENTS

As cloud computing gains a firm foothold as an information technology (IT) business solution and data is being centralized in the cloud, criminal elements have made data centers and cloud providers a serious target. Conventional digital forensic methodologies are not completely suitable for cloud computing environments because of the application of virtualization technologies and remote storage. The task of portraying possible evidence is convoluted by dynamism of cloud environments and services such as infrastructure as a service (IaaS), Software as a service (SaaS), and Platform as a service (PaaS). This chapter explores the essence of cloud computing and its various models. Also, it suggests some methods by which cloud forensic investigations can be improved.

5.1 INTRODUCTION TO CLOUD PLATFORM

Cloud, in simple words, means providing scalable resources remotely to software using the Internet. It is a sub-network of a network providing access to remotely access the resources. However, the most dependable and universally recognized definition of cloud computing is provided by the National Institute of Standards and Technology (NIST), which states that cloud computing is a model for enabling ubiquitous, convenient, on-demand network access to a shared pool of configurable computing resources, for example, networks, servers, storage, applications, and services, that can be rapidly provisioned and released with minimal management effort or service provider interaction. Cloud forensics is a cross-discipline of cloud computing and digital forensics. Cloud computing is the sharing of resources (e.g., networks, servers, storage, applications, and services) via an organized networking that can be restructured with less effort. Cloud forensics is a subset of network forensics. Cloud computing is based on broad network access. Therefore, cloud forensics follows the main phases of network forensics with techniques tailored to cloud computing environments. The information on cloud is stored in a physical server connected to Internet where the subscribed devices can connect for the on-demand services. There are various clouds available on the Internet serving different purposes having their own finite boundaries. The Internet serves as a common medium for accessing a cloud resource for a particular system. Hence, it can be said that the Internet is a broad scale public resource cloud where there are various other private clouds hosted by different cloud owners serving a variety of purposes. The cloud resources are accessed using the Internet using any protocols used for accessing resources remotely. The aim of the cloud is to perform more work at a lower cost. Another name of cloud computing is on-demand service, that is, pay per use services. All the maintenance of the service is being carried out by the Cloud Service provider and hence, the end user or the consumer is provided with the maintenance-free services. One major difference between traditional forensics and cloud forensics is that in traditional forensics, law enforcement will check in and physically seize forensics artifacts such as hardware and logs in order to gain full control over it whereas everything is remote in cloud forensics. The table below shows a comparative analysis between the traditional and cloud forensics.

Table 5.1: Comparison of traditional vs. cloud forensics

Traditional forensics	**Cloud forensics**
Physical access to resources	Decentralized resources with no access
Ownership of resources and logs	CSP owns resources and logs
Resources and data segregated among users	Multi-tenancy
Established forensic tools	Limitation of available tools
Non-cloud environment	Dependence on cloud services
Data access and established	Multi-user access policies, various geographical legal standards

Source: https://www.semanticscholar.org/paper/Cloud-forensics-challenges-from-a-service-model-and-Freet-Agrawal/84b0ab3570270d37dec3ec2ce4adf7869cc6d5ed

5.2 TYPES OF CLOUD

Liu et al. classified cloud deployment models into four types (2011). This section comprehensively analyzes the types of existing cloud.

5.2.1 Public Cloud

A public cloud refers to a cloud service delivery model in which a service provider makes massively scalable IT resources, such as CPU and storage capacities, or software applications, available to the general public over the Internet. Public cloud services are typically offered on a usage-based model. Public cloud is the first deployment model of cloud services to enter the IT industry's vocabulary. The concept of public clouds has clearly demonstrated the long-term potential of the cloud computing model and lit up the imagination of the industry and the research community. There are many public cloud service providers in place today, offering various services. Amazon EC2, Force.com, and Google App Engine are among some of the best-known examples of public clouds, but the market now bristles with competition. The public cloud offers a clean, infrastructure-less model for end users to benefit from IT services, and intrigues the research community with its disruptive nature. However, migrating the majority of today's IT services, such as the various business applications in an enterprise environment to a public cloud model is not realistic. Data security, corporate governance, regulatory compliance, and performance and reliability concerns prohibit such IT applications to be moved out of the "controlled domains" (i.e., within the corporate firewalls) while the public cloud infrastructure, government regulation, and public acceptation continue to improve.

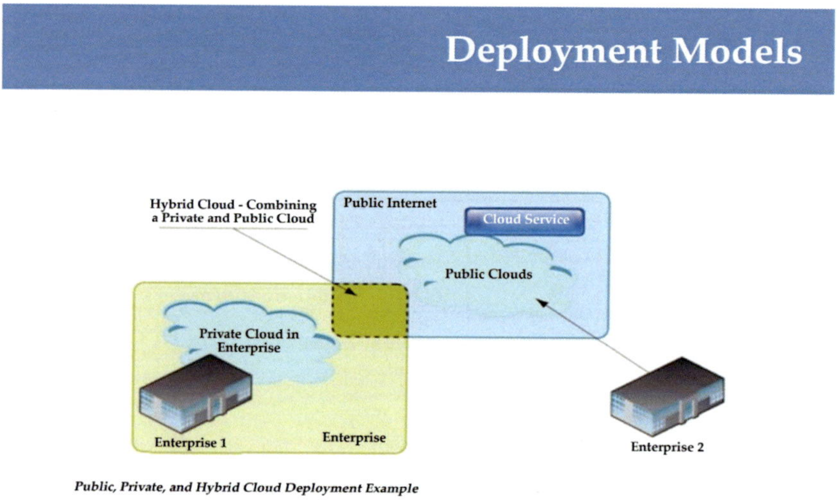

Figure 5.1: Cloud Deployment Models. *Source: http://slideplayer.com/slide/6258634/.*

5.2.2 Private Cloud

Private cloud, in contrast, represents a deployment model where enterprises (typically large corporations with multi-location presence) offer cloud services over the corporate network (can be a virtual private network) to its own internal users behind a firewall-protected environment. Recent advances in virtualization and data center consolidation have allowed corporate network and datacenter administrators to effectively become service providers that meet the needs of their customers within these corporations. Private clouds allow large corporations to benefit from the "resource pooling" concept associated with cloud computing and their very own size, yet in the meantime addressing the concerns on data security, corporate governance, government regulation, performance, and reliability issues associated with public clouds today. Critics of private clouds point out that these corporations "still have to buy, build, and manage clouds" and as such do not benefit from lower up-front capital costs and less hands-on management, essentially "lacking the economic model that makes cloud computing such an intriguing concept." While these criticisms are true from a conformist's perspective, private clouds are viable and necessary deployment model in the overall adoption of cloud computing as a new IT model. It is believed that without large corporations embracing it, cloud computing will never become the mainstream computing and IT model. Private cloud represents an enabling as well as a transitional step towards the broader adoption of IT services in public clouds. As the public cloud infrastructure, government regulation, and public acceptance continue to improve, more and more IT applications will be first offered as services in a private cloud environment and then migrated to the public cloud. The migration path of Email service in a corporation environment—from initially multiple departmental email servers to today's single corporate level email cloud to a public email cloud—offers an exemplary representation. While conformists might argue in black and white terms, we believe private cloud as a viable deployment model for cloud computing will exist for a long time and deserves the attention from both business and research communities.

5.2.3 Hybrid Cloud

Hybrid clouds are more complex than the other deployment models since they involve a composition of two or more clouds (private, community, or public). Each member remains a unique entity but is bound to others through standardized or proprietary technology that enables application and data portability among them. A hybrid cloud is a composition of at least one private cloud and at least one public cloud. A hybrid cloud is typically offered in one of two ways: a vendor has a private cloud and forms a partnership with a public cloud provider, or a public cloud provider forms a partnership with a vendor that provides private cloud platforms. Hybrid cloud infrastructure is a composition of two or more clouds that are unique entities, but at the same time are bound together by standardized or proprietary technology that enables data and application portability. In hybrid cloud, an organization provides and manages some resources in-house and some out-house. For example, organizations that have their human resource (HR) and customer relationship management (CRM) data in a public cloud like Saleforces.com but have confidential data in their own private cloud. Ideally, the hybrid approach allows a business to take advantage of the scalability and cost-effectiveness that a public cloud computing environment offers without exposing mission-critical applications and data to third-party vulnerabilities. This type of hybrid cloud is also referred to as hybrid IT. While public and private clouds represent the two ends of the cloud computing spectrum in terms of ownership and efficiency of shared resources—and each is finding acceptance in accordance to the services offered and customer segments targeted—a third deployment model of cloud computing, the hybrid cloud model that merges the characteristics of public and private clouds, is emerging. A hybrid cloud is a deployment model for cloud services where an organization provides cloud services and manages some supporting resources in-house and has others provided externally. For example, an organization might store customer data within its own data center and have a public cloud service, such as Amazon's EC2, to provide the computing power in an on-demand manner when data processing is needed. Another example is the concept of "public cloud as an overflow for private clouds" where an IT manager does not need to provision its enterprise private cloud for the worst case workload scenario but to leverage a public cloud for overflow capacities to move less-mission-critical workloads on and off-premise dynamically and transparently to accommodate business growth or seasonal peak load demands. One can find different variations of the "overflow" scenario, such as "follow-the-sun" operations in a global organization where workloads are moved around the globe based on the time zones of the working teams. Architecturally, a hybrid cloud can be considered a private cloud extending its boundary into a third-party cloud environment (e.g., a public cloud) to obtain additional resources in a secure and on-demand manner. Adoption of cloud services is a gradual process. Enterprise IT (which represents the majority of IT industry spending and service consumption) needs a migration path to move today's on-premise IT applications to the services offered by public cloud providers through a utility model. As such, the hybrid cloud represents a prevalent deployment model. Large enterprises often have substantial investments in the IT infrastructure required to provide resources in-house already. Meanwhile, organizations need to keep sensitive data under their own control to ensure security and compliance with government regulations. The tantalizing possibility offered by the hybrid cloud model—enterprise IT organizations managing an internal cloud that meshes seamlessly with a public cloud, which charges on a pay-as-you-go basis—embodies the promise of the amorphous term "cloud computing." To enable hybrid clouds, virtualization, seamless workload mobility, dynamic provisioning of cloud resources, and transparent user experience, are among the critical technical challenges to be resolved. **Advantages:** (a) Reduces capital expenses as part of the organization's infrastructure, needs are outsourced to public cloud providers. (b) Improves resource allocation for temporary projects at a vastly reduced cost because the use of public cloud removes the need for investments to carry out these projects. (c) Helps optimize the infrastructure spending during different stages of the application lifecycle. Public clouds can be tapped for development and testing while private clouds can be used for production. (d) More importantly, public clouds can be used to retire applications, which may be no longer needed because of the move to SaaS, at much lower costs than dedicated on-premise infrastructure. (e) Offers both the controls available in a private cloud deployment along with the ability to rapidly scale using public cloud. (f) Supplies support for cloud-bursting. (g) Provides drastic improvements in the overall organizational agility, because of the ability to leverage public clouds, leading to increased opportunities.

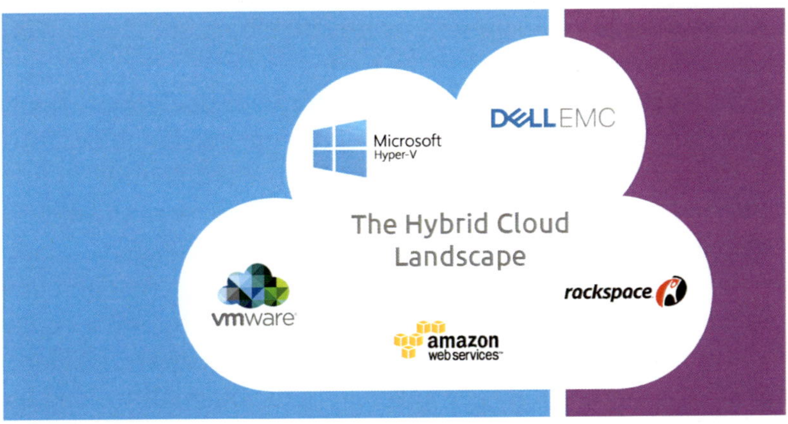

Figure 5.2: Hybrid Cloud Providers. *Source: https://www.loomsystems.com/blog/hybrid-cloud-providers-comparison-who-will-win-your-2018-it-budget.*

Drawbacks of hybrid cloud: (a) As a hybrid cloud extends the IT perimeter outside the organizational boundaries, it opens up a larger surface area for attacks with a section of the hybrid cloud infrastructure under the control of the service provider. (b) An easier approach to solving the identity, needs of hybrid clouds is to extend the existing enterprise identity and access management to the public clouds. This opens up concerns about how this approach will affect the enterprise identity and its impact on the organization's security. (c) When organizations manage complex hybrid cloud environments using a management tool, either as a part of the cloud platform or as a third-party tool, organizations should consider the security implications of using such a tool. For example, the management tool should be able to handle the identity and enforce security uniformly across hybrid cloud environments. (d) A hybrid cloud makes the data flow from a private environment to a public cloud much easier. There are privacy and integrity concerns associated with such data movement because the privacy controls in the public cloud environment vary significantly from the private cloud. (e) There are risks associated with the security policies spanning the hybrid cloud environment such as issues with how encryption keys are managed in a public cloud compared to a pure private cloud environment.

5.2.4 Community Cloud

In a community cloud, services are shared by organizations with similar data processing requirements and a common approach to privacy. A community cloud falls between public and private clouds with respect to the target set of consumers. It is somewhat similar to a private cloud, but the infrastructure and computational resources are exclusive to two or more organizations that have common privacy, security, and regulatory considerations, rather than a single organization. The community cloud aspires to combine distributed resource provision from grid computing, distributed control from digital ecosystems and sustainability from green computing, with the use cases of cloud computing, while making greater use of self-management advances from autonomic computing and essentially replacing vendor clouds by shaping the underutilized resources of user machines to form a community cloud, with nodes potentially fulfilling all roles, consumer, producer, and most importantly coordinator. The advantages of community cloud include: (a) Cost of setting up a communal cloud versus individual private cloud can be cheaper due to the division of costs among all participants. (b) Management of the community cloud can be outsourced to a cloud provider. The advantage here is that the provider would be an impartial third party that is bound by contract and that has no preference to any of the clients involved other than what is contractually mandated. (c) Tools residing in the community cloud can be used to leverage the information stored to serve consumers and the supply chain, such as return tracking and just-in-time production and distribution. Drawbacks of community cloud: (a) Costs higher than public cloud. (b) Fixed amount of bandwidth and data storage is shared among all community members. Information is accessible to all parties within the community and is distributed among them securely. Community clouds can be hosted on- or off-site and are managed by one or more of the participating organizations or by a third party provider. Costs are shared across the group, so those involved get some of the profits of a private cloud at a lower price. In this model, responsibility for control of the cloud can prove challenging. The concept of community cloud is still in its early stages, but picking up speedily among start-ups and small and medium term businesses.

Importance of Cloud Computing

Traditionally, organizations have their own network storage servers where all the data and related services provided reside. This incurs hefty costs in terms of expense as well as performance and efficiency. Taking an example of Google, where there are millions of requests at a time coming to the server. If the server is hosted locally then there would be a large amount of load on the server serving all the clients efficiently. People nowadays expect the response from the server to be as quick as possible and the expectation is not even in seconds but in milliseconds or even less. In order to fulfill such requests using a physical data store is difficult where the entire load in on the server hosted. Using cloud we can eliminate the need for physical equipment and entire server can be hosted on the web where we can have more throughout for the services and with reasonable cost and increased efficiency and minimal maintenance. Every organization can have their private/public cloud hosted on the Internet. Flexibility, lower cost, and fast performance are the factors contributing to the success of cloud computing.

5.3 SERVICE MODELS

Cloud service models describe how cloud services are made available to clients. Most fundamental service models include a combination of IaaS (infrastructure as a service), PaaS (platform as a service), and SaaS (software as a service). These service models may have synergies between each other and be interdependent—for example, PaaS is dependent on IaaS because application platforms require physical infrastructure.

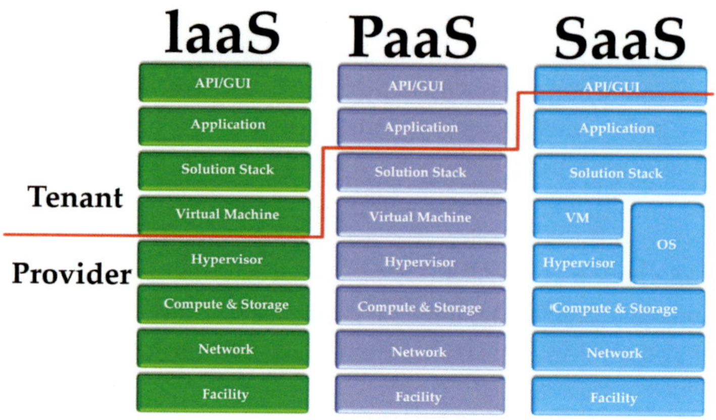

Figure 5.3: The delineation of responsibility within the cloud service models. *Source: https://pen-testing.sans.org/blog/2012/07/05/pen-testing-in-the-cloud.*

5.3.1 Software as a Service

Customers rent readymade applications running in the cloud service provider (CSP) premises: office productivity, customer relationship management, sales, business intelligence and many more. Access can be granted from a variety of client devices or by means of a program interface. Users are offloaded from any management task and are thus able to focus on their core business, but conversely there is little or no capacity to influence key features like the format in which information is stored, with possible issues of data transfer back at a later time. SaaS provides ready online software solutions. The SaaS software provider has complete control of application software. SaaS application examples include online mail, project-management systems, CRMs, and social media platforms. Salesforce is just an example of SaaS. Software as a Service Software-as-a-Service (SaaS) is based on licensing software use on demand, which is already installed and running on a cloud platform. These on-demand applications may have been developed and deployed on the PaaS or IaaS layer of a cloud platform. SaaS replaces traditional software usage with a Subscribe/Rent model, reducing the user's physical equipment deployment and management costs. The SaaS clouds may also allow users to compose existing services to meet their requirements. This section presents some SaaS clouds and applications.

Table 5.2: Service Models

Cloud Service Models	Description	Examples
SaaS Software as a Service	Applications that are deployed over a network, typically the web, accessible via browser or program interface; sometimes referred to as software on demand.	Facebook, Google Apps (email, calendar, documents), Sales-force.com, Twitter, ZenDesk, Zoho Office
PaaS Platform as a Service	A platform on which users can build applications using lan-guages, libraries, services and tools supported by the provider.	Force.com, Google App Engine, Red Hat OpenShift, Windows Azure
IaaS Infrastructure as a Service	Processing and storage capacity, networking and other computing resources where the user has control over operating systems and deployed applications; sometimes referred to as utility computing.	Amazon Web Services (EC2, S3, DynamoDB, others), GoGrid, ServePath, FlexiScale, Rackspace Mosso

The SaaS model incorporates a number of unique characteristics: (a) Although the consumer loses some level of control, the SaaS model shifts the burden of getting and keeping an enterprise application up and running from the consumer to the vendor. It permits users to leverage the software functionality without the burden of deploying and managing the software themselves. The applications are accessed through a web-based interface typically run from a web browser. This delivery mechanism allows for easy scalability as new users are added. (b) Generally, rather than licensing, installing and maintaining software on clients' computers or servers, the SaaS model lets users access the vendors software via the Internet on a pay-as-you-sell basis. (c) Each consumer can opt either to share access to the software with other consumers (multi-tenancy), thus enabling shared total costs and creating economies of scale, or decide to be a single tenant, thus providing greater control and security. (d) The SaaS model includes systematic support of the software, rather than annual maintenance and upload of fixes and patches, to all subscribers. (e) The SaaS model enables every consumer to benefit from the vendor's latest technological features without the disruptions and costs associated with software updates and upgrades. (f) The SaaS model eliminates the added costs and complexities of deploying additional hardware and software or dedicating additional staff resources to support an enterprise application on an ongoing basis. The traditional method of purchasing software requires the consumer to locally install an application on their computer and use licenses to authorize the usage. With SaaS, the consumer pays for the software on a subscription level and does not need to install any software on their computers. The software, application, is instead accessed via the Internet through a web browser. An example of this is Google Docs, a word processing application offered online.

5.3.2 Desktop as a Service

Desktop as a Service is a special variant of Software as a Service that provides a virtualized desktop-like personal workspace and sends its image to the user's real desktop. Instead of a local desktop, the user can access their own desktop-on-the cloud from different places for convenience, and receive the benefit of SaaS at same time. The "Global Hosted Operating SysTem" (G.ho.st) (2010) is a free and complete Internet-based Virtual Computer (VC) service suite including a personal desktop, files, and applications (G.ho.st, 2009). It offers users an operating system image simulated in a web browser using Flash and Javascript, which can be accessed through any browser. The G.ho.st application services are hosted by the Amazon Web Services (AWS) platform, so users can utilize EC2 and S3 resources through their G.ho.st desktops. One limitation of G.ho.st is, as a lightweight desktop service, it only supports online applications, and users cannot run legacy programs on it. Unlike G.ho.st's browser-based desktop image, the Desktone Virtual-D Platform (2010) implements a desktop as a service by encapsulating a virtual machine based desktop, called Virtual Desktop Infrastructure (VDI), into a service. The advantage of VDI is that it can offer the same environment as a native operating system, and allows users to install their own software. The Desktone Virtual-D Platform integrates all desktop virtualization layers and simplifies desktop management, improving security and compliance (The Desktone Virtual-D Platform—Fact Sheet, 2009). This solution delivers desktops as a cost-effective subscription service deployed on cloud.

(1) Google Apps

Google Apps (2010) is a simple SaaS implementation. It provides a variety of web applications with similar functions, such as traditional office programs (word processing, spreadsheets, etc.), but also allows users to interact, create, and work together easily and efficiently. Since all the apps are stored on the web and work through a web browser, users can access their accounts from any Internet connection and there is no need to install anything else locally. Google Apps has numerous components. The components of communication include Google Mail and Google Talk, which allow email, instant messaging, and voice calls. Office components include documents and spreadsheets being utilized by users to create online documents that facilitate search and collaboration. Google Calendar is an adjustable calendar app for structuring meetings and events. With "Web pages," Google's administrators can effortlessly publish web pages while "web pages" provide users with a wide range of content and applications that can be customized. Google Apps has many important features. First, it provides a flexible control panel which accelerates the most common administration tasks such as enabling/disabling applications, running accounts, and modifying interfaces. Second, although hosted on Google, the user can control the branding on all interfaces—email addresses will have only the user's domain name with no mention of Google in the message body (Wikipedia, Google App, 2010), and users can customize interfaces of their web, layouts, and colors on web and start pages. Third, administrators can incorporate existing platforms as well as extend the functionality of the core Google Apps applications with the Application Programming Interfaces (APIs) that are offered. There are APIs available for provisioning, reporting, and migration, as well as manipulating data in Calendar and Spreadsheets, and integrating with Single Sign-On (SSO) systems (Google Apps Products Overview, 2010).

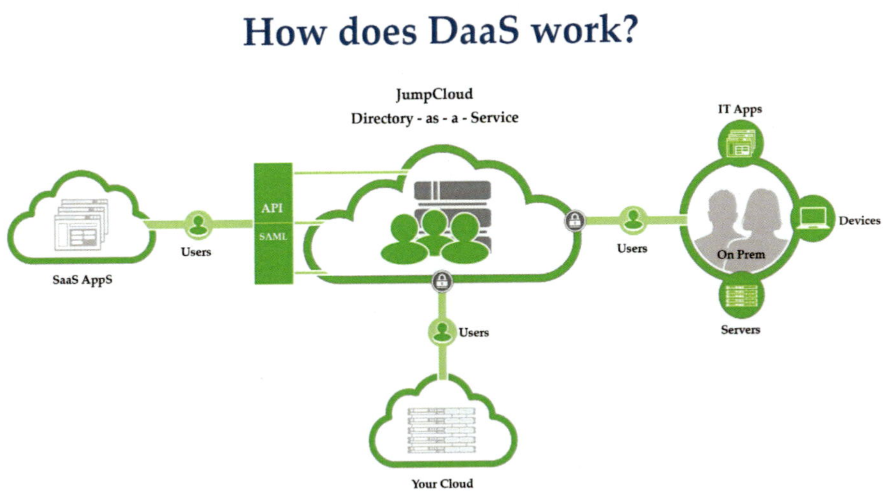

Figure 5.4: JumpCloud Interaction. *Source: https://jumpcloud.com/daas-glossary/the-benefits-of-moving-to-a-hosted-ldap-solution/*

(2) Salesforce

Salesforce (2010) is a business SaaS cloud platform that provides customizable applications, mostly Customer Relationship Management (CRM) services, to consumers. There are two major products presented by Salesforce. Sales Cloud is a group of comprehensive applications to improve the convenience and efficiency of business activities; and Service Cloud is provided to integrate social network applications like Facebook and Twitter, to construct a users' customer service community. Saleforce CRM services are deployed on the Force.com cloud platform, which operates a multi-tenancy oriented metadata-driven architecture (Force.com, 2009b). Multi-tenancy enables sharing the same version of an application among many users, but each user can only access their own private data, which keeps their activities isolated. All applications' functionalities and configurations are described with metadata, so users can customize applications as they want. Although the shared application model could cause interference between users, the Salesforce SaaS cloud has these advantages: (a) Service providers can develop only one version of application, and don't need to worry about heterogeneous execution environments; (b) The sharing of the physical computing resource, operating system and runtime environment lowers the cost of the application service; and (c) Service consumers are free to choose their preferred version of the application and customize it to fit their business.

5.3.3 Platform as a Service

It is the possibility for users to develop applications from scratch with high-level programming languages like Java or C# that leverage CSP's hardware resources by mean of an Application Programming Interface exposed by the provider (usually proprietary). There are still no management tasks that are not related to application maintenance. PaaS model delivers a pre-built application platform to the client; clients needn't spend time building underlying infrastructure for their applications. On the backend, PaaS automatically scales and provisions required infrastructure components depending on application requirements. Typically, PaaS solutions provide an API that includes a set of functions for programmatic platform management and solution development. Google AppEngine is a popular PaaS provider, and Amazon Web Services also provides some PaaS solutions in addition to IaaS offerings. Microsoft Azure and Google App Engine are an example of PaaS.

(1) Google App Engine

Google App Engine (GAE)'s main goal is to efficiently run users' web applications. It maintains Python and Java runtime environments on application servers, along with some simple APIs to access Google services. The front ends spread HTTP requests with load balancing and routing strategies based on the contents. Runtime systems running on application servers deal with the logic processing of applications and provide dynamic web content, while static pages are served by the shared Google infrastructure (Alon, 2009). To decouple the persistent data from application servers, GAE puts them into the Datastore instead of a local file system. Applications can integrate data services and other Google App Services, such as email, image storage and so on through APIs provided by the GAE. In addition to the services, Google also provides some tools for developers to help them build web applications easily on GAE. However, since they are tightly connected to the Google infrastructure, there are some restrictions that limit the functionality and portability of the applications.

(2) Microsoft Azure

Microsoft's cloud strategy is to construct a cloud platform that users can move their applications to in a seamless way, and ensure its managed resources are accessible to both cloud services and on-premises applications. To achieve this, Microsoft introduced the Windows Azure Platform (WAP), which is composed of a cloud operating system named Windows Azure, and a set of supporting services, as shown in the figure below. Windows Azure is the main part of the WAP. It employs virtual machines as its runtime environments. The applications in Microsoft's cloud offerings are divided into two types: Web role instances, which can serve web requests via the Internet information services (IIS); and Worker role instances, which can only receive messages from other Web role instances or on-premises applications (David, 2009a). Windows Azure employs a "fabric controller" to manage all virtual machines and storage servers on the physical machines in a Microsoft data center. Similar to the GAE's datastore, WAP also provides a database service called SQL Azure, to store data in the cloud. One feature of SQL Azure is that it provides a tool for data synchronization across on-premises and/or off-premises databases. Infrastructure services supported by WAP through. NET services currently include access control and exposing services. Both are available for cloud and on-premises applications.

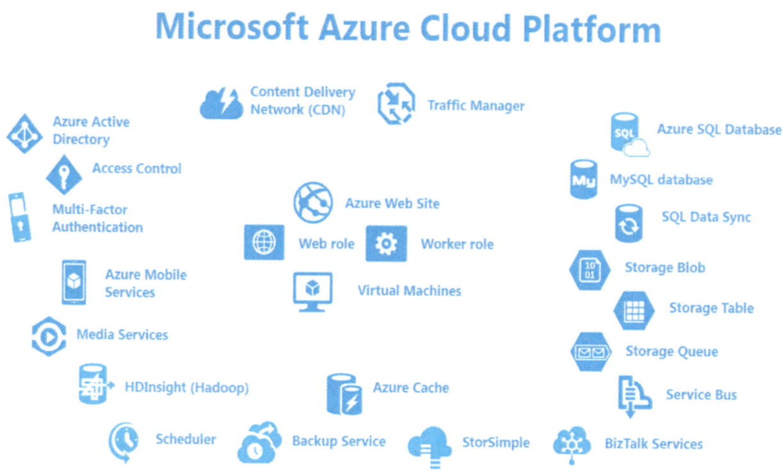

Figure 5.5: Windows Azure Cloud Services. *Source: http://oniwebblog.blogspot.com.ng/2016/01/windows-azure-cloud-computing-part-1.html*

Characteristics of PaaS

There are a number of different takes on what constitutes PaaS but some basic characteristics include; (a) Services to develop, test, deploy, host and maintain applications in the same integrated development environment. All the varying services needed to fulfill the application development process. (b) Web-based user interface creation tools help to create, modify, test and deploy different UI scenarios. (c) Multi-tenant architecture where multiple concurrent users utilize the same development application. (d) Built-in scalability of deployed software including load balancing and failover. (e) Integration with web services and databases via common standards. (f) Support for development team collaboration—some PaaS solutions include project planning and communication tools. (g) Tools to handle billing and subscription management.

5.3.4 Infrastructure as a Service

The Infrastructure as a Service (IaaS) providers supplies computing infrastructures such as virtual server space, bandwidth, network connections, IP addresses, and load balancers. With this service model, your enterprise is responsible for managing applications, data, operating systems, middleware, and runtime. Physically, your hardware resources are drawn from multiple servers and networks, typically in different data centers. In this way, the IaaS service model minimizes your hardware expenses while maximizing scalability. In addition to enterprise infrastructure, organizations use IaaS to host websites on virtual servers. When a website is subjected to unexpected demands, there is no single point of failure since cloud hosting uses a redundant network of physical servers. IaaS is also used with virtual data centers (VDC), virtualized networks of interconnected virtual servers within a public or private cloud. The physical security of each data center is the responsibility of the service provider, and your organization pays only for what it uses. IaaS model provides infrastructure components to clients. Components may include virtual machines, storage, networks, firewalls, load balancers, and so on. With IaaS, clients have direct access to the lowest-level software in the stack—that is, to the operating system on virtual machines, or to the management dashboard of a firewall or load balancer. Amazon Web Services is one of largest IaaS providers.

Characteristics of IaaS

As with the two previous sections, SaaS and PaaS, IaaS is a rapidly developing field. That said there are some core characteristics which describe what IaaS is. IaaS is generally accepted to comply with the following: (a) Resources are distributed as a service (b) Allows for dynamic scaling (c) Has a variable cost, utility pricing model (d) Generally includes multiple users on a single piece of hardware **Components of IaaS**

Infrastructure of cloud has multiple components which are used in infrastructure service model. They are the shared resources among the users, so they have multiple challenges for service providers. Some components are: (1) Service Level Agreements (2) Cloud Software (3) Platform Visualization (4) Network and Internet Connectivity (5) Computer Hardware

Figure 5.6: Examples of IaaS Providers. *Source: https://www.slideshare.net/ibahram1/cloud-computing-20829494*

(a) Service Level Agreements; Before deploying the service providing architecture of cloud computing, one of the desired concerns of the customers is the reliability and quality of the offered services. The expectations of these services changes from customer to customer so a consensus is needed between service provider and the customer. This agreement about the quality and reliability of service is called Service-Level Agreement. It aims at defining, describing and negotiating on terms and conditions of contract between service provider and customers to reach a final verdict. QoS attribute is also part of SLA and it needs to be defined properly. Quality of services (QoS) may include feature like response time, memory usage, throughput, etc. and they need to be monitored closely. It is very critical part because if any term or condition is skipped or not discussed, it will create problems for the users and service providers. SLA includes other features like services measurement, service condition evaluation, and management services appropriate cost for the usage. It also ensures that the scalability of infrastructure of cloud is managed properly. It allows the service provider to enhance the system without quitting the services, as the number of users is increased.

(b) Cloud Software; Cloud software is used to integrate different components of cloud infrastructure and make them synchronized. There are many open source software available in the market, that is, Eucalyptus and Nimbus, but they are not clear from bugs and vulnerabilities which can harm the cloud system. Furthermore, cloud service provider develops and use APIs (Application

Programming Interfaces), that is, SOAP, REST and HTTP with XML, for performing different functions, that is, access control, etc.

(c) Platform Virtualization; Virtualization is the basic task in cloud infrastructure because it provides multiple virtual systems on a single system so that multiple tasks are performed simultaneously. It reduces the hardware maintenance because it shared the hardware resources. In the described way it reduces the complexity and enhances the scalability of cloud resources.

(d) Network and Internet Connectivity; Cloud infrastructure is distributed on different locations to minimize the delay and damage of resources. These cloud infrastructure components are locally connected with LANs and then these components are connected with each other via high-speed Internet. These individual components construct the overall cloud infrastructure.

(e) Computer Hardware; An interface is provided by IaaS to its customers or users to access the distributed resources of cloud infrastructure. These resources are CPU, storage, and network connecting components. These cloud resources need a high-level security measure; as if they are vulnerable then the whole cloud is under threat. Any damage to of flaw in hardware will result in failure of services. Examples of IaaS are described below.

(1) Amazon Elastic Compute Cloud (EC2)

Amazon has provided a popular universal and comprehensive solution to cloud computing called the Amazon Elastic Compute Cloud (EC2). This solution was released as a limited public beta on August 25, 2006, but grew rapidly in the following years. After Amazon added many important and powerful features to EC2, it dropped the beta label on October 23, 2008. Today EC2 provides complete control over a customer's computing resources, so new server instances can be set up and booted in minutes, and their capacity can be scaled quickly through a simple web service interface. EC2 provides many useful features for customers, including a mature and inexpensive billing system able to charge for computing at a very fine-grained level (memory usage, CPU usage, data transfer, etc.), deployment between multiple locations, elastic IP addresses, connection to a customer's existing infrastructure through a Virtual Private Network, monitoring services by Amazon Cloud Watch, and elastic load balancing.

EC2 has deployed such fine granularity and precision that it has become a benchmark and model in cloud computing. Amazon's EC2 provides virtual machine based computation environments. It uses the Xen hypervisor (2010) to manage their Amazon Machine Image (AMI) instance. AMI is "an encrypted machine image that contains all information necessary to boot instances of your software" (Amazon EC2, 2010). Using simple web service interfaces, users can launch, run, monitor and terminate their instances. Moreover, they can, on-the-fly, add any of the abovementioned features to their configuration as they desire.

(2) GoGrid

GoGrid shares many common characteristics with Amazon in the classic cloud computing areas: supporting multiple operating systems through its own image management, and supporting load balancing, cloud storage, and so on. In addition, GoGrid provides customers with a user-friendly web service interface, comprehensible video demonstrations, and a strict but inexpensive billing system. Thus both EC2 and GoGrid provide basic and common features of cloud computing. The difference between the services they provide mainly derives from their respective business models. For example, GoGrid provides free cloud and persistent storage, slightly different from Amazon. GoGrid also provides Hybrid Hosting, which is a distinguishing feature. Many applications simply do not run well in a pure multitenant server environment. Databases perform better on a dedicated server where they do not have to compete for input/output resources, and the situation is similar with web server applications. GoGrid provides these special applications with dedicated servers that also have high-security assurance.

(3) Amazon Simple Storage Service (S3)

The Amazon Simple Storage Service (S3) is an online storage web service offered by Amazon Web Services. S3 is accessible to users through web services, REST-style HTTP interfaces or by involving a SOAP interface. Like other cloud computing services, users can request small or large amounts of storage on the fly, providing a highly scalable storage system. Amazon S3 organizes the storage space into many "buckets," with each bucket being given a globally unique namespace to help locate data addresses, identify the user account for payments, and gathering usage information (ASSSDG, 2010). S3 deals with all type of data as objects and stores them with their metadata into the bucket chosen by the data owner. An object can be accessed through a URL composed of its key and version ID with its bucket namespace as the prefix. Amazon S3's users are spread across countless fields, for example, SmugMug, Slideshare and Twitter use Amazon S3 to host images, Apache Hadoop uses S3 to store computation data, and online synchronization utilities such as Dropbox and Ubuntu One use S3 as their storage and transfer facility.

(4) Rackspace Cloud

Rackspace Cloud was initially launched on March 4, 2006 under the name "Mosso." In the following three years, it has changed his name from "Mosso LLC" to "Mosso: The Hosting Cloud," and then finally "Rackspace Cloud" on June 17, 2009. This company provides services including a cloud server, cloud files, and cloud site. The cloud files service is a cloud storage service providing unlimited online storage and a Content Delivery Network (CDN) for media on a utility computing basis. In addition to the online control panel, this company provides an API service that can be accessed over a RESTful API with open source client code. Rackspace solves the security problem by replicating three full copies of data across multiple computers in multiple zones, with every action protected by Secure Sockets Layer (SSL).

5.4 CHALLENGES TO THE ADOPTION OF CLOUD COMPUTING IN FORENSICS

Cloud computing, with its assets and limitations, can also be a tough environment for traditionally trained information security professionals to understand that the network has loopholes and that traditional forensics does not fit completely into a globally distributed cloud computing environment. This section identifies the most important issues pertaining to the cloud forensics.

5.4.1 Data Security

Data security is by far the most challenging barrier to cloud adoption. Data is the most precious corporate asset, and companies want to know that their data is safe. Companies feel confident when they store data internally because they have full control over it. Although there is no guaranty that data is better protected internally comparing to public cloud. In fact, there is a possibility that data could be even safer in the public cloud because public cloud providers may pose higher level of data security expertise comparing to their customers. When stored at public cloud, data can be compromised at several different data-lifecycle stages: during transfer from the internal company network to the public cloud, when data is stored in the public cloud, and during data backup and restore processes.

5.4.2 Loss of Control

Overall, there is a general loss of control over the forensic investigation process simply due to the data being stored elsewhere, where it is inaccessible. This, in turn, hinders crime scene reconstruction as the lack of knowledge of where data is actually stored means that it is difficult to piece together a sequence of events and create a timeline. Loss of control factors can be subdivided into two types: technical loss of control, and organizational loss of control. Organizational loss of control is instead related mostly to human factors that may create barriers for the transformation to cloud computing. These factors may include the fears of some individuals of losing influence in the organization, the fear of job loss if the cloud transformation will functionally affect specific positions, and the simple inability to embrace change. The fear of losing control is common and applies not only specifically to the cloud computing shift but also to many other organizational changes as well. Technical loss of control includes such factors as access control, software versions and updates, and control over the timing of technical operations such as data backups and restores, and is partially related to the data security issues discussed above. To address technical loss of control challenges, a cloud provider should offer company tools that provide full visibility into all cloud operations related to the company's assets.

5.4.3 Service-Level Agreements

A service-level agreement (SLA) is a contractual document between a cloud service provider and a cloud customer that defines the terms of use of cloud resources. Most current service level agreements do not incorporate provisions regarding forensic investigations and the recovery of evidence from cloud environments. Some provisions regarding the forensic retrieval of evidence from a cloud environment should be incorporated in the agreements. These include data access during forensic investigations and stipulations regarding investigations in multi-jurisdictional and multi-tenant environments, including legal regulations, confidentiality, and privacy. At this time, the terms of service are typically prescribed by the cloud provider and are generally non-negotiable. The customer thus has little or no voice regarding the data that the cloud service provider may and may not divulge. Ultimately, the onus is on the customer to negotiate a suitable service level agreement with the provider that addresses evidence retrieval from cloud environments as well as thorny issues such as multiple jurisdictions, data ownership and the establishment of a chain of custody.

5.4.4 Performance

Most cloud provider SLA agreements cover only infrastructure availability, not performance. If company applications have specific performance-related requirements, the company should discuss these requirements with cloud providers and confirm that these requirements can be supported. It is a good idea to include these requirements in an SLA contract, and it is standard practice to negotiate the SLA contact with the cloud service provider. It is the responsibility of the cloud customer to monitor cloud performance and ensure that it is compliant with requirements and SLAs. Also, collected performance metrics should be repeatedly analyzed. If cloud-hosted applications are used globally, it is important to monitor performance parameters such as network latency across all major customer locations.

5.4.5 Cost Uncertainty

There are hundreds of different cloud offerings on the market, and their pricing models vary considerably. This creates uncertainty and makes it difficult to estimate the real financial benefits of cloud computing. This uncertainty is particularly troublesome for non-technical people within organizations, who could be confused and scared away by the complexity of pricing models. Pricing differences across cloud providers may include charges for data storage, CPU, memory, IP address, domain name service, and load balancing, among others. There is no single standard for cloud services pricing, and it can be complicated to compare prices between providers. It is also difficult to predict future prices with specific provider—and, once company is locked in with one cloud provider, it is not easy to move an entire infrastructure to other clouds.

5.4.6 Data Portability/Integration

It can be technically difficult to integrate data in a company's internal data center with data located in a public off-premises cloud. Organizations that consider using a hybrid cloud where data is spread across both private and public clouds may face data integration problems: (a) Security issues (data governance, network connectivity, etc.) (b) Problems with transaction integrity (inability to support transactions across clouds) (c) Difficulties handling large data volumes (d) Lack of mechanisms to detect changes to data (e) Data quality control issues (f) Problems determining the origins of data (g) Lock-In Challenges Each cloud provider offers a unique set of services and tools for operating and controlling its cloud. Learning a new cloud environment is similar to learning a new technology: it takes time and effort to master. This can be easier with IaaS based cloud services, to which companies can install their own software on a provided infrastructure platform, but with PaaS or SaaS cloud platform, customers must learn the provider's specific interfaces and APIs in order to interact and manage these platforms. There are no uniform cloud management software standards across different providers, and once a company invests time and resources to establish operations on one cloud platform, it can be difficult to switch. It is not recommended that a company become locked-in with a specific cloud provider, because this dependence may limit control over costs and technical cloud hosting options. It is not uncommon for cloud providers to raise service prices or alter their technology offerings.

5.4.7 Legal issues

The final problem stems from the legal/people aspect of computer forensics in that whatever digital evidence is acquired from an investigation it must still be presented to a jury, who will pass judgment on a case. In conventional computer forensics investigators have to present their findings to the jury and this often requires that the investigator needs to explain, using technical jargon, how the evidence was acquired and what exactly the evidence means. This can prove challenging when dealing with conventional localized computer systems, let alone cloud data centers which may be several thousand miles away, running 40,000 VMs across 512 servers accessed by 1000 tenants of which the accessed is one. This may prove far too much for a jury member to comprehend, given that on average the jury will only have a basic grasp of using a home PC.

REFERENCES

1. Foster, I., Zhao, Y., Raicu, I., & Lu, S. (2008). *Cloud computing and grid computing 360-degree compared* (pp. 1-10). Grid Computing Environments Workshop, GCE'08.
2. Gorelik, E. (2013). *Cloud computing models*. Cambridge, MA: Massachusetts Institute of Technology.
3. Ruan, K., Carthy, J., Kechadi, T., & Crosbie, M. (2011). Cloud forensics. In G. Peterson, & S. Shenoi (Eds.), *Advances in Digital Forensics VII* (pp. 35-46). Berlin, Heidelberg: Springer.

CHAPTER 6

MOBILE DEVICE FORENSICS

"Certainly going back to Sherlock Holmes we have a tradition of forensic science featured in detective stories."

—Jeffery Deaver

CONTENTS

All but the most basic phones provide individuals with some ability to load additional applications, store and process personal and sensitive information independently of a desktop or notebook computer, and optionally synchronize the results ata later time. As digital technology evolves, the capabilities of these devices continue to improve rapidly. When cell phones or other cellular devices are involved in a crime or other incident, forensic examiners require tools that allow the proper retrieval and speedy examination of information present on the device. This chapter gives an overview of the current forensic software, designed for acquisition, examination, and reporting of data discovered on cellular handheld devices, and an understanding of their capabilities and limitations.

6.1 INTRODUCTION

Mobile devices are becoming an integral part of our lives that describe every aspect of our daily life. With the continued development of mobile devices, including smartphones and tablets, we can store a lot of information. The mobile forensics is just a method of collecting evidence from a digital data trace, which is often difficult to delete, which can be used in the law court. With the evolving data setting, traces of digital data are easily left on these devices. Mobile devices are generally defined as devices that can connect and operate on mobile networks, including mobile phones, wireless modems, and pagers. A core network of similar components, network service providers will retain usage logs and billing records and investigators can intercept network traffic from mobile devices. As a result, it is necessary for investigators to understand the principal technologies behind networks, types of databases that may exist in the mobile network, and how to collect and analyze the sources of digital evidence. The types of mobile forensics media include telephone calls, digital photos, text messages for mobile phones or email, phone numbers, GPS locations, websites, and sometimes digital video recordings on mobile phones. When evidence is collected for legal purposes, they may be retained and maintained to prevent cancelation or damage to the significant digital material. More often, mobile device forensics is applied to digital data retrieval of deleted communications. They can help legal groups or police cops to create and prove legal evidence. The basic principle of a sound forensic investigation of digital evidence is that the original evidence should not be altered. This is particularly difficult for mobile devices. Some forensic tools require mobile communication; this standard *write* protection will not work during the process of forensic acquisition. Other forensic acquisition methods may involve removing a chip or installing a bootloader on the mobile device before extracting data for forensic examination. In the event that the examination or data collection is not possible without modifying the configuration of the device, the processes, and the changes must be tested, authenticated, and recorded. Following proper methodology and guidelines are important when inspecting mobile device because it provides the most treasured data. As with any acquisition of evidence, if proper procedure is not followed during the examination, it can lead to loss or damage to the evidence or cause it to be inadmissible in court.

Figure 6.1: Advanced Mobile Forensics Station. *Source: http://www.ftforensics.com/cell-phone-forensics.html*

6.2 SUBSCRIBER IDENTITY MODULE

A SIM is removable card designed for insertion into a device, such as a handset. SIMs originated with a set of specifications originally developed by the Conference of European Posts and Telecommunications and continued by the European Telecommunications Standards Institute for the GSM networks. One useful way to classify cellular devices is by whether they use a SIM. The GSM standards mandate the use of a SIM for the operation of the phone. Without it, a GSM phone cannot operate. In contrast, contemporary Code Division Multiple Access (CDMA) phones do not require a SIM. Instead, SIM functionality is incorporated directly within the device. A SIM is an essential component of a GSM cell phone that contains information particular to the user. A SIM is a special type of smart card that typically contains between 16 and 64 KB of memory, a processor, and an operating system. A SIM uniquely identifies the subscriber, determines the phone's number, and contains the algorithms needed to authenticate a subscriber to a network. A user can remove the SIM from one phone, insert it into another compatible phone, and resume use without the need to involve the network operator. The hierarchically organized file system of a SIM is used to store names and phone numbers, received and sent text messages, and network configuration information. Depending on the phone, some of this information may also coexist in the memory of the phone or reside entirely in the memory of the phone instead of the SIM. While SIMs are most widely used in GSM systems, compatible modules are also used in iDEN phones and UMTS user equipment (i.e., a USIM). Because of the flexibility, SIM offers GSM phone users to port their identity and information between devices, eventually, all cellular phones are expected to include SIM capability. Though two sizes of SIMs have been standardized, only the smaller size shown at left is broadly used in GSM phones today. The module has a width of 25 mm, a height of 15 mm, and a thickness of 0.76 mm, which is roughly the size of a postage stamp. Its eight-pin connectors are not aligned along a bottom edge as might be expected, but instead form a circular contact pad integral to the smart card chip, which is embedded in a plastic frame. Also, the slot for the SIM card is normally not accessible from the exterior of the phone as with a memory card. When a SIM is inserted into a phone and pin contact is made, a serial interface is used to communicate with the computing platform using a half-duplex protocol. SIMs can be removed from a phone and read using a specialized SIM card reader and software. A SIM can also be placed in a standard-size smart card adapter and read using a conventional smart card reader. As with any smart card, its contents are protected and a PIN can be set to restrict access. Two PINs exist, sometimes called PIN1 and PIN2 or CHV1 and CHV2. These PINs can be modified or disabled by the user. The SIM allows only a preset number of attempts, usually three, to enter the correct PIN before further attempts are blocked. Entering the correct PIN unblocking key (PUK) resets the PIN number and the attempt counter. The PUK can be obtained from the service provider or the network operator based on the SIM's identity, for instance, its Integrated Circuit Card Identification (ICCID). If the number of attempts to enter the PUK correctly exceeds a set limit, normally 10 attempts, the card becomes blocked permanently. Besides other personal information, the SIM card also holds information about where the subscriber last registered the system, charge information, and the services enabled on the device. The table below gives a comparison of standard features on three levels of mobile phone devices: basic, advanced, and smart. The type of mobile phone will affect what type of evidence will need to be retrieved and analyzed.

Table 6.1: Software Characterization

	Basic	Advanced	Smart
OS	Proprietary	Proprietary	Linux, Windows Mobile, RIM OS, Palm OS, Symbian
PIM	Simple phonebook	Phonebook and calendar	Reminder list, enhanced Phonebook and calendar
Applications	None	MP3 player	MP3 player, office document viewing
Messaging	Text messaging	Text with simple embedded images and sounds (enhanced text)	Text, enhanced text, full multimedia messaging
Chat	None	SMS chat	Instant messaging
Email	None	Via network operator's service gateway	Via POP or IMAP server
Web	None	Via WAP gateway	Direct HTTP
Wireless	IrDA	IrDA, Bluetooth	IrDA, Bluetooth, Wi-Fi

Source: http://www.ccsc.org/southcentral/E-Journal/2009/Papers/AllynStottFinalVersion.pdf

Figure 6.2: Close up of a SIM card for mobile phones. *Source: http://www.alamy.com/stock-photo-close-up-of-a-sim-card-subscriber-identity-module-card-for-mobile-78998374.html*

6.3 FORENSIC SOFTWARE TOOL KITS

Features of professional forensic tools vary greatly depending on what aspect of forensic analysis they target and what market they are aimed at. There are large digital forensics frameworks and software solutions, alongside countless smaller utilities. The former group includes Digital Forensics Framework, Open Computer Forensics Architecture, Computer-Aided Investigative Environment, X-Ways Forensics, SANS Investigative Forensics Toolkit, EnCase, Sleuth Kit, and so on. However, many professional forensic specialists prefer to build their own customized toolboxes from individual tools and utilities that exactly fit their needs and preferences. This section describes some of the common forensics tools used by investigators.

6.3.1 Personal Digital Assistants Seizure

Paraben's PDA Seizure version 3.0.3.89 is a forensic software toolkit that allows forensic examiners to acquire, search, examine, and report data associated with personal digital assistants (PDAs) running Palm OS, Windows CE, and RIM OS. Though able to be used with smartphones running these operating systems, the toolkit is oriented toward non-cellular devices and omits cell phone-oriented features, such as SIM acquisition for GSM phones. PDA Seizure's features include the ability to perform a logical and physical acquisition, providing a view of internal memory and relevant information concerning individual files and databases. PDA Seizure uses the MD5 hash function to protect the integrity of acquired files. Additional features include bookmarking of information to be filtered and organized in a report format, searching for text strings within the acquired data, and automatic assembly found images under a single facility.

Pilot-link is an open source software suite originally developed for the Linux community to allow information to be transferred between Linux hosts and Palm OS devices. It runs on several other desktop operating systems besides Linux, including Windows and Mac OS. About 30-command line programs comprise the software suite. To perform a physical and logical dump, pilot-link establishes a connection to the device with the aid of the HotSync protocol. The two programs of interest to forensic examiners are pi-getram and pi-getrom, which, respectively, retrieve the physical contents of RAM and ROM from a device. Another useful program is pilot-xfer, which allows the installation of programs and the backup and restoration of databases. pilot-xfer provides a means to acquire the contents of a device logically. The contents retrieved with these utilities can be manually examined with either the Palm OS Emulator, a compatible forensics tool such as EnCase, or a hex editor. Pilot-link does not provide hash values of the information acquired. A separate step must be carried out to obtain needed hash values.

6.3.2 Cell Seizure

Paraben's Cell Seizure version 2.0.0.33660 is a forensic software toolkit that allows forensic examiners to acquire, search, examine, and report data associated with cell phones operating over CDMA, Time Division Multiple Access (TDMA), and GSM networks. To acquire data from cell phones using Paraben's Cell Seizure software, the proper cable must be selected from either the Cell Seizure Toolbox or a compatible cable (e.g., DataPilot) to establish a data-link between the phone and the forensic workstation. The type of phone being acquired determines the cable interface. Serial RS-232 and USB data-link connections are established via the phone data port or the under-battery interface connection. Additional features include bookmarking of information to be filtered and organized in a format report, searching for case-sensitive whole word text and hexadecimal values, and automatic assembly of found images under a single facility. The following data can usually be found on most cell phones with the tool; (a) SMS history: inbox/outbox (b) Phonebook: SIM-Card, own numbers, speed dialing, fixed dialing (c) Call logs: dialed numbers, received calls, missed calls (d) Calendar: reminder, meeting, memo (e) Logos: caller logos, startup logos, welcome notes (f) Graphics: wallpaper, picture camera images, EMS template images (g) WAP: WAP settings, WAP b(h) SIM: GSM specific data.

6.3.3 Oxygen Phone Manager

The forensic version of Oxygen Phone Manager (OPM) is available for police departments, law enforcement units, and all government services that wish to use the software for investigation purposes. The forensic version differs from the non-forensic version of OPM by prohibiting any changes in data during acquisition. OPM allows examiners to acquire data from the device and export the acquired data into multiple supported formats. The Oxygen software is tailored toward mobile phones and smartphones manufactured by Nokia, Sony Ericsson, Siemens, Panasonic, Sendo, BenQ and some Samsung models. Oxygen software provides software libraries, ActiveX libraries and components for Borland Delphi to software developers.

6.3.4 GSM.XRY

Micro Systemation's SoftGSM: XRY is a forensic software toolkit for acquiring data from GSM, CDMA, 3G phones and SIM/USIM cards. The XRY unit is able to connect to cell phone devices via infrared (IR) port, Bluetooth, or a cable interface. After establishing connectivity, the phone model is identified with a corresponding picture of the phone, the device name, manufacturer, model, serial number (IMEI), subscriber ID (Mobile Subscriber Identity [IMSI]), manufacturer code, device clock, and the PC clock. Data acquired from cell phone devices are stored in the. XRY format and cannot be altered but can be exported into external formats and viewed with third-party applications. After a successful acquisition, the following fields may be populated with data, depending on the phone's functionality: summary screen, case data, general information, contacts, calls, calendar, SMS, pictures, audio, files, notes, tasks, MMS, network information, video, and so on. Additionally, graphic files, audio files, and internal files present on the phone can be viewed internally or exported to the forensic workstation for safekeeping or further investigation.

Figure 6.3: XRY Software application. *Source: http://www.alzomar.com/products.asp? ID=32&Page=Digital%20Investigation*

6.3.5 Forensic SIM

Radio Tactic's Forensic SIM Toolkit consists of the following components: acquisition terminal, control card, data storage cards, analysis application, and the card reader. The acquisition terminal is a stand-alone unit that guides the examiner through each step of the acquisition process. The Forensic SIM toolkit deals with two processes: acquisition of data and analysis of data. Data acquisition is carried out using the acquisition terminal. Data analysis is carried out using the Forensic SIM card reader, attached to a PC running the Forensic SIM analysis application. The terminal's primary function is to capture copies of the data from the target SIM to a set of data storage cards. A control card is used to provide the examiner access to the acquisition terminal, thwarting unauthorized use. The data storage cards consist of a master data storage card, a prosecution data storage card, a defense data storage card, and a handset access card. The toolkit allows examiners read-only access to SIMs and generates textual reports based on the contents acquired. Reports can be viewed internally, saved to disk, or printed for presentation purposes.

6.3.6 Forensic Card Reader

The Forensic Card Reader (FCR) consists of a smart card reader with USB connection and the FCR software that gives examiners the ability to acquire data from SIM cards without modification. The examiner has the ability to select specific data elements that can be later stored and displayed in a finalized report. Operations details like case number, evidence number, and examiner can be automatically merged into the report and its file name. All usual data elements are acquired (e.g., phone directory, abbreviated dialing numbers, fixed dialing numbers, and SMS messages), as well as the identifiers of the SIM and the subscriber. Special elements such as deleted SMS messages can also be acquired. The FCR stores a complete report in an XML format. SIM cards for GSM mobiles and also SIM cards for 3G mobiles can be used with the FCR. Extended phone book entries can be acquired, including additional numbers and email addresses. The supplied FCR reader allows examiners to use either small or large SIM cards without the need for an adapter.

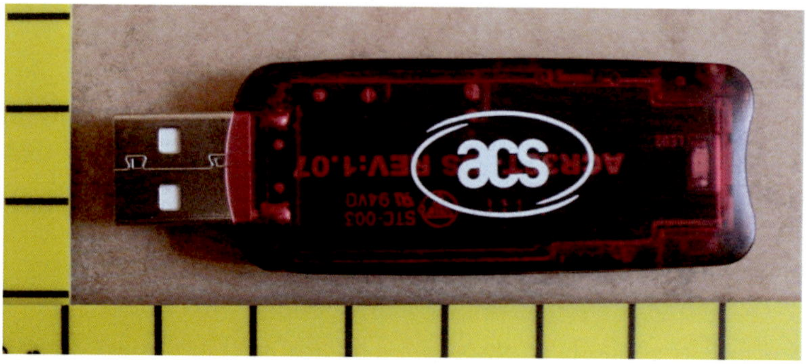

Figure 6.4: A SIM card reader.

Source: https://www.digitalforensics.com/blog/sim-cards-forensic-analysis-with-oxygen-software/

6.3.7 MOBILedit!

MOBILedit! Forensic is an application giving examiners the ability to acquire logically, search, examine and report data from GSM/CDMA/PCS cell phone devices. MOBILedit! is able to connect to cell phone devices via an IR port, a Bluetooth link, or a cable interface. After connectivity has been established, the phone model is identified by its manufacturer, model number, and serial number International Mobile Equipment Identifier (IMEI) and with a corresponding picture of the phone. Data acquired from cell phone devices are stored in themed file format. After a successful acquisition, the following fields are populated with data: subscriber information, device specifics, phonebook, SIM phonebook, missed calls, last numbers dialed, received calls, inbox, sent items, drafts, files folder. Items present in the files folder, ranging from graphics files to camera photos and tones, depend on the phone's capabilities. Additional features include the myPhoneSafe.com service, which provides access to the IMEI database to register and check for stolen phones.

6.3.8 TULP 2G

TULP2G (2nd generation) is an open source, forensic software tool originated by the Netherlands Forensic Institute that allows examiners to extract and read data from mobile cell phones and SIMs. TULP2G requires a forensic workstation running either Windows 2000 or XP, preferably with the latest patches and service pack installed, along with. NET 1.1 SP1. In order to take advantage of recently released 1.1 plug-ins, Windows XP SP2 is required. TULP2G acquires data from mobile phones using a proper data cable, Bluetooth or IrDA connection and a compatible protocol plug-in. Reading SIMs requires a PC/SC-compatible smart card reader and possibly an adapter to convert a small-sized SIM to the standard-size smart card format.

6.3.9 BitPIM

BitPIM is a phone program that runs on Windows, Linux, and Mac OS and allows the viewing and management of data on mobile phones. This data includes the phone book, calendar, wallpapers, ringtones, and the embedded file system. To acquire data successfully using BitPIM, examiners must have the proper driver and cable to form a connection between the phone and the forensic workstation. BitPIM provides detailed information contained in the help file, outlining supported phones, suggested cables to use with specific phone models, and notes and technical know-how about specific situations. BitPIM is distributed as open source software under the GNU General Public License.

6.4 DATA STORAGE

A mobile phone contains diverse set of information and a smartphone contains more than simply email or files. A mobile device can contain videos, web browsing, location, and social networks. All of these components are used in Mobile Forensics to uncover useful evidence.

6.4.1 Data Stored in Mobile Phones

The following contents of modern mobile phones can have value as evidence: IMEI, short dial numbers, text messages, settings (language, date/time, tone/volume, etc.), stored audio recordings, stored computer files, Logged incoming calls and dialed numbers, stored executable programs, stored calendar events, GPRS, WAP, and Internet settings. Most of this information is available through cable and manufacturer specific software.

However, direct analysis of the memory could potentially reveal other hidden information, such as deleted text messages. Such analysis has to the authors knowledge not yet been performed

6.4.2 Data Stored in SIM Cards

The SIM card, used in GSM phones, is a smart card which enables connection to GSM networks and enables the subscriber to be uniquely identified in the network. The SIM card contains a number of files, which contain the user's subscriber information, and personal information, such as (a) The IMSI, which is the SIM card's globally unique identifier. (b) Language preferences and network (service provider) information. (c) Currency information, such as call charge counters. (d) Information about the current (or most recent) location of the mobile phone. (e) Phonebook entries. (f) Sent and received SMS messages. (g) Recently dialed numbers. Many of the features available on a SIM card are optional, and therefore may not be implemented by every handset or service provider (ETSI 2004a).

6.4.3 Data Stored in Phone Memory

In addition to the SIM memory, memory is available within the phone to store phone software and additional data. This space can be used to extend the SIM memory, to store additional phone book data, call logs and so forth. The following are some examples of the additional information which may be found in a phone's memory: (a) Phone settings (b) Calendar information (c) SMS/MMS messages (d) Call log entries (e) Time and date (f) Ringtones (g) Data required for/produced by the phone's extra features, such as audio and video recordings, and images. (h) Generic data stored in the phone's memory. (i) Application executables (Willassen 2005, ETSI 2004b). Many modern phones come with a relatively large amount of onboard memory. For example, the Nokia 9300 has 80MB onboard memory, with the option to extend it with a removable memory card (Nokia 2005b). These removable cards are generally used to store multi-media files, such as audio, video, images, and MMS messages, and are not used for phone-related information (phonebook entries, etc.) (Willassen, 2005). However, the cards can be used for transfer and storage of any form of data. OBEX capable phones will typically allow the user to store any form of data in the phone's memory.

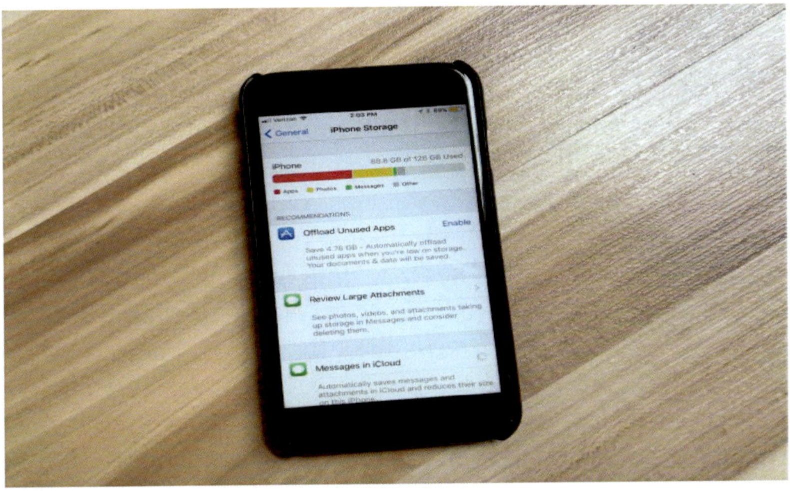

Figure 6.5: iPhone Storage. *Source: https://techcrunch.com/2017/06/06/ios-11-will-help-you-free-up-storage-on-your-iphone-through-personalized-suggestions/*

6.4.4 Data Stored by the Service Provider

Data retained by the service provider includes subscriber database. The database usually contains the following information about each customer such as customer name and address, billing name and address (if other than customer), username and address (if other than customer), billing account details, telephone number (Mobile Station International Subscriber Directory Number [MSISDN]), IMSI, SIM serial number (as printed on the SIM card), PIN and/or PUK for the SIM, and services allowed. Whenever a call is made or a text message is sent, a "call data record" is created and stored, containing, amongst other information, the sending and receiving phone numbers, the length of the call, and the initial and final location of the two parties.

6.5 ATTACKS ON THE SIM MODULE

It is important for the investigator to understand that the SIM can be attacked by crafty criminals. In a forensic context, the most obvious attack method is the removal of evidence. Since the files on the GSM card can be accessed in raw, an attacker can remove evidence by overwriting storage space. For instance, a person knowing that deleted text messages are still accessible on the card could use the card editor in Sim-Surf Profi to overwrite the messages with other information. Of more interest to a criminal would be to attack the SIM to impersonate another subscriber. If this could be done, a criminal would be able to make calls on other subscriber's accounts, and impersonate other subscribers, as their caller identification would show up at the called party. In the GSM system, the subscriber identity is only stored on the SIM, so the protection against impersonation only rely on the SIM security features. The only information that identifies a user is the user IMSI and the secret encryption key Ki. Both are stored on the SIM and in the HLR in the network. As we have seen, the IMSI can be read directly from the SIM card if the user knows the PIN or PUK code. IMSI or other valid subscribers could also be obtained by listening to unencrypted network traffic on the air interface since the IMSI will be transferred unencrypted across the air interface whenever a mobile registers with a new network. But how can the criminal obtain the encryption key Ki? Since the Ki is stored only internally in the SIM card it is not accessible directly, but only through usage of the encryption algorithms stored on the card. However, since the user of a SIM card can feed the algorithm with known numbers, the Ki can be found in the algorithms contain weaknesses that allow such analysis. Such an attack is commonly known as a chosen-plaintext attack. The algorithms in GSM do indeed have such a weakness. A tool to extract Ki from a SIM has been implemented in the program Sim-Scan, available on the Internet [SIMSCAN]. Both IMSI and Ki can, therefore, be obtained by anyone with access to a SIM card and knowledge of PIN or PUK. The next step for the criminal is to produce a new SIM card with the IMSI and Ki implemented. This cannot be done on SIM cards in use since IMSI is locked through the SIM access mechanism, and Ki is only internally stored. The attacker, therefore, needs to get hold of a fresh card without any subscriber information. These cards can be ordered from the same source where network providers get their cards. The card must then be programmed with a special tool for programming of fresh cards. Such a tool is distributed together with the SimScan package. An attacker could also get hold of a generic smart card and smart card programmer, and then program the card to act as a SIM.

6.6 MOBILE PHONE EVIDENCE EXTRACTION PROCESS

It is important to realize that there are a number of basic requirements for a handset or SIM card to interface with a computer. Once these requirements are met, the manufacturer is free to implement any other features in any way it wishes. This means that a forensic tool for mobile phones will not be able to target every feature on every type of phone, in other words, evidence extraction and forensic examination of each mobile device may differ. Furthermore, the different technologies upon which mobile networks are based, such as TDMA, CDMA, and more recent 3G technologies, such as WCDMA, each require the handsets to implement different standards. If a forensic examiner is able to follow a consistent examination process, this will assist in ensuring that the evidence extracted from each phone is well documented and that the results are repeatable and dependable. There are a number of different methods for obtaining the data. However, there is no accepted standard, as the freedom which manufacturers have when designing their phones means that every phone must be considered separately. However, the following figure provides an overview of process considerations for extraction of evidence from mobile devices.

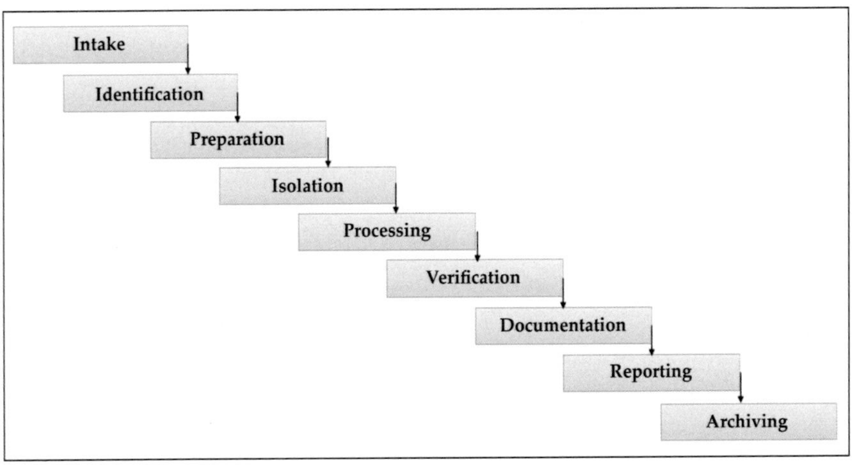

Figure 6.6: The mobile phone evidence extraction process. *Source: https://www.safaribooksonline.com/library/view/practical-mobile-forensics/9781786464200/ch01s03.html*

6.6.1 Evidence Intake Phase

The evidence intake phase involves the procedure by which requests for examinations are handled. This phase is very important in digital forensics because it collects the digital evidence provided in the mobile device. In this phase, the investigator preserves the device in its original stage. Also, the cell phones are seized that are involved in the activity so that there should not be any change in the evidence. Seize the mobile device means to cut off all the wireless networks. Any failure in this stage will result in the failure of all the rest stages. The goal of seizure is to preserve the evidence as it avoids shut down the device. The evidence intake phase generally entails request forms and intake paperwork to document the chain of custody, ownership information, and the type of incident the phone was involved in and outlines general information regarding the type of data the requester is seeking to have extracted or documented from the phone. A critical aspect at this phase of the examination is the development of specific objectives for each examination. This not only serves to document the examiner's goals but also assists in the triage of examinations and begins the documentation of the examination process for each individual phone examined. This information allows the examiner to triage cellular phones.

6.6.2 Identification Phase

For every examination, the examiner should identify the following: (a) The legal authority to examine the phone (b) The goals of the examination (c) The make, model, and identifying information for the cellular phone itself (d) Removable and external data storage (e) Other sources of potential evidence

(1) **Legal authority** Case law surrounding the search of data contained within cellular phones is in a nearly constant state of flux. It is imperative that the examiner determines and documents what legal authority exists for the search of the cellular phone, as well as what limitations are placed on the search of the phone prior to the examination of the device: (a) If the cellular phone is being searched pursuant to a warrant, the examiner should be mindful of confining the search to the limitations of the warrant. (b) If the cellular phone is being searched pursuant to consent, any possible limitations of the consent (such as consent to examine the call history only) and should determine whether consent is still valid prior to examine the phone. (c) In cases where the phone is being searched incident to arrest, the examiner needs to be particularly cautious, as current case law in this area is particularly problematic and in a state of constant change. Particular questions as to the

legal authority to search a cellular phone should be directed to a knowledgeable prosecutor or legal advisor in the examiner's local area.

(2) **The goal of the examination** While the general process used to examine any given cellular phone should be as consistent as possible, the goal of the examination for each phone may be significantly different. It is unlikely that any given forensics lab has neither the capability nor the capacity to examine every cellular phone that contains data of evidentiary value in every kind of case. For this reason, it can be useful to identify what level of examination is appropriate for any given cellular phone. The first of two main considerations is who will be responsible for the process of documenting the data. The second main consideration is how in depth the examination needs to be. Of those phones that are submitted to the lab for examination, there will be differences in the goals of each examination based upon the facts and circumstances of the particular case. In some cases, evidence from cellular phones may be documented in the field either by hand or photographically. A smaller subset of cellular phones may be submitted for examination with the goal of targeted data extraction of data that has evidentiary value. Specifically targeted data, such as pictures, videos, call history, text messages, or other specific data may be significant to the investigation while other stored data is irrelevant. It also might be the case that only a certain subset of the data can be examined due to legal restrictions. In any event, limiting the scope of the exam will likely make extraction and documentation of the data less time-consuming. The goal of the exam may alternatively include an attempt to recover deleted data from the memory of the phone. This is only possible if a tool is available for a particular phone that can extract data at a physical level. If such a tool is available, then the examination will involve traditional computer forensic methods such as data carving and hex decoding, and examination process may be a time consuming and technically involved endeavor, as deeper levels of examination necessitate a more technically complex and time-consuming process.

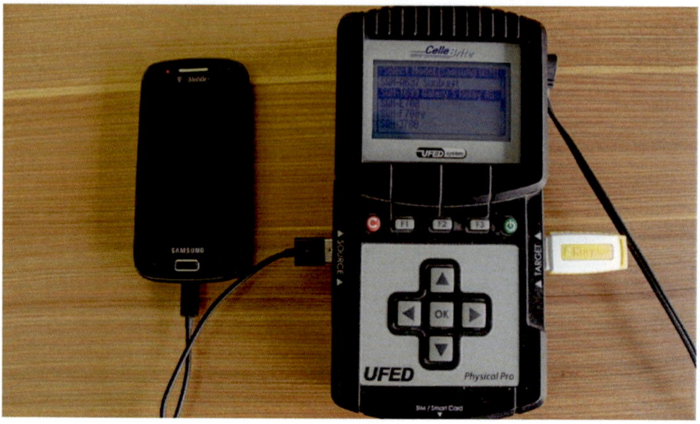

Figure 6.7: Extraction of data from Samsung Galaxy S Relay 4G using Cellebrite UFED. *Source: https://www.magnetforensics.com/mobile-forensics/ief-and-cellebrite-on-android/*

(3) The make, model and identifying information for the cellular phone: As part of the examination of any cellular phone, the identifying information for the phone itself should be documented. This enables the examiner not only to identify a particular phone at a later time but also assists in the determination about what tools might work with the phone as most cellular phone forensic tools provide lists of supported phones based on the make and model of the phone. For all phones, the manufacturer, model number, carrier and the current phone number associated with the cellular phone should be identified and documented. Depending upon the cellular phone technology involved, additional identifying information should be documented, if available, as follows: **(a) CDMA cellular phones** The Electronic Serial Number (ESN) is located under the battery of the cellular phone. This is a unique 32-bit number assigned to each mobile phone on the network. The ESN may be listed in decimal (11 digits) and/or hexadecimal (8 hex digits). The examiner should be aware that the hex version of the ESN is not a direct numeric conversion of the decimal value. An ESN converter can be found at http://www.elfqrin.com/esndhconv.html. The Mobile Equipment ID (MEID), also found under the battery cover, is a 56-bit number which replaced the ESN due to the limited number of 32 bit ESN numbers. The MEID is listed in hex, where the first byte

is a regional code, next three bytes are a manufacturer code, and remaining three bytes are a manufacturer-assigned serial number. CDMA phones do not generally contain a SIM card, but some newer hybrid phones contain dual CDMA and GSM technology and can be used on either CDMA or GSM networks. Inside these dual technology phones are located a slot for a SIM card. The identifying information under the battery of these phones may list an IMEI number in addition to the ESN/MEID number. CDMA phones also have two other identifying numbers, namely, the Mobile Identification Number (MIN) and Mobile Directory Number (MDN). The MIN is a carrier-assigned, carrier-unique 24-bit (10-digit) telephone number. When a call is placed, the phone sends the ESN and MIN to the local tower. The MDN is the globally unique telephone number of the phone. Prior to wireless number portability, the MIN and MDN were the same but in today's environment, the customer can keep their phone number (MDN) even if they change carriers.

Figure 6.8: JIVI CDMA Cell Phone JV C300. *Source: https://www.indiamart.com/magicon-impex/cdma-phones.html*

(b) **GSM cellular phones** The IMEI is a unique 15-digit number that identifies a GSM cellular phone handset on its network. This number is generally found under the battery of the cellular phone. The first 8 digits are a Type Allocation Code and the next 6 digits are the Device Serial Number. The final digit is a check digit, usually set to 0. On a GSM phone, there will be at least a SIM card slot which is also generally located under the battery.

The SIM card may be branded with the name of the network to which the SIM is registered. Also located on the SIM card is the ICCID, which is an 18 to 20 digit number (10 bytes) that uniquely identifies each SIM card. The ICCID number is tied to the IMSI which is typically a 15-digit number (56 bits) consisting of three parts including the Mobile Country Code (MCC; 3 digits), Mobile Network Code (MNC; 3 digits in the U. S. and Canada, and 2 digits elsewhere), and Mobile Station Identification Number (9 digits in the U. S. and Canada, and 10 digits elsewhere) which are stored electronically within the SIM. The IMSI can be obtained either through analysis of the SIM or from the carrier. The MSISDN is the phone's 15-digit, globally unique number. The MSISDN follows the International Telecommunication Union Recommendation E.164 telephone numbering plan, composed of a 1–3 digit country code, followed by a country-specific number. In North America, the first digit is a 1, followed by a 3-digit area code.

Figure 6.9: Original Nokia 105 GSM Cell Phone. *Source: https://www.dhgate.com/product/refurbished-original-nokia-105-gsm-cell-phone/398981757.html*

(c) **iDen cellular phones** iDen cellular phones contain an IMEI that identifies an iDen cellular phone on its network. This number is generally found under the battery of the cellular phone. iDen cellular phones also contain SIM cards, with the identifying information described above, though they are based on different technology than GSM SIM cards and are not compatible with GSM cellular phones. Unique to iDen cellular phones is the Direct Connect Number which is also known as the MOTOTalk ID, Radio-Private ID or iDen Number. The DCN is the identifying number used to communicate directly device-to-device with other iDen cellular phones. This number consists of a series of numbers formatted as ###*###*##### where the first three digits are the Area ID (region of the home carrier's network), the next three digits are the Network ID (specific iDen carrier) and the last five digits are a subscriber identification number which sometimes corresponds to the last five of the cellular phone number. (Punja & Mislan, 2008)

(d) **Removable/external data storage** Many cellular phones currently on the market include the ability to store data to a removable storage device such as a Trans Flash Micro SD memory expansion card. In the event that such a card is installed in a cellular phone that is submitted for examination, the card should be removed by the examiner and processed using traditional digital forensics techniques. The processing of data storage cards using cellular phone forensic tools while the card remains installed within the phone may result in the alteration of date and time stamp data for files located on the data card. Additionally, cellular phones may allow for the external storage of data within network-based storage areas accessible to the phone's user by computer. Accessing this data, which is stored on the cellular phone service provider's network, may require further legal authority and is generally beyond the scope of the examination of a cellular phone handset. However, the potential existence of network-based data storage should be taken into account by the examiner. Many feature phones and smartphones are also designed to sync with a user's computer to facilitate access to and transfer of data to and from the cellular phone. Full backups of the data from a phone may be found on the phone owner's computer. The potential for the existence of these alternative storage areas should be considered by the examiner as additional sources of data originating from cellular phones.

(e) **Other potential evidence collection** Prior to the beginning examination of a cellular phone, consideration should be given to whether or not other evidence collection issues exist. Cellular phones may be good sources of DNA, fingerprint, or other biological evidence. Collection of DNA, biological and fingerprint evidence should be accomplished prior to the examination of the cellular phone to avoid contamination issues.

6.6.3 Preparation Phase

Within the Identification phase of the process, the examiner has already been involved in significant preparation for the examination of the phone. However, the preparation phase involves particular research regarding the phone in question, the proper tools to be used during the examination and preparation of the examination machine to ensure that all of the necessary equipment, cables, software, and drivers are in place for the examination. Once the make and model of the phone have been identified, the examiner can then research the specific phone to determine what available tools are capable of extracting the desired data from the phone. Resources such as phonescoop.com and mobileforensicscentral.com can be invaluable in identifying information about cellular phones and what tools will work to extract and document the data from specific phones. The SEARCH toolbar (available as a free download from www.search.org) contains additional and regularly updated resources for cellular phone examinations. Other resources that should not be overlooked are cellular phone manufacturer's and cell phone carrier's websites. They can contain links to electronic versions of manuals for almost every make and model of phone as well as cable and phone driver downloads. Manufacturers will also sometimes provide free software designed for users to access and synchronize the data on their phones with their computers. While these tools are not designed specifically for extraction and documentation of evidence, they may be useful when other tools do not work. Caution should be used when utilizing these tools, as they are generally designed to access and write data back to a cellular phone.

6.6.4 Isolation Phase

Cellular phones are by design intended to communicate via cell phone networks. They are also sometimes capable of connecting to each other and to other networks via Bluetooth, infrared, and wireless (Wi-Fi) network capabilities. For this reason, isolation of the phone from these communication sources is important prior to the examination. Isolation of the phone prevents the addition of new data to the phone through incoming calls and text messages as well as the potential destruction of data through a kill signal or accidental overwriting of existing data as new calls and text messages come in. Isolation also prevents overreaching of the legal authority of warrant or consent that covers data on the phone. If the phone is isolated from the network, the examiner cannot accidentally access voicemail, email,

Internet browsing history or other data that may be stored on the service provider's network rather than on the phone itself. Isolation of a cellular phone in the field can be accomplished through the use of Faraday bags or radio frequency shielding cloths which are specifically designed for this purpose. Other available items such as arson cans or several layers of tinfoil may also be used to isolate some cellular phones. One problem with these isolation methods however is that once they are employed, it is difficult or impossible to work with the phone as you cannot see through them or work with the phone's keypad through them. Faraday tents, rooms, and enclosures exist, but are cost prohibitive. Additionally, some laboratories within the US federal government may use signal jamming devices to curtail radio signals from being sent or received for a given area. The use of such devices is illegal for many organizations and their use should only be implemented after verifying the legality of the use of such devices for a given organization. Additional information about the FCC exceptions can be found at www.fcc.org. Another viable option is to wrap the cellular phone in radio frequency shielding cloth and to then place the phone into airplane mode (also known as standalone, radio off, standby, or phone off mode). Instructions for how to place a phone into Airplane mode can be found in the manufacturer's user manual for the particular make and model of cellular phone. Unfortunately, not all phones have an airplane mode, and sometimes even the most seemingly foolproof isolation methods can fail.

6.6.5 Processing Phase

Once the phone has been isolated from the cell phone and other communication networks, the actual processing of the phone may begin. The appropriate tools to achieve the goal of the examination have been identified in the steps described previously, and they can now ideally be used to extract the desired data from the phone. Accessing data stored on these cards through use or processing of the cellular phone may alter data on the data storage card thus any installed data storage/memory cards should be removed from the cellular phone and processed separately using traditional computer forensics methods to ensure that date and time information for files stored on the data storage/memory card are not altered during the examination. Similarly, SIM cards should be processed separately from the cellular phone they are installed in to preserve the integrity of the data contained on the SIM card. Consideration should be given to the order of the software and hardware tools used during the examination of the cellular phone. There are advantages to consistency in order of tools used during examination of a cellular phone. This consistency may help the examiner to remember the order of tools used in the examination at a later time.

6.6.6 Verification Phase

After processing the phone, it is imperative that the examiner engages in some sort of verification of the accuracy of the data extracted from the phone. Unfortunately, it is not unusual for cellular phone tools to erroneously or incompletely report data or to have different tools report conflicting information. Verification of extracted data can be accomplished in several ways. (1) *Comparison of Extracted Data to the Handset* Comparison of the extracted data to the handset simply means checking to be sure the data which was extracted from the cellular phone matches the data displayed by the phone itself. This is the only authoritative way to ensure that the tools are reporting the phone information correctly. (2) *Use of More than One Tool, Compare Results* Another way to ensure the accuracy of extracted data is to use more than one tool to extract data from the cellular phone and to cross verify the results by comparing the data reported from tool to tool. If there are inconsistencies, the examiner should use other means to verify the accuracy of the data extracted from the phone. Even if two tools report information consistently, verification via manual inspection of the handset is authoritative. (3) *Use of Hash Values* If file system extraction is supported, traditional forensic tools can be used for verification of extracted data in several ways. The forensic examiner can extract the file system of the cell phone initially, and then hash the extracted files. Any individually extracted files can then be hashed and checked against the originals to verify the integrity of individual files. Alternatively, the examiner could extract the file system of the cell phone initially, perform the examination and then extract the file system of the phone a second time. The two file system extractions can then be hashed and the hash values compared to see what data on the phone, if any, has been altered during the examination process. Any changed files should then be examined to determine if they are system files or user files to potentially determine the reason for the changes to the files. It should be noted that hashing only validates the data as it exists after it has left the phone. Cases where the data extraction process actually modifies data have been documented in other papers. In some cases, a combination of verification techniques may be employed to validate the integrity of the data extracted from the phone.

6.6.7 Documentation and Reporting Phase

Documentation of the examination should occur throughout the process in the form of contemporaneous notes regarding what was done during the examination. Examination worksheets can be helpful in the examination process to ensure that basic information is recorded. The examiner's notes and documentation should include information such as: (a) The date and time the examination was started (b) The physical condition of the phone (c) Pictures of the phone and individual components (e.g., SIM card and memory expansion card) and the label with identifying information (d) The status of the phone when received (off or on) (e) Make, model, and identifying information (f) Tools were used during the examination (g) What data was documented during the examination. Most cellular phone tools include reporting functions, but these may not be sufficient for documentation needs. At times, the cellular phone tools may report inaccurate information such as the wrong ESN, MIN/MDN numbers, model, or erroneous date and time data, and so care must be taken to document the correct information after data verification. For law enforcement purposes, the process used to extract data from the phone, the kinds of data extracted and documented and any pertinent findings should be accurately documented in reports. Even if the examiner is successful in extracting the desired data using available tools, additional documentation of the information through photographs may be useful, especially for court presentation purposes.

6.6.8 Presentation Phase

Consideration should be given throughout the examination as to how the information extracted and documented can clearly be presented to another investigator, prosecutor and to a court. In many cases, the receiver may prefer to have the extracted data in both paper and electronic format so that call history or other data can be sorted or imported into other software for further analysis. The investigator may also want to provide reference information regarding the source of date and time information, EXIF data extracted from images or other data formats, in order that recipients of the data are better able to understand the information. For court purposes, pictures or video of the data as it existed on the cellular phone may be useful or compelling as exhibits. Extracted text messages may be great evidence, but pictures of the same text messages may be more familiar and visually compelling to a jury. It is often very useful to present a series of pictures of text messages and call history logs in chronological order via a simple PowerPoint presentation so that the progression of communications is shown clearly to the audience, whether the audience is an investigator, prosecutor, or jury. This is especially effective if there are a number of cellular phones involved in a case.

6.6.9 Archiving Phase

Preservation of the data extracted and documented from the cellular phone is an important part of the overall process. It is necessary to retain the data in a useable format for the ongoing court process, future reference, and for record keeping requirements. Some cases may endure for many years before a final resolution, and most jurisdictions require that data be retained for varying lengths of time for the purposes of appeals. Due to the proprietary nature of the various tools on the market for the extraction and documentation of cell phone data, consideration should be given to the ability to access saved data at a later date. If possible, store data in both proprietary and non-proprietary formats on standard media so that the data can be accessed later even in the event that the original software tool is no longer available. It may also be a good practice to retain a copy of the tool itself to facilitate the viewing of the data at a later date.

6.7 CHALLENGES OF MOBILE FORENSICS

Knowing the importance of the forensics of mobile phone devices, it is essential to understand the current known challenges facing investigators. Here are some of the challenges militating against mobile forensics.

6.7.1 Carriers and Manufacturers

In an investigation of a mobile phone, the first action must be the identification of the phone. Given that there are multiple network carriers (at least seventeen in the US alone) and device manufacturers (over 30 in the United States), identifying a phone by sight alone is extremely difficult even for trained investigators. A given model from a single hardware manufacturer may be marketed using many different names from the various carriers. A good example of this is the recently popular Motorola RAZR which is marketed under at least 24 different product names. It is not until an investigator removes the device's battery that the true hardware model can be determined, but removing batteries can cause the phone to lose the information stored in volatile memory, or even worse, force a handset lock code on power up.

6.7.2 Data Preservation

For a mobile phone investigation, it is important to prevent the device from receiving any further data or voice communication. As text messages are stored in a "First In, First Out" order, any new incoming text messages could delete older stored text messages. Likewise, incoming calls could erase call history logs, and some devices (such as the RIM Blackberry) can be wiped of all data remotely if not protected from incoming communications. Therefore, upon initial acquisition, these mobile phones must be placed in some sort of wireless preservation container. Multiple technologies can be used for this with various levels of success. These tools range from three layers of common aluminum foil to a tri-weave mesh material shield of nickel, silver, and copper, to an anodized aluminum shielded enclosure made to withstand wireless devices from radio frequencies.

6.7.3 Power and Data Connectors

Another challenge facing investigators is how to preserve power to the phone. If left unplugged for a long enough period of time, a phone's battery will eventually lose all power. Because many mobile phones store information in volatile memory, a complete loss of power may mean a loss of information, thus a loss of crucial evidence. Therefore, it is desirable to keep a phone in a charging state. Frustratingly, there currently is no standard for power requirements for mobile phones. This lack of power standards is compounded by the fact that there is also no standard for cable connectors. There are literally hundreds of different mobile phone power connectors currently in use. So even if two phones require the same voltage to remain charged, they likely will not have compatible power connectors.

6.7.4 Operating Systems and Communication Protocol

Another challenge impeding the development of forensics tools is the various operating systems used on mobile phones. Mobile phones have evolved into full-fledged computing platforms requiring vendors to use sophisticated operating systems so that various software applications can be run on them. Several of the common operating systems in include RIM's Blackberry, iDEN, Palm, Symbian, Windows Mobile, Macintosh OS X, and various versions of the Linux open-source operating system. Some operating systems are also proprietary to the hardware manufacturer. For example, Nokia has the ISA platform for the Series 30 and 40 phones.

REFERENCES

1. Casey, E. (2000). *Digital evidence and computer crime: Forensic science, computers and the internet*. London: Academic Press. Retrieved March 20, 2018, from https://epdf.tips/forensic-computer-crime-investigation.html
2. Kessler, G. (2010). *Cell phone analysis: Technology, tools, and processes. Mobile Forensics World*. Chicago: Purdue University.
3. McCarthy, P. (2006). *Forensic analysis of mobile phones*. Retrieved March 20, 2018, from http://esm.cis.unisa.edu.au/new_esml/resources/publications/forensic%20analysis%20of%20mobile%20phones.pdf
4. Understanding the cloud computing stack SaaS, PaaS, IaaS. Retrieved March 21, 2018, from http://broadcast.rackspace.com/hosting_knowledge/whitepapers/Understanding-the-Cloud-Computing-Stack.pdf

CHAPTER 7

COMPUTER INTRUSIONS AND DETECTION

"You are absolutely deluded, if not stupid, if you think that a worldwide collection of software engineers who can't write operating systems or applications without security holes, can then turn around and suddenly write virtualization layers without security holes."

—Theo De Raad, 2007

CONTENTS

A computer system should provide confidentiality, integrity, and assurance against denial of service, however, due to increased connectivity more and more systems are subject to attack by intruders. Therefore, it is essential that the security mechanisms of a system are designed so as to prevent unauthorized access to system resources and data. Intrusion detection (ID) takes over where preemptive security fails. It is designed to identify, and in some cases limit the occurrence and effect of intrusions into computer systems. Such intrusions are difficult to prevent by traditional access control techniques as they typically evade access control by exploiting flaws in the implementation. This chapter discusses ID, ID systems and methods of intrusive investigations. The last section elaborates on challenges involved in intrusion forensics.

7.1 INTRODUCTION TO COMPUTER INTRUSIONS

In the digital age, data on computer systems can have substantial value, and criminals are taking advantage of the fact that businesses and individuals have become dependent on computers. Organizations use computers to store all forms of information including medical and financial data. The exposure of such information can lead to financial loss, and integrity damage. For instance, over $10 million was embezzled from the Royal Bank of Scotland as a result of a violation of security measures. In 2008, the Heartland Payment Systems Company experienced a data breach that uncovered over 100 million credit card records. Individuals are also being targeted when they use their computers to make purchases and conduct online banking and to store private data including tax documents and other business records as well as health information. The disclosure of such sensitive information can lead to financial loss and identity fraud. Criminals break into computers for a wide range of purposes, including stealing valuable information, eavesdropping on users' communications, harassing administrators or users, launching attacks against other systems, storing toolkits and stolen data, and defacing websites. Some individuals view computer intrusions as victimless crimes. However, whether a computer intruder purloins proprietary information from an organization, steals an individual's credit card or banking details, or deletes the contents of an individual's hard drive, people are affected in a very real way. For instance, if computer intruder changes prescription information in a pharmacy database, interferes with critical systems at an airport, disables an emergency telephone service, or destroys other critical systems, the implications can be fatal. As another example, it can take victims of identity fraud many years to regain their financial strength. Computer intruders have been categorized as teenagers with social problems. Stereotypes of computer intruders being antisocial adolescents do not address the extensive range of criminals who gain unlawful access to computers. An increasing number of intrusions are committed by criminal organizations and state-sponsored groups. New techniques to interfere with and break into computers seem to be developed every day with changing degrees of sophistication. Although it takes a specific degree of skill to find new ways to execute these attacks, once a new method of attack is developed, it is often made available on the Internet. Programs that spontaneously exploit vulnerability are commonly called *exploits*, and many of them are generously available at sites like SecurityFocus. With a little knowledge of computer networks, almost anyone can obtain and use the required tools to be a nuisance by breaking into a computer and erasing its contents. It takes skill and experience, however, to break into a computer system, commit a crime, and conceal one's cover one's tracks.

7.2 STANDARD COMPUTER INTRUSION TACTICS

A typical computer intrusion might follow the following steps:

(a) Gather information about the target computer.
(b) Probe the computer for vulnerabilities and attempt to exploit them.
(c) Gain unauthorized access into the computer.
(d) Escalate from an unprivileged account to privileged account.
(e) Hide tracks and instantiate a persistent reentry.
(f) Extend unauthorized access to other areas of the network.
(g) Pursue the goal of intrusion (e.g., steal information or destroy data). While specific tactics and techniques have evolved overtime, there is a classic set of methods that can be followed within the phases of an attack, against a single computer.

7.2.1 Direct Attack Methods

There are a number of ways that intruders can acquire information about a computer that can be useful for launching an attack. Knowing the operating system and services that are running on a computer is often all that is required—because some services on certain operating systems are known to be susceptible. Computer intruders may be able to guess passwords or exploit vulnerability in the remote system to gain unlawful remote access.

7.2.2 Social Engineering

When intruders cannot get through a system through known security holes, they use less technical methods to gain access. Intruders sometimes even dig through garbage for valuable information. Intruders also try to get information using social engineering and reverse social engineering. Social engineering refers to any attempt to contact real users of the target system and trick them into giving out information that can give the intruder a clue of how to break into the system. For example, calling someone and pretending to be a new employee who does not understand the operations of the company can result in useful information like computer names, operating systems, and even some information about employee accounts. Alternatively, pretending to be a computer technician who is trying to fix a problem can also result in the acquisition of beneficial information. There are many different ways to do this, including calling people claiming to be looking into a problem or going into the organization to look around. Some people will even make the mistake of giving out their passwords. Reverse social engineering is any attempt by intruders to have someone in the target organization to contact them for assistance. Instead of contacting them, they contact the intruder. For example, sending a memo with a "new" technical support email can result in ample flow of information. The advantage of reverse social engineering is that the user is less likely to be suspicious and report the incident. When people seek help from an intruder who resolves their problems, they are less likely to be suspicious and are unlikely to have any reason to report the incident to anyone.

7.3 EXISTING COMPUTER INTRUSION TACTICS

Overtime, the preferred tactics of computer intruders have evolved. While direct attacks against Internet-facing systems and applications were once common, security measures have made this tactic more difficult. As a result, computer intruders have developed approaches to attacking client systems more indirectly through email or via the web browsers that visit a compromised web server.

7.3.1 Phishing

Phishing attacks typically rely on social networking techniques applied to email or other electronic communication methods, including direct messages sent over social networks, SMS text messages, and other instant messaging modes. Phishers may use social engineering and other public sources of information, including social networks like LinkedIn, Facebook and Twitter, to gather background information about the victim's personal and work history, his interests, and his activities. Pre-phishing attack reconnaissance can uncover names, job titles, and email addresses of potential victims, as well as information about their colleagues and the names of key employees in their organizations. This information can then be used to craft a believable email. Targeted attacks, including those carried out by advanced persistent threat groups; typically begin with a phishing email containing a malicious link or attachment.

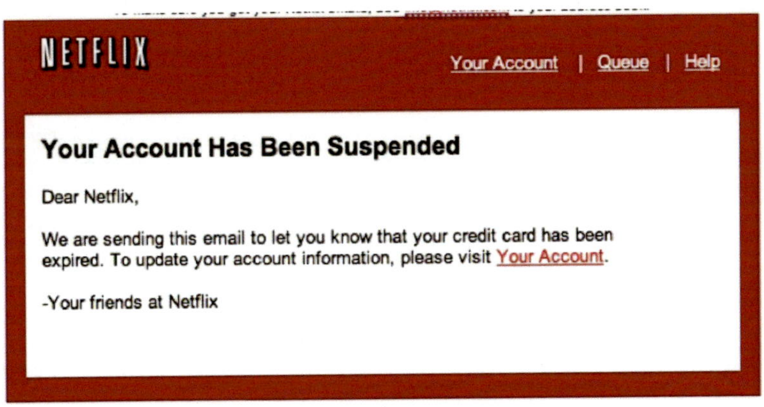

Figure 7.1: Phishing Scam message. *Source: http://resources.infosecinstitute.com/category/enterprise/phishing/#gref*

7.3.1.1 Types of phishing

As defenders continue to educate their users in phishing defense and deploy anti-phishing strategies, cybercriminals continue to hone their skills at existing phishing attacks and roll out new types of phishing scams. Some of the more common types of phishing attacks include the following: (a) Spear phishing attacks are directed at specific individuals or companies, usually using information specific to the victim that has been gathered to more successfully represent the message as being authentic. Spear phishing emails might include references to coworkers or executives at the victim's organization, as well as the use of the victim's name, location or other personal information. *Whaling* attacks are a type of spear phishing attack that specifically targets senior executives within an organization, often with the objective of stealing large sums. Those preparing a spear phishing campaign research their victims, in detail, to create a more genuine message. Using information relevant or specific to a target increases the chances of the attack being successful. A typical whaling attack targets an employee with the ability to authorize payments, with the phishing message appearing to be a command from an executive to authorize a large payment to a vendor when, in fact, the payment would be made to the attackers.

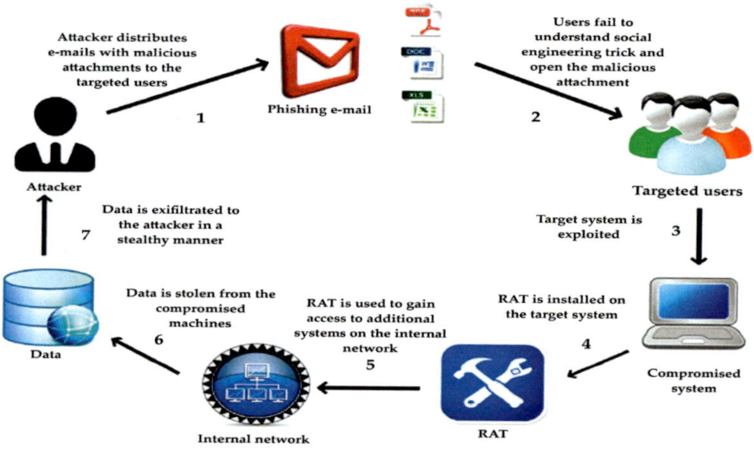

Figure 7.2: Spear phishing attack model. *Source: https://searchsecurity.techtarget.com/feature/Targeted-Cyber-Attacks*

(b) Pharming is a type of phishing that depends on DNS cache poisoning to redirect users from a legitimate site to a fraudulent one, and tricking users into using their login credentials to attempt to log in to the fraudulent site. (c) Clone phishing attacks use previously delivered, but legitimate emails that contain either a link or an attachment. Attackers make a copy or clone of the legitimate email, replacing one or more links or attached files with malicious links or malware attachments. Because the message appears to be a duplicate of the original, legitimate email, victims can often be tricked into clicking the malicious link or opening the malicious attachment. This technique is often used by attackers who have taken control of another victim's system. In this case, the attackers leverage their control of one system to pivot within an organization using email messages from a trusted sender known to the victims. Phishers sometimes use the evil twin Wi-Fi attack by standing up a Wi-Fi access point and advertising it with a deceptive name that is similar to a legitimate access point. When victims connect to the evil twin Wi-Fi network, the attackers gain access to all the transmissions sent to or from victim devices, including user IDs and passwords. Attackers can also use this vector to target victim devices with their own fraudulent prompts for system credentials that appear to originate from legitimate systems. (d) Voice phishing, also known as vishing, is a form of phishing that occurs over voice communications media, including voice over IP or plain old telephone service. A typical vishing scam uses speech synthesis software to leave voicemails purporting to notify the victim of suspicious activity in a bank or credit account, and solicits the victim to respond to a malicious phone number to verify his identity thus compromising the victim's account credentials. (e) SMS phishing also sometimes called SMishing or SMShing is another mobile device-oriented phishing attack which uses text messaging to persuade victims to disclose account credentials or to install malware.

7.3.2 Drive-by download

This is a term sometimes used to refer to an attack where a user happens to visit a website hosted on an infected or malicious web server through otherwise innocuous web browsing. For example, an individual might be web browsing on social networking sites, and a malicious advertisement might direct that user to an infected web server that would then infect or compromise the web browsers through the exploitation of a vulnerability or misconfiguration. (a) Cross-site scripting also written as "XSS," cross-site scripting is a general set of techniques whereby an attacker is able to execute malicious code on another system through an intermediary web application. In addition, attacks against Internet-facing systems have transitioned from attacks against underlying services and primary service applications (IIS, Apache, etc.) to attacks versus custom databases and web applications. A primary example of this is SQL injection attacks. (b) SQL injection is the placement of SQL control characters as input into an application with a database back end, where the application was not expecting SQL control characters. If those characters are placed properly and accepted by the database server, they can be used to cause the database server to supply or modify information that should not have been accessible by the user account in question or through the particular interface in use.

7.4 ATTACK DETECTION

Attack detection assumes that an attacker can obtain access to her desired targets and is successful in violating a given security policy. Mechanisms in this class are based on the optimistic assumption that, most of the time; the information is transferred without interference. When undesired actions occur, attack detection has the task of reporting that something went wrong and to react in a proper way. Additionally, it is often necessary to ascertain the exact type of attack. An essential facet of attack detection is recovery. Often it is adequate to just report that malicious activity has been detected, but some systems require that the effects of an attack be reverted or that an ongoing and discovered attack is stopped. On one hand, attack detection has the benefit that it operates under the worst-case theory that the attacker gains access to the communication channel and is able to use or modify the resource. On the other hand, detection is not effective in providing confidentiality of information. When the security policy specifies that interception of information has a serious security impact, then attack detection is not an appropriate mechanism. The most important members of the attack detection class are IDSs.

7.5 INTRUSION DETECTION SYSTEMS (IDS)

Here, we need to understand the meaning of intrusion first before we proceed. An intrusion is defined as a sequence of related actions performed by a malicious adversary that results in the compromise of a target system. It is assumed that the actions of the intruder violate a given security policy. The existence of a security policy that states which actions are considered malicious and should be prevented is a key requirement for IDS. Violations can only be detected when actions can be compared against given rules. ID is the process of recognizing and responding to malicious activities aimed at computing and network resources. This definition introduces the concept of ID as a process, which involves technology, people, and tools. ID is an approach that is complementary with respect to mainstream approaches to security, such as access control and cryptography. The adoption of IDSs is motivated by several factors: (1) Surveys have shown that most computer systems are flawed by vulnerabilities, irrespective of manufacturer or purpose (Landwehr et al., 1994), that the number of security incidents is continuously accumulating and that users and administrators are generally very slow in applying fixes to vulnerable systems. As a consequence, many experts believe that computer systems will never be absolutely secure. (2) Deployed security mechanism, for example, authentication and access control, may be disabled as a consequence of misconfiguration or malicious actions. (3) Users of the system may abuse their privileges and perform damaging activities. (4) Even if an attack is not successful, in most cases it is useful to be aware of the compromise attempt. IDSs help computer systems prepare for and deal with attacks. They collect information from a selection of vantage points within computer systems and networks and analyze this information as indications of security problems. IDSs are software applications dedicated to detect intrusions against a target network. IDSs have been designed to address the issues described above. As such, they are not intended to replace traditional security methods, but rather to complete them. Dacier states that IDS has to fulfill the following requirements (1999); (a) Accuracy: An IDS must not identify a legitimate action in a system environment as an anomaly or a misuse (a legitimate action which is identified as an intrusion is called a false positive). (b) Performance: The IDS performance must be sufficient enough to carry out real time ID (real time means that an intrusion has to be detected before significant damage has occurred. (c) Completeness: An IDS should not fail to detect an intrusion (an undetected intrusion is called a false negative). One has to admit that it is rather difficult to fulfill this requirement because it is almost impossible to have a global knowledge about past, present, and future attacks. (d) Fault Tolerance: An IDS must itself be resistant to attacks. (e) Scalability: An IDS must be able to process the worst-case number of events without dropping information. This point is especially relevant for systems that correlate events from different sources at a small number of dedicated hosts. As networks grow bigger and get faster, such nodes become overwhelmed by the increasing number of events. There are, generally speaking, three kinds of commercially available analysis engines: (a) Event or signature-based analysis (b) statistical analysis (c) adaptive systems. The event, or signature-based, systems function much like the anti-virus software with which most people are familiar. The vendor produces a list of patterns that it deems to be suspicious or indicative of an attack; the IDS merely scans the environment looking for a match to the known patterns. The IDS can then respond by taking a user-defined action, sending an alert, or performing additional logging. This is the most common kind of IDS. A statistical analysis system builds statistical models of the environment, such as the average length of a telnet session, and then looks for deviations from "normal." After over 10 years of government research, some products are just beginning to incorporate this technology into marketable products.

The adaptive systems start with generalized rules for the environment, then learn, or adapt to, local conditions that would otherwise be unusual. After the initial learning period, the system understands how people interact with the environment, and then warns the operators about unusual activities. There is a considerable amount of active research in this area.

7.5.1 Network IDS

Network-based IDSs are most common, and examine passing network traffic for signs of intrusion (see figure 7.3 below). Host-based systems look at user and process activity on the local machine for signs of intrusion. The network IDS usually has two logical components: the sensor and the management station. The sensor sits on a network segment, monitoring it for suspicious traffic. The management station receives alarms from the sensor(s) and displays them to an operator. The sensors are usually dedicated systems that exist only to monitor the network. They have a network interface in unrestrained mode, which means they receive all network traffic—not just that destined for their IP address—they capture passing network traffic for analysis. If they detect something that looks unusual, they pass it back to the analysis station. The analysis station can display the alarms or do additional analysis. Some displays are simply an interface to a network management tool, like HP Openview, but some are custom GUIs designed to help the operator analyze the problem.

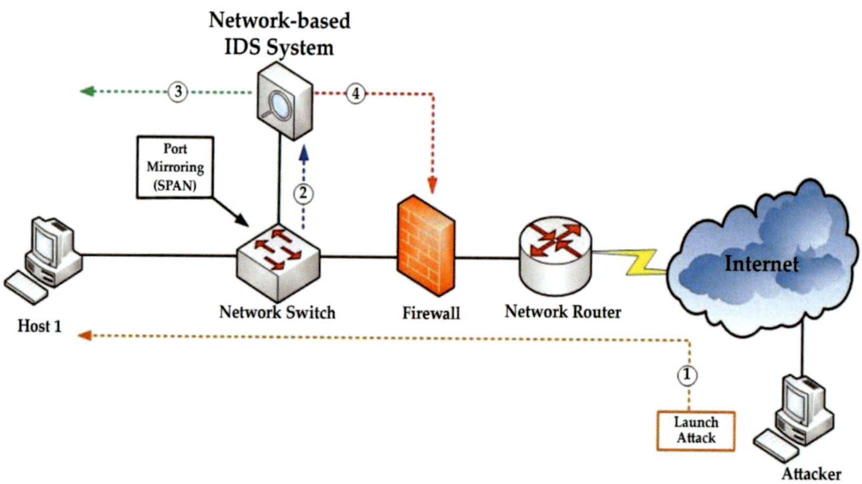

Figure 7.3: Network Intrusion Detection System. *Source: http://www.anses.net.in/index.php/network-and-data-security/technology-for-internet-security/intrusion-detection-systems/*

Pros The network IDSs can detect some of the attacks that use the network. They are good for detecting access without authority or some kinds of access in excess of authority. A network-based IDS does not require modification of production servers or hosts. This is an advantage because production servers frequently have close operating tolerances for CPU, I/O, and disk capacity; installing additional software may exceed the systems capacities. The IDS is not on a critical path for any production services or processes because a network-based IDS does not act as a router or other critical device. System failure does not have a significant impact on the business. A side benefit of this is that you are likely to encounter less resistance from other people within your organization; the risk to existing critical processes is lower with a network system than with a host system. Network-based IDS systems tend to be more self-contained than host-based systems. They run on a dedicated system that is simple to install; merely unbox the device, do some remedial configuration, and plug it into your network in a location that permits it to monitor sensitive traffic.

Cons Network IDS, on the other hand, only checks the network traffic of a segment that is directly connected but does not detect attacks that cross the network. This is a localized version, especially in the transferred Ethernet environment. This may require the organization to purchase a number of sensors to meet their coverage targets. Wide coverage with IDS sensors can be disabled because each device is expensive. The network IDS tends to use signature analysis to meet the need for deployment. This will detect attacks that are usually organized by external sources, but it is not enough to look for more complex information threats. This requires a robust opportunity to test the environment. The network IDS may transfer large volumes of data back to the central scanning system. Sometimes every checked package provides a lot of analytics traffic. Many of these systems use aggressive data reduction to reduce the number of communications traffic. They also press the decision-making process in their own sensors and use the central station as a status display or communication center, not for real analysis. The downside is that it provides very little coordination between the sensors; the sensor is oblivious of the fact that the other has detected an attack. Such a system cannot detect complicated attacks or complications. Network IDS may find it difficult to resolve attacks in encrypted sessions. Fortunately, there were very few attacks that happened in encrypted traffic than attacking weaker web servers. This will be a problem when organizations move to IPv6.

7.5.2 Host IDS

The host-based IDS looks for signs of intrusion on the local host system. These frequently use the host system's audit and logging mechanism as a source of information for analysis. They look for unusual activity that is confined to the local host such as logins, improper file access, unapproved privilege escalation, or alterations on system privileges. This IDS architecture generally uses rule-based engines for analyzing activity; an example of such a rule might be, "superuser privilege can only be attained through the su command." Therefore successive login attempts to the root account might be considered an attack.

Pros

Host-based IDS can be the most powerful tool for analyzing attacks. For example, sometimes you can say exactly an attacker did with the command line, which file is opened, and what the system calls he execute instead of making unclear allegations that he tries to implement the dangerous command. Host-based IDS provides more detailed information and important information than any network IDS. Host-based systems tend to have lower false positive rates than the network-based systems. This is because the range of commands running on a host is more important than the type of traffic that is running on the network. This feature can reduce the complexity of host-based analytics. This host-based system can be used in environments where it is not necessary to discover a wide range of intrusion or where there is a lack of communication bandwidth from the sensor to analyze. Host-based systems can be entirely self-contained. This also allows machine-based systems to run in some cases by the media being read-only. This protects an attacker from closing the IDS. Finally, in a host-based system, there are fewer risks in configuring an active response such as termination of service or logging off an offending user. A host-based system is more problematic to spoof into controlling access from legitimate sources.

Cons

In host-based system, you have to install the specific device you want to protect. For example, if you have a human resource server and you want to protect it, you need to install the IDS on this server. As already mentioned, this can create a problem of capacity. In some cases, this issue can create security problems because security staffs do not have access to the server. Another problem associated with a host-based system is that they tend to rely on the internal capacity for recording and monitoring of the server. If this server is not configured in practice and insufficiently controllable, you have to change the configuration of a production engine. How do you predict the results of summing that logging capability up? The host-based system is fairly expensive. Many organizations do not have the financial assets to secure the entire network, using host-based systems. These organizations must be careful about which system to protect. This may leave a big gap in identity issues, for example, an attacker on an adjacent but unsecured system can sniff authentication data or other sensitive material from the network. Finally, host-based systems suffer, to an even greater degree, from local-vision restrictions. They are almost completely unaware of the network environment. Thus, the analysis time required to assess damage from a potential intrusion rises linearly with the number of protected hosts; that is, if a human takes time t to examine an incident on one system, it will take 2t to examine two systems, 3t to examine three systems, and so forth.

7.5.3 File Integrity Checkers

A file integrity checker examines the files on a computer to determine whether they have been altered since the last time the integrity checker was run. The integrity checker keeps a database of hash values for each file. Each time the checker runs, it recalculates the hash value and compares it to the stored value. If the hash values are different, the file has changed. If the values are not different, the file has not changed. A hash function is a mathematical process for reducing the sequence of bytes in a file to a fixed-length number. The same file will always produce the same hash value and any change in the file is supposed to produce a different value. Unlike encryption, a hash is a one-way function; you cannot produce the original source file from the hash value. Some hashes are more secure than others. Very secure hashes, which meet special mathematical requirements, are called cryptographically secure hashes. One of the requirements for a cryptographically secure hash is that it is very hard (the technical term is computationally infeasible) to calculate a collision—two inputs that hash to the same number. That means that even if an attacker changes a file, he cannot change the file in a way that fools the integrity checker into thinking the file has not been changed.

Pros

It is computationally infeasible to defeat the mathematics in an integrity checker. This makes it a very, very strong tool for detecting changes to files on a computer. It is so strong, in fact, that it is one of the most important tools you can use to detect misuse of computer systems. Integrity checkers can be configured to watch everything on the system, or only important files. They are extremely flexible. Once attackers compromise a system, they like to do two things. First, they like to cover up their tracks, which mean that they will alter system binaries, libraries, or log files to hide the fact that they are or have been on the system. Second, they will make changes to ensure they will have continued access to the system. A properly configured file integrity checker will detect both activities.

Cons

Integrity checkers rely on data stored on the local computers. Like log files, this data (the database of hash values) is vulnerable to modification on the system. Say an attacker gains superuser privileges on your system. The attacker can find the integrity checker, make any hostile changes to the system, and rerun the integrity checker to recreate the database of hash values. When the system administrator runs the tool, it will not report any changes to the system. One way around this problem is to keep your database on read-only media such as a writable CD. This works for most stable and unchanging systems, but for most production machines it is incredibly inconvenient. The integrity checker must be configured for each system. Usually, this is a laborious and complicated task. If the operating system is not good at enforcing system integrity, installation becomes even more complex. Once the checker is configured, it must be run frequently. Depending on the operating system, simple changes or normal operation can report from tens to thousands of changes. For example, an integrity checker run just before upgrading MS-Outlook on a Windows NT system, then just after the installation, reported over 1800 changes. Finally, integrity checkers consume a considerable number of system resources. They can chew CPU, memory, and disk space. Many administrators will not want to run integrity checkers frequently. This limits their functionality because a checker run once a month will report so many changes that a real attack has a good chance of going unnoticed.

7.6 VULNERABILITY SCANNERS

A vulnerability scanner differs from IDS, as mentioned earlier, in that the vulnerability scanner looks for static configurations and the IDS looks for transient misuse or abnormalities. A vulnerability scanner may look for a known NFS vulnerability by examining the available services and configuration on a remote system. An IDS, managing the same vulnerability, would only report the existence of the vulnerability when an attacker attempted to exploit it. Vulnerability scanners, whether network or host scanners, give the organization the opportunity to fix problems before they arise, rather than reacting to an intrusion or misuse that is already in progress. An IDS detects intrusions in progress, while a vulnerability scanner allows the organization to prevent the intrusion in the first place. Vulnerability scanners may be helpful in organizations without a good incident response capability.

Figure 7.4: Vulnerability Scanners and Vendors. *Source: https://avleonov.com/2016/12/07/zeronights16-enterprise-vulnerability-management/*

7.6.1 Network vulnerability scanner

A network vulnerability scanner operates remotely by examining the network interface on a remote system. It will look for vulnerable services running on that remote machine, and report on a possible vulnerability. For example, it is well-known that rexd is a weak service; a network vulnerability scanner will attempt to connect to the rexd service on the target system. If the connection succeeds, the scanner will report rexd vulnerability. Since a network vulnerability scanner can be run from a single machine on the network, it can be installed without impacting the configuration management of other machines. Frequently, these scanners are used by auditors and security groups because they can provide an "outsider's view" of security holes in a computer or network.

Pros

Network vulnerability scanners can report on a variety of target architectures. Some work with routers, some with UNIX systems, and some with NT or other Windows platforms. Network vulnerability scanners are, in general, very easy to install and begin using (from a technical standpoint). Unlike host-based systems, which usually require software installation or reconfiguration, a network-based system can be dropped into place on a network. Simply plug the interface into the switch and boot up the machine. The GUI with a network system tends to be quite intuitive, which means that junior personnel can monitor the system and call more senior analysts if something unusual crops up.

Cons

Network vulnerability scanners are almost exclusively signature-based systems. Like a signature-based IDS, a signature-based vulnerability scanner can only detect those vulnerabilities it is programmed to recognize. If a new vulnerability comes into play, as they frequently do, there is a window of opportunity for the attacker before the vendor updates the signatures (and the customer downloads and installs the new signatures). If the vulnerability remains closely held, systems can remain vulnerable to attack for long periods of time. If customers are as negligent with their vulnerability scanner signatures as history shows they are with virus signatures, then many organizations will be vulnerable to attack, even though they run vulnerability scanners at regular intervals. A recent analysis showed that 90% of web servers running IIS is still vulnerable to critical security vulnerability which is well documented, for which the vendor has produced a patch and a security advisory. A vulnerability scanner can only point out possible problems; the organization must still fix them. Another potential problem with a network vulnerability scanner is that the output still requires skilled interpretation. Every environment has different operating requirements and different security vulnerabilities. In fact, the concept of "vulnerability" embodies other loosely defined concepts, such as risk, threat, acceptability, and expected attacker skills. Since each of these varies with each organization, the degree to which a particular configuration represents "vulnerability" also varies with each organization. When the vulnerability scanner reports a particular vulnerability, the organization's network or operations personnel must evaluate that report within the context of the organization's operating environment. The vulnerability may not pose an unacceptable risk in that organization's environment, or the risk may be forced upon the organization by business requirements. This may seem silly in the context of a security discussion, but in the real-world security concerns frequently fall prey to business justifications. Vulnerability scanners have been known to take down the target system. Some IP implementations are not robust enough to handle many simultaneous connections or IP packets with unusual flag combinations. The traffic generated by an aggressive port scan, for example, can sometimes crash a machine. Finally, network vulnerability scanners tend to contain a huge amount of vulnerability data. If anyone ever breaks into the scanner system, compromise of most other machines on the network can become child's play. Protect the scanner to prevent unauthorized use of scanning data.

7.6.2 Host Vulnerability Scanner

A host vulnerability scanner differs from a network vulnerability scanner in that it is confined entirely to the local operating system. A network vulnerability scanner requires the target machine be accessible from the network in order for it to operate; a host vulnerability scanner does not. Host vulnerability scanners are software packages that are installed on particular operating systems. Once the software is installed it can be configured to run at any time of the day or night. Usually, the scans performed by this type of tool are scheduled to run at a low priority to reduce the impact of the scan on production work.

Pros

Host vulnerability scanners tend to be much more tuned and accurate for a given operating system. They can frequently tell the user which patches to apply to fix identified vulnerabilities, while network scanners sometimes only provide general guidelines. When considering which product to purchase, look at sample reports for your specific operating systems to determine how much information is contained in the reports. The depth and accuracy of reporting should be a selection criterion. Host vulnerability scanners do not consume network bandwidth when they run. All processing is restricted to the local host system. Host vulnerability scanners are not as likely as network scanners to cause the IP stack on the target system to hang. Some operating systems have weak or poorly implemented IP stacks associated with their network interfaces; sending a high volume of traffic (as a port scanner would do) or unusual TCP header flags may cause the interface to hang, which would necessitate a reboot. Host vulnerability scanners are less likely to be used against you by a successful intruder. A hacker who breaks a system and finds a network vulnerability scanner, or reports from such a scanner, is likely to use the tool or the reports to attack other systems within your organization. A host-based tool provides much less useful information for extending an attack; that is, it is better compartmentalized than a network-based tool.

Cons

Host vulnerability scanners are, again, signature-based. They look for known dangerous system configurations and report on a cookbook approach to mitigating those particular threats. Local system procedures and operating requirements may require flexibility in finding and applying solutions to any given vulnerability. Installing host vulnerability scanners requires the cooperation of system administrators. Since the software usually runs with privilege, the system administrator for each machine should agree to the purpose and configuration of the tool. In many organizations, this can be a difficult coordination task. As with any host-based system, attackers can modify the vulnerability scanner so it does not report on the vulnerabilities the attackers wish to exploit. There is an important outcome here, that is, the vulnerability scanner cannot protect a system that was compromised when the scanner was installed.

7.7 INTRUSION INVESTIGATION

Sources of evidence with respect to intrusion investigation fall into three broad categories: host-based evidence, network-based evidence and the first person (direct) evidence of witnesses. Appropriate collection of data generated by the system, network, application and user activities is essential to detecting signs of intrusion, conducting real-time investigations and preserving evidence so that it is admissible in court. Maintaining proper records of what has been observed or discovered is highly important. A written chronological event log of the intruders suspected activities and site responses should be maintained. The log should detail what is suspected, what actions were taken, who was contacted as a result and what evidence of the intruders activities was located. Resource utilization including man-hours and equipment used to reestablish the system and locate the perpetrator should also be detailed to assist in later developing a victim impact statement.

7.7.1 Intrusion Detection Methods

ID falls into two categories, manual ID, such as log analysis and manual correlation, and the use of automated IDS. The optimal solution is normally a combination of both mechanisms as IDS do not and will not detect all possible attacks.

(1) Manual intrusion detection methods

Knowledge of, and the ability to competently apply, manual ID techniques is essential to comprehensive network security. IDS, which rely on various techniques including attack signature recognition and system/network anomaly detection, can lull management and administrators into a false sense of security. Firewalls may engender a similar false sense of security, particularly if they are not managed properly. Manual ID relies on the extensive knowledge an administrator has about his or her network. Applying manual ID methods in a time critical environment such as a post-intrusion scenario requires the sysAdm/ISSO to be familiar and competent with the tools they will utilize to conduct their examinations and have a consistent set of procedures for conducting their analyses. Manual ID is conducted by: (a) identification of anomalous entries in system logs, (b) verification of the integrity of critical system files, (c) identification (and preservation) of suspicious users, processes, files and other intruder remnants, (d) analysis of network transaction records, and (e) correlation of all relevant data to develop a picture of what has occurred. Not all attacks or suspicious activities need to be investigated in the same way, so tools utilized to assist in an investigation must allow the user to access various levels of detail according to their needs.

(a) **System log analysis** Log files contain information about what activities have occurred overtime. They are often the only record of suspicious behavior making them probably the most crucial form of evidence in an intrusion investigation. There must be recognized at a high level within an organization that system log files are in fact crucial records for an organization and they must be treated as such. Different systems provide different types of logging information and some systems do not provide adequate logging in their default configuration. Some "trusted" operating systems, however, such as those accredited by national security agencies for classified use, produce a much larger quantity of logs with a consequently higher degree of detail. Sysadms/ISSOs should identify, prior to any intrusion, the types of logs and logging mechanisms available to each system (file access logs, process logs, network logs, application specific logs, etc.) and identify the data recorded within each log. These logging mechanisms should then be enabled to the maximum extent possible. Failure to enable these mechanisms may seriously impact on a site's ability to determine whether or not an intrusion has been attempted or in fact succeeded. Simply enabling logging is not enough, however. A site must have the essential procedures and tools available to process and analyze the products of logging. There are many tools that can assist in this process.

(b) **File integrity assessment** Intruders, as part of their normal Modus Operandi, will alter the configuration of a system to allowed continued access, conceal their presence and carry out their goals on the system. If no record of the system's baseline configuration is maintained determination of what modifications have been made by an intruder to the system will be difficult. File integrity assessment (FIA), through the use of cryptographic checksums, creates a baseline database of a system, and then allows the administrator to monitor files for unauthorized changes. System files should not change, except when updated or patched, and log files should only grow in size. Forensic application of FIA allows administrators to build a complete list of what has been altered on a system. The FIA of the altered system will form an essential part of the evidence supporting prosecution, particularly where legislation imposes greater penalties for the insertion, alteration or deletion of data in a system as is the case with Australian Commonwealth law. The most well-known automated tool for carrying out FIA is Tripwire, which is available for both UNIX and NT systems.

(c) **Intruder artifacts** Intruders often leave all sorts of files on the systems that they compromise. These can range from sniffer log files, stolen password files, exploit scripts, and source code to various programs. Smarter and more experienced intruders will often only leave processes running in memory. Generically, programs that have been left behind by intruders are called remnant files. Potentially malicious scripts, source code, and programs are referred to as artifacts. Some of these files may not, in fact, be malicious however they must always be treated as such until they have been comprehensively analyzed. Intruders normally replace system files with other files that differ in operation from the original program but have the same name. These Trojan programs are popular among intruders as they offer a method of concealment for their activities. The Trojan programs themselves may also provide valuable information or functionality to support further intrusions. Many Trojan programs are identical to their original namesake with respect to all file system attributes except content, meaning that only a proper cryptographic checksum analysis can detect a difference between files. Keeping off-line, read-only lists of checksums of system files and important programs is therefore essential. Cryptographic checksums of the artifact(s) on the original system are also essential when giving copies to LE in order to validate the integrity of the copy of the artifact provided. If artifacts have been recovered from a compromised system, LE may sometimes request a site assist them by analyzing the artifact to determine its function. This may prove particularly important if a search warrant is later executed on a suspect and uncompiled Trojan code recovered from their computer system. Artifacts should not be analyzed on compromised system(s). Care should be taken to make a copy of the artifact(s) plus surroundings that, where possible, exactly mirror the original environment. Ideally, artifacts should be analyzed on an isolated system.

(d) **Network transaction auditing** Network transaction auditing is a useful tool in determining what is happening on your network both in real-time and from a historical perspective. Like ID (which transaction auditing supports), network transaction auditing can be separated into methods and tools that support historical and/or real-time analysis.

7.7.2 Automated IDS

The IDS marketplace is very volatile given the movement of commerce to the Internet and the race to market network security products to protect and support Internet connectivity and commerce. Some of the better known commercial IDS include RealSecure from Internet Security Systems, Sessionwall-3 from Platinum Systems, Netranger from Cisco Systems, and Cybercop Monitor from Network Associates. There are also a number of free IDS available on the Internet for non-commercial use. These systems include SHADOW and Network Flight Recorder. These freely available systems are not as user-friendly as the commercial systems but they are much more customizable. Automated IDS are useful for perimeter defense, however, they cannot keep up with the fact that security threats are constantly changing and may differ from enterprise to enterprise. Network-based IDS do not address the issue of internal threats to the network and, like firewalls, automated IDS need to be properly monitored and maintained.

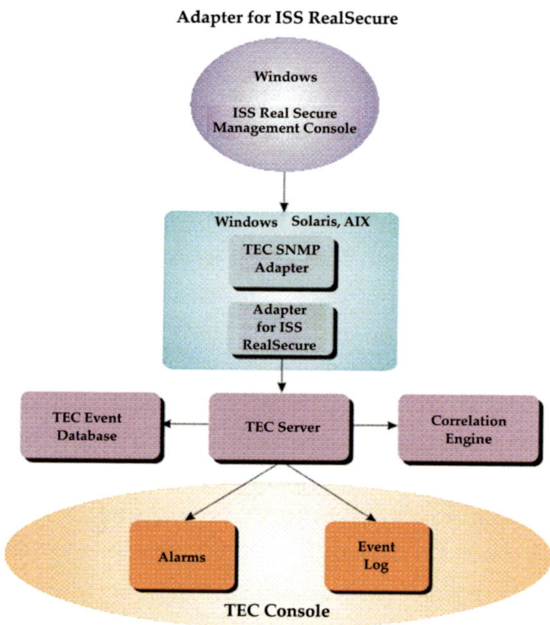

Figure 7.5: Adapter for ISS RealSecure IDS. *Source: http://publib.boulder.ibm.com/tividd/td/TRM/SC23–4823–00/en_US/HTML/adapter_guide06.htm*

7.8 CHALLENGES OF INTRUSION INVESTIGATION

At the core, an intrusion investigation is a digital forensic investigation, and as such, it should conform to the scientific method and scientific principles. However, there are special challenges to intrusion digital investigators that should be noted as they are not as common in other forms of digital forensics. Some of the more prominent challenges are described below.

7.8.1 Connection of events to an actual person

It is important to remember that linking events to an actual person is a concern for all digital investigations, and especially so with computer intrusions. Tracing events to a specific computer system is not sufficient to claim that a specific person was using that computer system during the time of those events and that that same person was responsible for the observed events.

7.8.2 Vulnerability of Compromised Systems

A common challenge that arises during intrusion investigations is the need to protect the target systems against further attack. Digital investigators may even be asked to remove a backdoor and repair the target system before they have collected evidence from the system. Whenever possible, evidence should be preserved prior to repairing the target system or altering its state in any other way. It is usually feasible to protect the target system by isolating it on the network while it is being processed as a source of evidence. In some cases, it may be viable to isolate a system simply by unplugging its network cable. However, when the system is a critical component of a network, it may be necessary to involve network administrators to reconfigure a router or firewall, partially isolating the system but permitting vital connections to enable an organization to remain in operation.

7.8.3 Monitoring the Progress of An Attacker

In many forms of criminal investigations, it can be beneficial for digital investigators to observe the suspect in the act of committing a crime. This will allow the digital investigator to gather additional information that can be used to identify and prosecute that suspect. This is also true for intrusion investigations, for multiple reasons: (a) Computer intrusions can be extremely complex, most especially those that extend across an enterprise network. Further observation may be necessary to determine the true scope of the incident. (b) Some intruders are skilled in hiding or erasing the traces of their activities. If they are not observed in action, there may not be enough evidence left behind to pursue investigative goals. (c) Many organizations are not architected and configured to retain the types of electronic records (log files, for example) that would enable an effective postmortem investigation. Therefore, observation of current events is much more critical. The problem with continued observation comes into play when the attacker is or may be causing damage to the target information systems, and the organization or individual who owns the information systems or who is reflected in the data that reside on those information systems. For example, an attacker may be actively removing sensitive data from a compromised system.

7.8.4 Response to Threat

A common problem for organizations that implement IDS is that they lack an appropriate incident response capability. Identifying a problem is half the battle, knowing how to respond appropriately and having the resources in place to do so is equally important. Effective incident response requires skilled security personnel with the knowledge of how to swiftly remediate threats, as well as robust procedures to address issues without impacting day-to-day operations. In many organizations there is a big disconnect between the people charged with monitoring alerts and those managing infrastructure, meaning that swift remediation can be difficult to achieve.

7.8.5 Management and Analysis of Malicious Code

In computer intrusions, more so than in other cybercrimes, digital investigators have to deal with unknown and/or malicious computer programs that are specifically related to events of interest. This means that, as opposed to there being spyware on a suspect's computer that is unrelated to the actual crime with which the suspect has been charged, there is malicious code in play that was specifically used to perpetrate the crime under investigation. A digital investigator will find some form of malicious computer program on the majority of compromised systems that he/she investigates. Furthermore, in order to successfully complete the investigation, the digital investigator will often need to analyze the malicious programs to learn more about what they do and how they operate. Analyzing malicious code to determine the answers to questions such as these often requires a deep understanding of computer programs, including the ability to read and interpret a disassembled or decompiled executable, as well as the ability to identify and circumvent defenses built into the code against disassembly and debugging.

REFERENCES

1. Casey, E. (2004). *Digital evidence and computer crime* (2nd ed.). London: Academic Press. Retrieved March 24, 2018, from http://index of.es/EBooks/Digital%20Evidence%20and%20Computer%20Crime%203rd%20Edition/Binder1.pdf
2. Casey, E. (2005). Case study: network intrusion investigation – lessons in forensic preparation. *Digital Investigation*, *2*, 254-460.
3. Farmer, D, & Venema, W. (2004). Forensic discovery. New Jersey: AddisonWesley. Retrieved March 24, 2018 http://www.fish2.com/security/wf-book.pdf
4. West-Brown, M., Stikvoort, D., & Kossakowski, K. (1998 December). *Handbook for Computer Security Incident Response Teams (CSIRTs).* CMU/SEI-98-HB-001.

CHAPTER 8

DIGITAL EVIDENCE AND LEGAL PROCEEDINGS

"In reality, those rare few cases with good forensic evidence are the ones that make it to court."

—Pat Brown

CONTENTS

Computers have become an important part of our lives and are becoming fundamental to activities in the home and workplace. State, federal, and local government agencies use the computer and Internet to create and access information. Similarly, digital systems have become the mainstay of criminal activity. Legal proceedings have always been influenced by tradition and court decisions and have necessitated the development of complex sets of rules that are used to assess forensic evidence in legal matters. However, not all evidence presented by digital forensic investigators in legal proceedings has been admissible. This chapter presents an overview of issues in the discipline of digital forensics and explores the workings of the law with regards to digital evidence. These include case jurisdiction, search and seizure, the requirement for search and seizure, criminal laws, and stages of a trial process.

8.1 INTRODUCTION

Digital evidence is more important in judicial procedures as a result of advances in information technology (IT) and telecommunications. Due to the cybercriminal nature of cybercrime and computer-assisted crime, digital claims, the process of digital evidence must be standard in order to ensure that the digital evidence submitted is admissible in legal proceedings. The different positions of law on matters of evidence in different authorities further complicate the international admissibility of digital evidence. Professional biologists can be engaged by diverse entities such as state or local federal laboratories or academic institutions. They may be called as expert witnesses or employed as consultants to provide practical and scientific advice. Forensic experts may be called or chosen by the court to assist a judge or jury in criminal or civil cases to help the accused or provide a third, poor criminal, ideas, and evidence that were formerly dealt with by prosecutors and defense experts. Regardless of how and why experts are called to testify, they must be prepared. They need to search for evidence or collect technical information related to this case. When testing the evidence, they must follow typical laboratory procedures. They are taken in a rational step in order to obtain correct test results, based on what the findings are based. After collecting information, expert witnesses needed to develop that information into an effective report in plain language, write this to reflect the use of scientific approaches and include valid documents. Expert witnesses and lawyers or courts who request them must collaborate to focus on the most significant issues of the case and to help each other comprehend the legal and technical terms. Preparation and organization help expert witnesses to gain skill and competence for their testimonies. It also helps in the investigative pretrial process decided by an attorney to learn basic facts about controversial issues. The findings relate to the information provided to members of the opposition that can help them clarify their case. It is structured and governed by a court-ordered period or procedural procedure.

8.2 FOURTH AMENDMENT

The Fourth Amendment creates a right to be free from "unreasonable" searches and seizures (US Constitution, Amendment IV). To be "reasonable," a search or seizure must be carried out either pursuant to a lawfully authorized search or arrest warrant or pursuant to one of the exceptions that the US Supreme Court has recognized to the warrant requirement (Annual Review of Criminal Procedure, 2008). A "search" constitutes an intrusion on an individual's reasonable expectation of privacy (Katz v. the United States, 1967). A "seizure" constitutes an interference with someone's possession and use of his/her property (Soldal v. Cook County, 1992). The sections below review how the Supreme Court has applied the Fourth Amendment to areas in which technology and privacy intersect. "The right of the people to be secure in their persons, houses, papers, and effects against unreasonable searches and seizures, shall not be violated, and no Warrants shall issue, but upon probable cause, supported by Oath or affirmation, and particularly describing the place to be searched and the persons or things to be seized." The US federal law relating to the collection of digital evidence by law enforcement agencies is administered by the Fourth Amendment and statutory privacy laws codified in the Wiretap Statute (18 USC Sections 2510–22), the Electronic Communications Privacy Act (ECPA) of 1986 (18 USC Sections 2701–02) and the Pen/Trap Statute (18 USC Sections 3121–27). The Fourth Amendment restricts the capability of government agents to acquire evidence without a warrant. A search warrant is a document signed by a judge that legalizes a police officer to conduct a search. According to the Fourth Amendment, there can be no search warrants without probable cause. Probable cause is a reasonable belief that a presumed detail is true. Sometimes, people consent to a search. In that scenario, the police may conduct a search without a warrant. A warrantless search does not infringe the Fourth Amendment if: (i) the agents' conduct does not violate an individual's "reasonable expectation of privacy," or (ii) the search falls within an exception to the warrant requirement. Therefore, agents must cogitate if a search violates the expectation of privacy. Even if a search does violate this expectation, it may still be reasonable if it falls within an exception to the warrant requirement. Determining what establishes a reasonable expectation of privacy is tough in cases involving computers. To support federal investigators, the US Justice Department recommends that agents treat a computer as a closed container (e.g., a file cabinet). The Fourth Amendment prohibits law enforcement agents such as police and other public employees or public officials from gaining access to and viewing computer information without a warrant if they would be prohibited from opening a closed container and inspecting its contents in the same situation. However, courts have reached different conclusions on whether or not individual computer files should be treated as separate closed containers. A private party cannot violate a suspect's Fourth Amendment rights unless acting as instructed by the police or another government agent. In other words, if a landlord searches a tenant's home or an employer searches an employee's office, it is not a violation of the Fourth Amendment. However, such a search could be a violation of privacy and a basis for a civil suit in some cases and not in others; for example, courts have held that an employee generally does not have an expectation of privacy in an office owned by the employer.

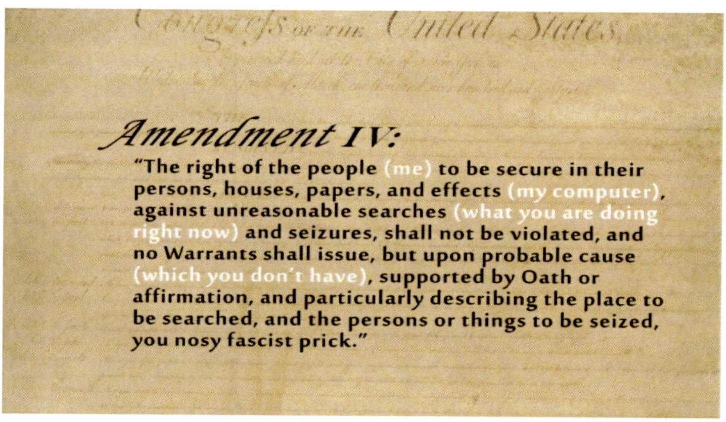

Figure 8.1: The Fourth Amendment. *Source: http://www.lataco.com/1984-day-defend-the-4th-amendment-los-angeles-84/*

8.3 PRIVACY LAWS

The US Privacy Protection Act (PPA) covers search and seizure of items that fall under the First Amendment (freedom of speech and freedom of the press) protections. The Privacy Act was intended to protect journalists, publishers, and other such people who might have evidence of criminal activity but are not suspected of having committed any criminal act. This law applies to materials that are created for the purpose of disseminating information to the public (which could apply to writings intended to be posted to websites, because this is a form of publishing to a public forum). If there is reason to suspect that the person who has the materials is committing the crime—that the materials pertain to or if there is a danger to some person of physical injury or death that could be prevented by seizing the evidence—then search and seizure is not a violation of the Privacy Act. Violation of the act is a civil rather than a criminal matter. Violators of the act are subject to civil lawsuit, but a violation does not mean that the evidence will be thrown out of court, as is the case with a violation of constitutional rights. The incidental seizure of certain materials may implicate the PPA or the ECPA. Under the PPA, law enforcement agents must take special steps when planning a search that may result in the seizure of First Amendment materials (e.g., materials posted on the web). The ECPA regulates how agents can obtain the contents of electronic communications stored by third-party service providers. To minimize liability under these statutes, agents should attempt to determine in advance the type of information that may be stored on the computer systems to be searched. Law enforcement agents can conduct "no-knock" warrants if they suspect that announcing their presence would lead to the destruction of evidence. Courts may also authorize "sneak-and-peek" warrants, which do not require agents to notify the person whose premises are searched. The USA PATRIOT Act amended 18 USC Section 3103a to allow a court to grant a delay of notice associated with the execution of a search warrant if it believes that providing immediate notification will have adverse effects. However, warrants issued under the amended statute still prohibit the seizure of electronic information unless specifically authorized by a court. In addition to physically seizing computers, agents frequently perform electronic surveillance. In these situations, it is important for agents to act in accord with the Wiretap Statute and the Pen/Trap Statute. The Wiretap Statute (Title III) governs real-time electronic surveillance in federal criminal investigations. Title III broadly prohibits the interception of oral, wire, and electronic communications. However, Title III contains dozens of exceptions and agents must be familiar with them before performing surveillance.

8.4 SEARCH WARRANT

A *search* was legally defined by the courts in *State versus Woodall* as "an examination of a man's house or other buildings or premises, or of his person, or of his vehicle, aircraft, etc., with a view to the discovery of contraband or illicit or stolen property, or some evidence of guilt to be used in the prosecution of a criminal action for some crime or offense with which he is charged" (according to *Black's Law Dictionary*). A *seizure* was defined in *Molina versus State* as "the act of taking possession of the property, for example, for a violation of law or by virtue of an execution" (of a warrant).

Figure 8.2: A Search Warrant. *Source: http://www.lawweb.in/2015/05/whether-court-can-issue-general-search.html*

A *search warrant* is a document signed by a magistrate giving law enforcement officers the authority to search a specified place for specific items that are particularly described in the warrant. A warrant must be based on another document called an *affidavit,* which is signed under oath by some person (a police officer or any other person) expressing the belief that certain items will be found at the location to be searched and giving facts that support the belief. Those facts must constitute *probable cause* that the objects of the search will be found at the described location. Only those items specifically named in the warrant can be searched for. A warrant can authorize the search and seizure of computer hardware, digital information, or both. Overly broad language (such as authorization to seize "all records" or "all computers") can result in the warrant being invalidated; the warrant must specify the crime(s) to which the evidence pertains. Because courts may or may not apply an exception, it is advisable to obtain a warrant before searching and seizing evidence. However, because computer files may be encrypted, misleadingly labeled, stored in unusual formats or commingled with innocuous files, agents cannot simply establish probable cause, describe the files they need, and then go and retrieve the data. In effect, they must understand the technical boundaries of different search methods; plan the search carefully and then draft the warrant in a manner that authorizes them to take the steps necessary to obtain the evidence. Agents should obtain multiple warrants if they have reason to believe that a network search will retrieve data stored in multiple locations. Also, agents should obtain a second warrant to search a computer seized pursuant to a valid warrant if the property targeted by the search is different from that specified in the first warrant. However, there are a number of other exceptions to the requirement for a search warrant, as established by statutes and court cases. These include

8.4.1 Consent Searches

If the party who has control over the premises or thing to be searched gives voluntary consent to the search, officers do not need a warrant. This is called a *consent search*. Officers do not need to show probable cause of a crime; they can legally search with consent even if there is no reason whatsoever to believe that a criminal offense has occurred. The key element here is that the consent must be voluntary. If consent is obtained under duress, threat, or intimidation, it is not voluntary and thus is not valid.

8.4.2 Abandoned Property

Law enforcement officers are generally allowed to search property that has clearly been abandoned without obtaining a warrant. For example, if a suspect is carrying a diskette and, upon observing that police are in the area, throws the diskette in a public trash can, officers can lawfully retrieve it.

8.4.3 Exigent Circumstances

Another situation in which searches can be conducted without a warrant is the case of *exigent circumstances*—that is, an emergency in which there is not time to get a warrant and the search is required immediately to save a life or prevent physical injury to some person, to keep the suspect from escaping, or to prevent evidence from being destroyed. This last situation is most applicable to digital evidence because of its fragile nature. It is very easy to destroy evidence that consists of computer data. In *United States versus David* and *United States versus Romero-Garcia,* the courts have held that seizure of electronic evidence without a warrant was legal because the evidence was about to be destroyed.

8.4.4 Plain View Searches

The idea of *plain view* (sometimes also referred to as the *open fields doctrine*) rests on the premise that the law enforcement officer is legally in a certain place where he or she can see observable evidence of a crime in plain view. Because the contents of a file stored on a computer are typically not in plain view (unless the officer lawfully entered the room where the suspect had the file open on the screen), this principle is not often applied to digital evidence. This issue has come into play when officers had a warrant to search for evidence of a crime (for example, child pornography) and during that legal search came across evidence of a different crime (for example, a photo indicating that the suspect had committed a murder). Courts have generally held that the plain-view doctrine applies, but upon finding the evidence of the second offense, officers should return with that evidence to the magistrate to establish probable cause for issuance of a search warrant to search for further evidence of the second crime.

8.5 SEARCH WITHOUT WARRANT

Warrantless searches that violate a reasonable expectation of privacy comply with the Fourth Amendment if they fall within an established exception to the warrant requirement. For example, agents may conduct a search without a warrant if an individual with authority has consented to the search, if there is an expectation that the evidence will be destroyed, or if the evidence is in plain view. Other exceptions occur during searches incident to a lawful arrest, inventory searches, and border searches. In some circumstances, Fourth Amendment protections do not apply because the action is deemed not to be a search. If the police take a vehicle into custody (for example, because they have arrested the person who was driving it), they are allowed to take record of the contents of the vehicle as a standard procedure as inventory. This does not constitute a search because it is not done for the purpose of looking for evidence of a crime but for the purpose of protecting the owner's property (and protecting the agency against claims of theft). However, this exception does not allow police to open locked containers, such as a briefcase, as part of the inventory process. To do so, they would generally need a warrant (unless some other exception, such as exigent circumstances, applies). A laptop or other computer that is in the vehicle when it is seized would generally be treated like a closed container in that in most cases law enforcement agents should obtain a warrant to open it and view the data on it.

Figure 8.3: Crime scene tape in front of police officers.

Source: https://securityintelligence.com/smart-forensics-for-the-internet-of-things-iot/

8.6 PEN REGISTERS/TRAP AND TRACE

The pen/trap Statute governs the use of pen registers and traps and trace devices. The statute authorizes a government attorney to apply for a court order authorizing the installation of a pen register and/or trap and trace device when the information sought is relevant to an investigation. As modified by the USA PATRIOT Act, it now applies to communications on computer networks in addition to telephone communications and gives nationwide effect to pen/trap orders. In addition to the applicable federal laws, state laws must also be considered. In particular, many states have laws regarding privacy, especially with regard to stored electronic information. Unfortunately, laws vary considerably from state to state, and a detailed discussion is beyond the scope of this book. Pen registers and trap and trace devices provide non-content information about the origin and destination of particular communications. Because this information does not contain the content of the communication, it is subject to lesser restrictions than actual content. The Supreme Court has long held that there is no reasonable expectation of privacy in this information because the telecommunications company has ready access to it; in fact, the company must utilize this information to ensure the communications are properly routed and delivered. The pen register Act covers pen registers/trap and trace. In the context of phone calls, pen registers display the outgoing number and the incoming number. Because email subject lines contain content, their use on emails, per revisions in the USA PATRIOT Act, must include the sender and addressee but avoid any part of the subject. IP addresses and port numbers associated with the communication are also fair game under the Act. The regulations specifically apply to "devices" that capture this information. Thus, ECPA generally prohibits the installation or use of any device that serves as a pen register or trap and trace. Amendments in the USA PATRIOT Act allow the term devices to also encompass software. Also, unlike provisions relating to the interception and access of communications, there is no statutory exclusionary rule that applies when the government illegally uses a pen register/trap and trace device. And there is no private cause of action against the government for violations of this law.

8.7 CRIMINAL LAW

One major cankerworm that has eaten deep into the fabric of the global society is crime. Crime is a violation of the criminal law. The elements of a crime are a wrongful act (the actus reus) and a wrongful intent (the mens rea). With the exception of strict liability crimes, these two elements are always necessary. In a strict liability crime, intent does not have to be shown. There are many different types of crimes: Some are directed against people, some against property, and some appear to be victimless crimes.

8.7.1 Crimes against Persons

Crimes against persons include homicide, rape, assault, and battery. There are many other crimes that result in harm done to a person. When a person dies, the first step is identifying the cause of death. If the death has been found to be due to natural causes, no investigation is necessary. Conversely, if the death has been found to be homicide, a police investigation will begin (Figure. Homicide is the act by which one person takes the life of another. There are several different types of homicide. The most seriously punished form of homicide is murder. For a homicide to be considered murder, several elements need to be present. Under the Model Penal Code, a murder is a homicide that includes malice aforethought, a legal term that refers to intentional killings that are committed purposely or knowingly with no justification or mitigation, situations in which the defendant purposefully inflicts serious harm or assaults with a deadly weapon, homicides committed recklessly "under circumstances manifesting extreme indifference to the value of human life," or felony murder. The Model Penal Code is a set of laws that many states have used as an example for their own laws. However, there are many variations among the states. In most states, murder is divided into several degrees. First-degree murder often includes homicide where there is not only intent but also premeditation. Premeditation can mean anything from simply intending to kill to have devised a plan for the killing, depending on the state. In some states, murders that occur during the commission of a felony, and those that include the use of poison or bombing, may be considered first-degree murder. Second-degree murder is defined differently in different states. Characteristics of second-degree murder that are common to all states are that there is no actual premeditation and that the crime does not qualify as manslaughter. For instance, in Florida, second-degree murder may be considered a homicide in which the defendant has a "depraved mind or heart." This means that: (i) A person of ordinary judgment would realize that the act will likely kill or cause serious injury. (ii) The act is done from ill will or hatred in such a way as to show indifference to human life. In other states, there are slightly different, but similar standards. When a jury believes that the defendant acted recklessly but did not intend to kill the victim, they will return a verdict of second-degree murder. Manslaughter is a homicide that is committed without any justification, but also without malice aforethought. Manslaughter may be considered voluntary or involuntary. *Voluntary manslaughter* is usually a homicide that was committed in the heat of passion. It occurs when the defendant was provoked by acts of the victim such as "to cause a reasonable man to act rashly and without reflection." This provocation can generally include violent assault and an unlawful arrest attempt, but not just insulting words. According to the Model Penal Code, there needs to be "extreme mental or emotional disturbance." *Involuntary manslaughter* is a killing in which there is no actual intent to kill. It occurs when the killing is the result of the commission of an act not likely to cause severe bodily harm, or during a crime that is not a felony. Also, it may be the result of a lawful act done in a criminal manner. This would be a case of negligence. A typical example of an involuntary manslaughter case is when a person is killed due to reckless and careless driving. However, in some states, such killing is a separate crime (vehicular homicide). Suicide is the intentional taking of a person's own life. In most states, it is a crime to assist someone who is committing suicide. For example, in New York, helping someone commit suicide is considered manslaughter. *Assault* and *battery* are two different offenses. The battery is when someone uses force to do bodily harm to another. Assault is an attempted battery. Battery needs to involve physical contact, whereas assault does not. Some examples of simple assault would be threatening someone with a weapon or threatening to strike the person. Some examples of simple battery would be hitting or pushing someone, or any other offensive touching of another person. A simple assault and battery is often a misdemeanor. Aggravated assault and battery can occur if there is an intent to commit a more serious crime (such as murder), or if a deadly weapon is used. If assault and battery are committed against a police officer, firefighter, or other public official, that could also be considered aggravated. Another very serious crime against a person is *rape*. Rape can be one of two types: forcible or statutory. Forcible rape is usually defined as someone having sexual intercourse with a person who did not give his or her consent. Statutory rape takes place if the victim of the rape is under a certain age (which may be 16, 17, or 18), or has a reduced mental capacity. For statutory rape, it is not necessary to show that force was used. Statutory rape is a strict liability crime, and mistake of age usually cannot be used as a defense. In recent years, several changes in rape laws have been enacted. For example, it is possible for there to be rape when the defendant and the victim are married. There are several different degrees of rape, depending on factors such as the force that was used and the age and mental capacity of the victim. *False imprisonment* and *kidnapping* are crimes that involve a victim being restrained without his or her consent. False imprisonment means confining someone against their will. Some states classify false imprisonment (without the use of violence) as a misdemeanor; some states do not have statutes regarding false imprisonment.

Kidnapping is a serious felony in all states and the federal government. The elements of the crime usually include the unlawful taking and carrying away of another person. Usually, force or coercion is involved. If the victim is a child or an incompetent person, then a show of force or coercion is not needed. There are two categories of kidnapping: simple kidnapping and kidnapping for ransom. Kidnapping, with the intention of receiving money as ransom, is considered first-degree kidnapping and is treated more seriously. Another type of kidnapping is *child-snatching*. This is when a parent kidnaps his or her own child away from the other parent. Child abuse is the physical or mental mistreatment or neglect of children by their parents or guardians. This can include physical injuries from beating or excessive discipline, sexual molestation, or neglect. There can also be emotional abuse, which can be committed through words. Other types of abuse are abuse against a spouse or against an elderly person.

8.8 CLASSES OF EVIDENCE

Legal evidence is classified based on the type of fact it is to prove, its form, the laws that govern its use and the role it has in the case. Major classes of legal evidence include: direct, circumstantial, documentary, hearsay, expert, scientific, inculpatory, and exculpatory evidence.

8.8.1 Direct Evidence

Direct evidence is not presumed or inferred it is directly related to the fact. According to the legal dictionary online, direct evidence is “evidence that if believed, proves the existence of the fact in issue without inference or presumption. Direct evidence proves or disproves a fact directly. Perhaps the most well-known type of direct evidence is eyewitness testimony, where a witness describes precisely what she saw, heard, or experienced. For instance, in a personal injury case, suppose that the injured plaintiff was crossing the street when the defendant hit her with his car. One type of direct evidence the plaintiff might use to prove that the defendant was the one driving might be the testimony of a bystander who saw the defendant clearly as his car hit the plaintiff. Exhibits and other pieces of real or documentary evidence may also provide direct evidence. For instance, in a breach of contract case, the contract itself is direct evidence of the existence of the contract. A products liability case may bring the actual defective product into court to show the judge or jury that the product did, in fact, break in the way that witnesses say it did.” Direct evidence is concrete or firsthand evidence of the fact being proven.

8.8.2 Circumstantial Evidence

Circumstantial evidence as defined as “…evidence that is drawn not from direct observation of a fact but from events or circumstances that surrounds it.” Circumstantial evidence is that which suggest or infer the existence of the fact. Circumstantial evidence, by contrast, is evidence that does not point directly to a fact. Instead, an inference must be made that links the circumstantial evidence to the fact the party using it is trying to prove. *For example*, suppose that in the car accident as described in "direct evidence," the injured plaintiff offers into evidence a photograph of the defendant's car, taken at the accident scene. The front of the car is crumpled. The plaintiff offers the photo to prove that the defendant hit her with the car. Unlike the plaintiff's direct testimony that "the defendant hit me with his car," the photograph is circumstantial evidence. It demonstrates that the defendant's car was at the accident scene at some point and that it had a damaged front end while it was there.

Figure 8.4: Fingerprints as Circumstantial evidence. *Source: http://thecreationclub.com/the-evidence-for-creation-part-2-the-evidence/*

8.8.3 Documentary Evidence

Documentary evidence includes any type of written evidence offered to support a fact that is being proven. The doctrine of documentary evidence may be explained thus: the onus is on the prosecution to show to the court that the evidence produced is no more and no less now than when it was first taken into the possession of the police.

8.8.4 Hearsay Evidence

Hearsay evidence is evidence that is not based on the personal account of an event but on the account of another and is not allowed under oath. It is essentially second-hand evidence. In hearsay, the evidence is given not about what one saw or heard personally but about what one was told by someone who saw or heard. Hearsay evidence consists of statements made by witnesses who are not present. While hearsay evidence is not admissible in court, it can be relevant and valuable in a workplace investigation where the burden of proof is less robust than in court. The rule against hearsay says that any assertion of fact other than one made by a person while giving oral evidence in the court proceedings is inadmissible as evidence of any fact asserted. Thus, any out of court statements including photographs, videotapes, and digital information produced and stored by a computer are hearsay and cannot be used as evidence. There are, however, multiple exceptions to the hearsay rule, which allow admission of hearsay coming from sufficiently reliable sources. In particular, data recorded by a machine in the normal course of operation is usually admissible as evidence of the recorded events if there was no human intervention in the recording process.

8.8.5 Expert Evidence

Expert evidence is given with regards to a scientific or technical subject. An expert in a case would give testimony based on specialized formal training and/or experience in a particular field. This type of evidence is usually required when there are parts of a case that are outside the capabilities of the trier/finder of the fact. It is expected that an expert witness is qualified in the particular field in which they are to give evidence.

8.8.6 Scientific Evidence

Forensic science refers to "the application of science expertise in the form of knowledge base and methodology within the court" (White, 2010). It is the use of scientific techniques in a legal investigation producing evidence to be used in court. Science is used in court to establish particular fact which may be out of the trier of the facts' field of expertise. This suggests that where scientific evidence is gathered, the objective is for it to be used in legal proceedings. Scientific evidence is evidence culled from a scientific procedure that helps the trier of fact understand the evidence or determine facts at issue in a judicial proceeding. Under rule 702 of the Federal Rules of Evidence (in the courts of the United States) and similar state court rules of evidence, "a witness qualified as an expert by knowledge, skill, experience, training, or education" may testify and offer opinions in court if "scientific, technical, or other specialized knowledge will assist the trier of fact to understand the evidence or to determine a fact in issue." Article VII of the Federal Rules of Evidence contain other rules on Expert testimony and scientific evidence.

All states have rules on expert testimony and scientific evidence that are similar to the rules in article VII. Expert testimony on scientific evidence is different from ordinary testimony from laypersons. A lay witness may testify to inferences and give opinions only if they are rationally based upon the witness's observations of the subject of the testimony. Experts, by contrast, may give opinions and testify about potential inferences based in part on information obtained from secondhand sources and not from observation of the object of the testimony. For example, a layperson would not be allowed to take the witness stand and offer an opinion on a plaintiff's injury unless the person had witnessed relevant information regarding the injury. However, a doctor who is certified as a specialist in the particular injury could take the stand and offer opinions on the injury based not only on an examination of the plaintiff but also on secondhand information that is normally relied on by experts in that particular field of medical study. One of the most important issues that arise in expert testimony in which scientific procedures a court should accept as evidence. Many scientific procedures are not seriously in dispute and are accepted by courts with little or no inquisition into their validity. Examples include fingerprint tests for purposes of identification, blood tests, breathalyzer tests for alcohol consumption, and ballistics tests of bullets and their impact areas. These scientific procedures are so widely accepted that a court may take judicial notice of the procedure's validity. Judicial notice means that the parties in the case do not have to present evidence to the court to establish the validity of the scientific procedure. In some instances, legislatures have specifically authorized the use of scientific tests, such as breathalyzer tests for suspected drunk drivers. Whether they are judicially noticed or legislatively mandated, scientific tests that are universally accepted must be presented by a qualified expert. A person is established as a qualified expert before the court through questioning by the attorney who is using the witness as an expert. The attorney asks a series of questions to establish that the witness has adequate education and training to testify as an expert—a process called laying a foundation for the witness. Once the court is convinced that the witness is an expert on the procedure or subject matter that will be presented as evidence, the witness gives an expert opinion to the exact procedures that were used or the factual circumstances that arose in the case at hand. For example, assume that a person sues a doctor for Medical Malpractice, arguing that the defendant failed to set a broken bone properly. If the plaintiff offers a bone specialist as an expert witness on the issues surrounding the care he received from the defendant, the expert witness must testify about the witness's credentials and give details about the plaintiff's treatment. Some scientific tests and examinations that are not universally accepted are nevertheless generally considered reliable. Some examples are neutron activation analysis to determine the identity of goods, voiceprints to determine a person's identity, and genetic testing or DNA analysis. These types of scientific procedures may be accepted in the medical communities, but they are not so established that they may be judicially noticed as automatically valid sources of scientific evidence. They may be admitted as evidence, but only after an expert witness has testified to the validity of the test. In determining whether to admit scientific evidence from procedures that are not universally accepted, a court must ask whether the test is reliable. A technique's reliability depends on a number of factors, including whether the technique can be or has been tested, whether it has been subjected to peer review, whether the test procedures have been published, whether the test has a margin of error and, if so, at what rate, and whether the technique, as applied, confirmed to existing standards for the test (Daubert v. Merrell Dow Pharmaceuticals, Inc., 509 U. S. 579, 113 S. Ct. 2786, 125 L. Ed. 2d 469 [1993]).

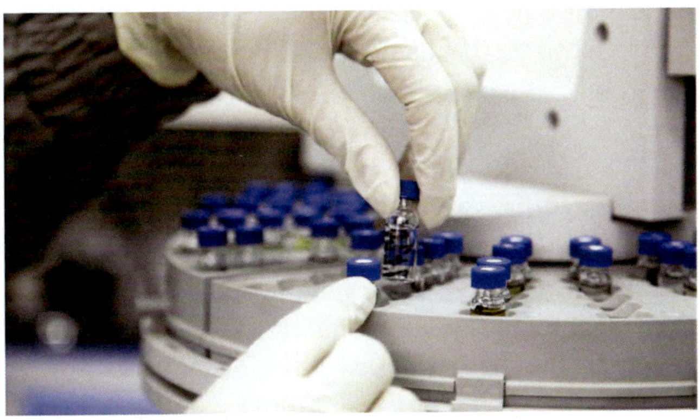

Figure 8.5: A forensic investigator at work in the forensic science department of Dubai Police. *Source: https://www.thenational.ae/uae/unidentified-torso-case-highlights-work-of-dubai-police-forensic-team-1.48771*

In its 1999 Kumho Tire v. Carmichael opinion, the US Supreme Court ruled that the Daubert standards govern not just the admissibility of scientific evidence in federal court, but should be applied to all witnesses seeking federal court approval to testify as an expert. Thus, the Supreme Court found that a purported expert on tire failure was subject to a Daubert inquiry before he could be permitted to testify on the subject in a products liability trial, even if some of his proffered testimony was not wholly "scientific." The lower court had attempted to draw a distinction between scientific expert for which the Daubert standards did apply and a technical expert for which the Daubert standards did not apply. By expanding the Daubert test, the Court reemphasized the trial court's broad discretion in matters of expert testimony. In some instances, courts are reluctant to admit certain scientific evidence because the procedures yield results that are not considered sufficiently reliable to be used as evidence. Such procedures include polygraph and chemical tests that have been created to determine whether a person is telling the truth. If all parties agree that testimony derived from such procedures shall be admissible, however, a court is free to allow the evidence to be introduced. In any case, regardless of the level of acceptance of a particular scientific procedure, the scientific evidence presented must be relevant to the issue at hand. Furthermore, the scientific evidence must have been obtained in a manner that is consistent with the way such evidence is normally obtained. For instance, assume that a physicist intends to testify to the speed of the defendant's vehicle in a personal injury case stemming from a car accident. If the physicist used different methods from those used by other physicists in determining a vehicle's speed, the court may refuse to allow the physicist to testify as to the vehicle's speed. An expert witness giving testimony on scientific evidence may offer opinions on issues related to that evidence. An expert witness may also give an opinion on the ultimate issue in the case. Under rule 704 of the Federal Rules of Evidence, however, an expert witness testifying with respect to the mental state or condition of a criminal defendant may not state "an opinion or inference as to whether the defendant did or did not have the mental state or condition constituting an element of the crime charged or of a defense thereto." The US Congress approved this rule, which is applied by courts only in criminal cases, in 1984, largely in response to the outcome of the criminal prosecution of John Hinckley, who attempted to assassinate President Ronald Reagan in 1981. Hinckley was charged with attempted assassination, assault on a federal officer, and use of a firearm in the commission of a federal offense, but was found not guilty by reason of insanity after the jury heard testimony from a psychiatrist who declared that Hinckley could not be found guilty because he lacked the knowing mental state required for a conviction on the charges. The weight given to scientific evidence may vary according to the particular test that yielded the evidence. One party's expert testimony may be convincing, but it may not be dispositive of the case because the other party may have experts from the same field who have studied the same evidence and come to different conclusions. Experts have become indispensable to the vast majority of litigated cases, and in many cases, civil and criminal alike, come down to a battle between experts. One notable exception to this trend is the Paternity case, in which blood test results or DNA test results can establish the ultimate issue in the case. This is true, however, only if the parties in the paternity case agree that the particular tests will be conclusive and if the tests show that the individual named as the father could not be a parent of the child in question. If the tests show that the individual named as the father could be the parent, the test results will not dispose of the case, and the parties will have to present further evidence. Courts have the discretion to appoint an expert witness to testify to scientific evidence. Under rule 706 of the Federal Rules of Evidence and similar state court rules of evidence, a court may appoint an expert to present evidence on a particular topic and order compensation for the expert's time and effort. Typically, in a civil case, the parties must allocate the costs as the court directs. In just compensation cases under the Fifth Amendment and in criminal cases, the court orders payment for the expert out of government funds.

8.8.7 Inculpatory and Exculpatory Evidence

The inculpatory and exculpatory evidence is directly related to the function the evidence plays in a case. *Inculpatory evidence* refers to evidence which can be used to establish the guilt of the person in question. It is that evidence that shows involvement in an act. The inculpatory evidence is any evidence that will directly or indirectly link an accused person to the offence being investigated. For an investigator, inculpatory evidence can be found in the victim's complaint, physical evidence, witness accounts, or the circumstantial relationships that are examined, analyzed, and recorded during the investigative process. It can be anything from the direct evidence of an eyewitness who saw the accused committing the crime, to the circumstantial evidence of a fingerprint found in a location connecting the accused to the victim or the crime scene. Naturally, direct evidence that shows the accused committed the crime is the preferred inculpatory evidence, but, in practice, this it is frequently not available. The investigator must look for and interpret other sources for evidence and information. Often, many pieces of circumstantial evidence are required to build a case that allows the investigator to achieve reasonable grounds to believe, and enables the court to reach their belief beyond a reasonable doubt. A single fingerprint found on the outside driver's door of a stolen car would not be sufficient for the court to find an accused guilty of car theft. However, if you added witness evidence to show that the accused was seen near the car at the time it was stolen, and a security camera recording of the accused walking off the parking lot where the stolen car was dumped, and the police finding the accused leaving the dump site where he attempted to toss the keys of that stolen car into the bushes, the court would likely have proof beyond a reasonable doubt. If an abundance of inculpatory circumstantial evidence can be located for presentation to the court that leads to a single logical conclusion, the court will often reach their conclusion of proof beyond a reasonable doubt, unless exculpatory evidence is presented by the defense to create a reasonable doubt. *Exculpatory evidence*, on the other hand, is evidence that is used to establish the innocence of the person in question. Exculpatory evidence is the exact opposite of inculpatory evidence in that it tends to show the accused person or the suspect did not commit the offence. It is important for an investigator to not only look for inculpatory evidence, but to also consider evidence from an exculpatory perspective. Considering evidence from the exculpatory perspective demonstrates that an investigator is being objective and is not falling into the trap of tunnel vision. If it is possible to find exculpatory evidence that shows the suspect is not responsible for the offence, it is helpful for police because it allows for the elimination of that suspect and the redirecting of the investigation to pursue the real perpetrator. Sometimes, exculpatory evidence will be presented by the defense at trial to show the accused was not involved in the offence or perhaps only involved to a lesser degree. In our previous circumstantial case of car theft, there is strong circumstantial case; but what if the defense produces the following exculpatory evidence where: (1) A tow truck dispatcher testifies at the trial and produces records showing the accused is a tow truck driver; (2) On the date of the car theft, the accused was dispatched to the site of the car theft to assist a motorist locked out of his car; (3) The accused testifies that he only assisted another male to gain entry to the stolen car because he could see the car keys on the front seat; (4) The accused explains that, after opening the car, he agreed to meet this male at the parking lot where the car was left parked; (5) He accepted the keys of the stolen car from the other male to tow the vehicle later to a service station from that location; (6) When approached by police, he stated that he became nervous and suspicious about the car he had just towed; and (7) He tried to throw the keys away because he has a previous criminal record and knew the police would not believe him. The court might dismiss the case against the accused, if provided with this kind of exculpatory evidence.

8.9 MOTIONS BEFORE TRIAL

At its most basic, a motion is a formal legal request made to the judge in a case. A pretrial motion is one made before trial. In criminal procedure, pretrial motions, and preliminary hearings take care of certain legal issues before the trial takes place, such as the admission of evidence and who will be allowed to testify as a witness. The pretrial motion and preliminary hearing phase of a case are often crucial. It can be a turning point. Depending on the facts and circumstances of the case, your criminal defense lawyer can bring a motion to exclude evidence at trial or a motion to dismiss the charges altogether.

Figure 8.6: Presentation of pre-trial motions in a US court. *Source: https://www.thoughtco.com/the-pre-trial-motions-stage-970830*

Examples of Pretrial Motions in Federal Cases;

Motion to Dismiss A motion to dismiss is a request to the judge that the federal charges be dismissed altogether for lack of evidence or other issues. It is otherwise an attempt to get a judge to dismiss a charge or the entire case. If may be used when there is not enough evidence or when the evidence or facts in the case do not equal a crime. It is also filed when the court does not have the authority or jurisdiction to make a ruling in the case. For example, if a will is being contested, the case would have to be decided by a probate court and not a small claims court. A motion to dismiss the case based on lack of subject matter jurisdiction would likely be filed.

Motion to Suppress A motion to suppress asks the judge to keep certain evidence or witness statements out of the trial. A motion to suppress evidence often addresses issues such as evidence seized illegally. Confessions wrongly obtained. Statements improperly obtained. If there was probable cause to make an arrest.

Motion for Change of Venue A motion for change of venue is a request that the case is moved to a different location because of concerns that the jury will be swayed by publicity (often done in high profile cases). Famous cases when changes of venue were granted; (a) The four Los Angeles police officers charged with assault of Rodney King in 1991, had their trial moved from Los Angeles County to Ventura County. (b) Oklahoma City Bomber Timothy McVeigh was granted a change of venue from Oklahoma to the US District Court in Denver, Colorado. (c) Beltway snipers Lee Boyd Malvo and John Allen Muhammad had their trials moved from northern Virginia to Chesapeake and Virginia Beach, in southeastern Virginia. Anyone of these motions, whether granted or denied, can have a significant impact on the case at hand.

8.9.1 Trial Process

In the United States, the trial is the principal method for resolving legal disputes that parties cannot settle by themselves or through less formal methods. The chief purpose of a trial is to secure fair and impartial administration of justice between the parties to the action. A trial seeks to ascertain the truth of the matters in issue between the parties and to apply the law to those matters. Also, a trial provides a final legal determination of the dispute between the parties. The two main types of trials are civil trials and criminal trials. Civil trials resolve civil actions, which are brought to enforce, redress, or protect individual rights. Generally, all types of actions other than criminal actions are civil actions. In a criminal trial, a person charged with crime is found guilty or not guilty and sentenced. The government, on behalf of the citizens, brings a criminal action in order to punish the violators of criminal laws.

8.9.2 Jury Selection

Although a trial does not technically begin until after the jury is seated, jury selection, or Voir Dire (pronounced vwahr DEER), is commonly referred to as the first stage of a trial. At the beginning of a trial, the jury is chosen from the jury pool, a group of citizens who have been randomly chosen form the community for the duty of a jury. The judge and the attorneys, on behalf of the parties, interrogate each of the potential jurors. If a potential juror is for any reason is biased in judging the evidence, he will not be allowed to sit on the jury. This is also known as a challenge for a cause. A potential juror may be confronted for conviction of a serious crime, a financial interest in the result of a controversy, participation in another proceeding concerning one of the parties, a business, personal, family relationship, professional, or any other reason that may show prejudice.

8.9.3 Opening Statements

After the judge gives the preliminary instructions, the attorneys for the parties give their opening statements to the jury. During opening statements, the lawyers outline the issues in the case and tell the jury what they expect the evidence will prove during the trial. The purpose of the opening statement is to give a general picture of the facts and issues to help the jury better understand the evidence. The opening statements usually last ten to thirty minutes, although sometimes they are much longer. The judge can limit the time for opening statements. Usually, an attorney will present her opening statement as a story, giving a chronological overview of what happened from the party's viewpoint. Although the attorneys will present the case in the best possible light for their clients, the opening statements should be factual, not argumentative. The opening statements are not evidence, and the attorneys should not offer their opinion of the evidence. Attorneys are not permitted to make statements that cannot be supported by the evidence they expect to present during the trial.

8.9.4 Plaintiff Testimony

The first part of the actual trial proceeding consists of the plaintiffs presenting their witnesses and experts to present the arguments and justifications for the complaint. The defense is permitted to cross-examine each witness in an attempt to dismiss, discredit, or disprove the witnesses' statements.

8.9.5 Defense Testimony

After the plaintiffs' case is presented, the defendants present their case in much the same way using witnesses and experts that present direct testimony, followed by cross-examination by the plaintiffs' counsel.

8.9.6 Redirection and Recall

At the discretion of the judge, each witness can be redirected after cross-examination by either the counsel. If critical information is not divulged during the initial testimony, counsel can request to recall a witness to the stand for additional questioning and cross-examination.

8.9.7 Closing Arguments

Counsel for the plaintiffs and defense summarize their clients' positions to remind the jurors of the facts presented in their case and to convince the jurors of the veracity of their cause. Closing arguments are typically intended to be dramatic and pointed for effect. In most jurisdictions, the plaintiff argues first and last. That is, the plaintiff argues first, then the defendant argues, and then the plaintiff makes a rebuttal argument. Actually, the party with the burden of proof usually argues first and last. This is almost always the plaintiff, but sometimes the only issues remaining for the jury to decide are affirmative defenses or counterclaims raised by the defendant. Also, a few jurisdictions allow only one argument per side, and in a few of these, the defendant argues first, plaintiff last.

8.9.8 Jury's Instructions

After closing arguments, the judge will instruct the jury. The purpose of jury instruction is to explain to the jurors the meaning of the law as it relates to the issues they are considering and to tell the jurors what facts they must determine if they are to give a verdict for one party or the other. Each lawyer will have prepared a set of written instructions that she hopes the judge will give to the jury. These will be tailored to advance her client's case. Many a verdict has been overturned on appeal because a trial judge has wrongly instructed the jury. The judge will carefully determine which instructions to give and often will use a set of pattern instructions provided by the state bar association or the supreme court of the state. These pattern jury instructions are often safer because they are patterned after language that appellate courts have used previously, and appellate courts are less likely to find reversible error in the instructions.

8.9.9 Jury's Deliberations and Verdict

After the judge has finished instructing the jury, the jury retires to the jury room to begin deliberations. At this time the alternate jurors are dismissed, although some jurisdictions allow the alternate jurors to participate in deliberations. The court bailiff brings the exhibits and written instructions to the jury room and safeguards the jury's privacy during deliberations. It is largely up to the jury to decide how to organize itself and conduct the deliberations. The judge usually only instructs the jurors to select a foreperson to preside over the deliberations and to sign the verdict forms that reflect their decisions. Jurors sometimes have questions during their deliberations. Usually, they write down their questions and give them to the bailiff, who takes them to the judge. The judge confers with the attorneys and sends a written response to the jury. A jury might deliberate anywhere from a few minutes to several days. Usually, the jury must reach a unanimous verdict, although majority verdicts are sometimes allowed in civil cases. If the jury tells the judge it cannot reach a verdict, the judge usually gives the jury some further instructions and returns it to the jury room for further deliberations. If the jury still cannot reach a verdict, however, the jury is deadlocked, and a mistrial is declared. The case must then be retried.

Figure 8.7: Jurors deliberating in jury room, taking vote on verdict. *Source: https://www.gettyimages.co.uk/detail/photo/jurors-deliberating-in-jury-room-taking-high-res-stock-photography/873180–008*

Usually, however, the jury reaches a verdict. When the jury reaches a verdict and signs the verdict forms, it notifies the judge that it has reached a decision. The attorneys, if they are not in the courtroom, are called, and everyone returns to the courtroom. The judge asks the foreperson if the jury has reached a verdict. The foreperson responds "yes," and the verdict forms are read aloud, usually by the court clerk. In most jurisdictions, the parties may poll the jury by asking each individual juror if he or she agrees with the verdict. Obviously, in a court trial without an advisory jury, there is no jury deliberation or verdict. The judge simply enters a judgment based on the applicable law and his own view of the facts. There is also a post-trial phase, sometimes a *collection (judgment enforcement)* stage, and occasionally an *appeals* phase.

REFERENCES

1. Andrea, C. (2000). *Forensic science: evidence, clues, and investigation*. Philadelphia, PA: Chelsea House Publishers.
2. Casey, E. (2004). *Digital evidence and computer crime* (2nd ed.). London. Academic Press.
3. Faigman, D. (2002). *Modern scientific evidence: The law and science of expert testimony* (2nd ed.). St. Paul, MN: West Group.
4. Guidotti, T., & Susan, R. (2001). *Science on the witness stand: Evaluating scientific evidence in law, adjudication, and policy*. Beverly Farms, MA: OEM Press.

CHAPTER 9

CYBERSTALKING

"In order to become a cyberstalker, one must either feel rejected, angry, powerful or misunderstood."

—Michael Nuccitelli, Psy. D.

CONTENTS

Cyberstalking is a relatively new kind of cyber terrorism crime. Although it often receives a lower priority then cyber-terrorism it is an important global issue. Due to new technologies, it is striking in different forms. Due to the Internet's provision of anonymity and security, it is proliferating quickly. Technology and tools available to curb it have many limitations and are not easy to implement. Legal acts to protect people from cyberstalking are geographically limited to the concerned state or country. This chapter reviews cyberstalking, how cyberstalkers operate, impacts, provision of legal acts, and actions taken to prevent it. There is an immediate need for research in the various dimensions of cyberstalking to assess this social problem.

9.1 INTRODUCTION

The advent of new technologies and innovations has enriched our lives in numerous ways. Also, increased dependence on IT and communication technology for dynamic and fast business solutions have its own side effect. The influence of digital information technologies on the world certainly poses endless benefits for the citizens of the growing global village. The dark side of it, not surprisingly, is the abuse of IT for criminal activities. Cyberstalking is a new kind of crime that existed since the late 1990s that emerged as major global criminological issues. In essence, cyberstalking describes the use of Information and Communication Technology in order to harass one or more victims (Bocij, 2006). In addition, harassment means any behavior that causes the victim distress, whether intentional or not. Cyberstalking often finds their victim online as they use computers and networks for criminal activities as these technologies can easily be abused to frighten, intimidate, bully, harass, and victimize unsuspecting users. Cyberstalking is analogous to traditional forms of stalking, in that it incorporates persistent behaviors that instill anxiety and fear. However, with the emergence of new technologies, traditional stalking has taken on entirely new form through various medium such as email and the Internet, that is, cyberspace. Cyberstalking radically signals the potential of the Internet to facilitate some types of crimes, as well as pointing to the existing interventions and likely to prove effective. Cyberstalking is an entirely new form of deviant behavior that makes use of technology to harass others in a variety of ways. In a decade, our reliance on the Internet, email, instant messaging, chat rooms, and other communications technologies has made cyberstalking a growing social problem that can affect computer users anywhere in the world. This chapter is devoted exclusively to an examination of cyberstalking, providing a synopsis of the problem, its causes and consequences, and global case studies. Although cyberstalking usually involves one person pursuing another, this is not always the case. As the behavior has developed, it has come to include such acts as stock market fraud, sexual harassment, data theft, impersonation, identity theft, consumer fraud, computer monitoring, and attacks by political groups on government services. At an alarming rate, pornographers and pedophiles have begun to use cyberstalking as a way of tracking down new victims. While cyberstalking has become a global problem, most cases emanates from the United States, making Americans the most vulnerable group of targets.

The California Penal code (1998) included electronic communications in their anti-stalking law. The important sections of the California Penal Code have strongly influenced all subsequent anti-stalking laws in the United States, clearly defining stalking and related terms.

Cyberstalking is one among of the cybercrime. Cyberstalking in a way is the use of the Internet to stalk someone—a kind of harassment targeted at computer users. The term is used interchangeably with online harassment and online abuse. A cyberstalked does not present a direct physical threat to a victim, but follows the victim's online activity to obtain information, make threats in different forms of verbal intimidation. The anonymity of online interaction reduces the chance of identification and makes cyberstalking more common than physical stalking. Though cyberstalking might seem relatively harmless, it can cause victims psychological and emotional harm. It may occasionally lead to actual stalking. Cyberstalking in the contemporary information society is becoming a prevalent scheme in racism, and other expressions of bigotry and hate.

Any person who willfully, maliciously, and repeatedly follows or harasses another person and who makes a credible threat with the intent to place that person in reasonable fear of death or great bodily injury is guilty of the crime of stalking … "harasses" means a knowing and willful course of conduct directed at a specific person that seriously alarms, annoys, torments, or terrorizes the person, and that serves no legitimate purpose. This course of conduct must be such as would cause a reasonable person to suffer substantial emotional distress, and must actually cause substantial emotional distress to the person.

(California Penal Code 646.9)

Figure 9.1: A Cyberstalker in action.

Source: https://cyberbullying.org/cyberstalking

9.2 TYPES OF CYBERSTALKING

Ellison suggests that cyberstalking can be classified by the type of electronic communication used to stalk the victim and the extent to which the communication is private or public (1999). Ellison has classified cyberstalking as either "direct" or "indirect." For example, direct cyberstalking includes the use of pagers, cell phones, and email to send messages of hate, obscenities, and threats to intimidate a victim. Direct cyberstalking has been reported to be the most common form of cyberstalking with a close resemblance to offline stalking (Wallace, 2000). Direct cyberstalking is claimed to be the most common way in which stalking begins. On the other hand, indirect cyberstalking includes the use of the Internet to display messages of hate, and threats or used to spread false rumors about a victim (Ellison and Akdeniz, 1998). Messages can be posted on web pages, within chat groups, or bulletin boards. Working to Halt Online Abuse (2003) statistics show chat rooms, instant messages, message boards, and newsgroups to be the most common way that indirect cyberstalking begins. Ogilvie claims indirect cyberstalking has the greatest potential to transfer into real-world stalking (2000). Messages placed within the public space of the Internet can encourage third parties to support their assault. Therefore, indirect cyberstalking can escalate the risk of victims by restraining the geographical margins of possible threats. Consequently, indirect cyberstalking have a greater potential than direct cyberstalking to transfer into the real world as it increases the potential for third parties to become involved (Maxwell, 2001).

However, depending on the use of the internet, there are three primary ways of cyberstalking (Ogilvie, 2000):

9.2.1 Email Stalking

This is direct communication through email which is the most easily available form of harassment. It is almost similar to traditional stalking in some aspects. One may send email of a threatening, hateful, or obscene nature, or even send spam or viruses to harass others. For example, in India in 2004 two MBA students sent emails to their female classmate to intimidate her. The free availability of anonymizers and anonymous remailers (which shield the sender's identity and allow the email content to be concealed) provide a high degree of protection for stalkers seeking to cover their tracks more effectively.

9.2.2 Internet Stalking

There is global communication through the Internet. Here, the domain is more wide and public in comparison to email stalking. Here, stalkers can use a wide range of activities to harass their victims. Internet cyberstalking is used to slander and endanger victims, taking on a public rather than private dimension. Harassment includes hacking, spoofing, the use of spyware, and the use of offensive content such as pornographic images and email bombs. A stalker will visit a chat room pretending to be his/her victim or post information about his/her victim on a bulletin board. The information most often contains the victim's name, address, and telephone number, and a message inviting strangers to join in the sexual activity. Internet cyberstalkers can follow their victims from place to place on the Internet, and can build and maintain websites dedicated to their victims, encouraging visitors to participate in degrading and harassing her/him. For example, a woman was stalked for a period of 6 months. Her harasser posted notes in a chat room that threatened to intimidate and kill her, and posted doctored pornographic pictures of her on the net together with personal details (Dean, 2000).

9.2.3 Computer Stalking

This is unauthorized control of another person's computer. In this type of stalking, the stalker exploits the working of the Internet and the Windows operating system in order to assume control over the computer of the targeted victim. In this form the offender is technocrat and he can take control of the computer of the victim as soon as the computer starts operating. The stalker gets control of the victims computer address and gets control over it. Here the cyberstalker can communicate directly with their target as soon as the target computer connects in any way to the Internet. The stalker can assume control of the victim's computer and the only defensive option for the victim is to disconnect and relinquish their current Internet "address." In this way, an individual Windows-based computer connected to the Internet can be identified, and connected to, by another computer connected to the Internet. This "connection" is not the link via a third party describing typical Internet interactions; rather, it is a computer-to-computer connection allowing the interloper to exercise control over the computer of the target. At present, a judiciously high degree of computer knowledge is required to undertake this form of exploitation of the Internet and the Windows operating system. However, instructions on how to use technology in this way are available on the Internet. It is likely that in the future, easier scripts will be made generously available for anyone inclined to download them. This form of cyberstalking requires high degree of computer knowledge to get access to the targets computer and the option available to the victim is to disconnect the computer and abandon the present Internet address. The term stalking is not new to the world because it existed for many centuries in the physical space. The stalking in the physical world is done by the former acquaintances, employees, or the person who wants to force his will over the target are the examples of stalkers. But after the advent of cyberspace, the reach of the stalker is extended, he can reach to any part of the world and threaten and harass the target. It is not necessary now to disclose his identity. Most of the stalkers are the dejected lover's, ex-boyfriends, colleagues, who failed to satisfy their desire and wants to harass the victim. Most stalkers are man and most victims are women. The common reason behind the cyberstalking is rejection in love or denial of affection, revenge, harassment, and show off by the offender.

9.3 CATEGORIES OF CYBERSTALKERS

Internet stalkers exhibit familiar patterns in their behaviors, acting out due to some type of rejection, jealousy, or criticism; the action of abandonment also feed the stalkers' obsession, with the victim, and most commonly turn the stalkers rage into a motive of anger. The stalker, usually a loner who is socially inept in today's society, will harass their victim(s) through a variety of unwanted and obsessive contact; such as messages, emails, comments, and even gifts. Psychologists have grouped the 21st century Internet stalker into six specific categories in connection to mental disorders.

9.3.1 The Obsessional Cyberstalker

These stalkers refuse to believe that their relationship is over. But the often the victim commits by believing that this stalker is harmlessly in love. These stalkers are also relatively common and tend to be a casual acquaintance or isolated "loner." They crave for a relationship with the victim and persist in their quest whether the victim reacts to it or not.

Elliot Fogel is an example of this. He met Claire Waxman at college. About 10 years later, she started receiving emails and cards from him. Fogel was then seen outside her home and police found her wedding photograph as a screensaver on his computer. During his 2012 trial, it was revealed that Fogel had researched her 40,000 times on Google in 1 year and had broken into her car. He made hundreds of late night phone calls to her and posed as a prospective parent at the nursery her children attended.

In May 2015, he was given a three and a half year imprisonment for breaching his restraining order for the third time. Waxman has stated that she suffered a miscarriage, developed an eating disorder and has had to move five times as a result of Fogel's campaign.

9.3.2 The Delusional Cyberstalker

Delusional stalkers are people who have had little, if any, time with his/her victim. Delusional stalkers may have major mental illnesses such as schizophrenia, manic depression, or erotomania. Erotomaniac stalkers believe that the victim is in love with him/her and they are having a relationship, even though they may have never seen each other before. Other delusional stalkers believe that they are destined to be with someone, and if they pursue the person long enough, love is inevitable. These stalkers know that they are not having relationships with their victims, but believe that 1 day they will. They assume that the victim loves them even though they have never met. A delusional stalker is usually a loner and most often chooses victims such as a married woman, a celebrity, a doctor, a teacher, and so forth. Those in the noble and helping professions like doctors, teachers, and so forth, are often at risk for attracting a delusional stalker. They are very difficult to shake off.

Figure 9.2: An Erotomaniac stalker.

Source: https://www.medicalnewstoday.com/articles/319145.php

9.3.3 The Vengeful Stalker

These cyberstalkers are angry at their victim due to some minor reason which may be either real or imagined. Vengeful stalkers are not motivated by love but by vengeance. Vengeful stalkers are also angry with their victims over some slight, real or imagined. In college and university communities, vengeful stalkers are likely to target members of the faculty or staff. Some of these stalkers are psychopaths, while some are delusional and truly believe that they are the victims. Vengeful stalkers stalk to get even. Typical example is disgruntled employee or ex-spouse, and so forth.

9.3.4 The Predatory Stalker

These Internet stalkers are classic sexual predators. The predatory stalkers are motivated by the desire for sexual gratification and power over the victim. Usually sexually deviant, this type of stalker may also have poor social skills, and lowered intelligence; they most commonly keep to themselves as sociopathic individuals and come from a troubled existence with past hardships. This type of stalker should be considered very dangerous; victims and observers are encouraged to contact local law enforcement in the protection of themselves and others. Sexual predators prey on those who appear to be weaker usually females and children; and may engage in behaviors such as surveillance, monitoring Internet activities, obscene phone calls, fetishism, voyeurism, sexual masochism, sexual sadism, and exhibitionism. Victims of this type of Internet stalker can be a known individual or complete stranger.

9.4 HOW CYBERSTALKERS OPERATE

Cyberstalking works in much the same way as stalking in the physical world. In fact, many offenders combine their online activities with more traditional forms of stalking and harassment such as telephoning the victim and going to the victim's home. Some cyberstalkers obtain victims over the Internet and others put personal information about their victims online, encouraging others to contact the victim, or even harm him/her. In general, stalkers want to exert power over their victims in some way, basically through fear. The crux of a stalker's power is information about and knowledge of the victim. A stalker's ability to frighten and control a victim increases with the amount of information that he or she can gather about the victim. Stalkers use information like telephone numbers, addresses, and personal preferences to impinge upon their victims' lives. Also, overtime cyberstalkers can learn what sorts of things upset their victims and can use this knowledge to harass the victims further.

9.4.1 Acquiring Victims

Previous studies indicate that many stalkers had prior social contact with their victims before the stalking behavior began. The implication of these studies is that investigators should pay particular attention to acquaintances of the victim. However, these studies are limited because many stalking cases are unsolved or unreported. Additionally, it is not clear if these studies apply to the Internet. After all, it is uncertain what constitutes an acquaintance on the Internet and the Internet makes it easier for cyberstalkers to find victims of opportunity.

Cyberstalkers can search the web, browse through ICQ and AOL profiles, and lurk in IRC and AOL chat rooms looking for likely targets. These are the vulnerable individuals with low self-esteem who will be easy to intimidate. As a rule, investigators should rely more on available evidence than on general studies. Although research can be useful to a certain degree, the evidence is the most reliable source of information about a specific case and it is what the courts will use to make a decision.

9.4.2 Anonymity and Secret Monitoring

The Internet has the added advantage of protecting a stalker's identity and allowing a stalker to monitor a victim's activities. For example, stalkers acquainted with their victims use the Internet to hide their identity, sending forged or anonymous email and using ICQ or AOL Instant Messenger to harass their victims. Also, stalkers can utilize ICQ or AOL Instant Messenger, and other applications (e.g., finger) to determine when a victim is online. Most disturbing of all, stalkers can use the Internet to spy on a victim. Although few cyberstalkers are skilled enough to break into a victim's email account or intercept email in transit, a cyberstalker can easily observe a conversation in a live chat room. This type of presurveillance of victims and amassing of information about potential victims might suggest intent to commit a crime but it is not a crime in itself and is not stalking as defined by the law.

9.4.3 Escalation and Violence

It is often suggested that stalkers will cease harassing their victims once they cease to provoke the desired response. However, some stalkers become aggravated when they do not get what they want and become increasingly threatening. Since stalkers have resorted to violence and murder, it is important for investigators to be extremely cautious when dealing with a stalking case. Investigators should examine the available evidence closely, protect the victim against further harm as much as possible, and consult with experts when in doubt. Most importantly, investigators should not make hurried judgments that are based primarily on studies of past cases.

9.5 INVESTIGATING CYBERSTALKING

There are several stages to investigating a cyberstalking case. These stages assume that the identity of the cyberstalker is unknown. Even if the victim suspects an individual, investigators are advised to explore alternative possibilities and suspects. Although past research suggests that most stalkers have prior relationships with victims, this may not apply when the Internet is involved as stranger stalking is easier. Therefore, consider the possibility that the victim knows the stalker, but do not assume that this is the case:

(1) Interview victim

An investigator should determine what evidence the victim has of cyberstalking and obtain details about the victim that can be used to develop victimology. The aim of this initial information gathering stage is to confirm that a crime has been committed and to obtain enough information to move forward with the investigation.

(2) Interview others

The investigator needs to interview other people that are involved in the case in order a get a clearer picture of the event.

(3) Victimology and risk assessment

The investigator should also determine why an offender chose a particular victim and what risks the offender was willing to take to acquire that victim. The primary aim of this stage of the investigation is to understand the victim–offender relationship and determine where additional digital evidence might be found.

(4) Search for additional digital evidence

As an investigator, you need to use what is known about the victim and cyberstalker to perform a thorough search of the Internet. Victimology is a major element at this stage, guiding investigators to locations that might interest the victim or individuals like the victim. The cyberstalker initially observed or encountered the victim somewhere and investigators should try to determine where. Consider the possibility that the cyberstalker encountered the victim in the physical world. The aim of this stage is to gather more information about the crime, the victim, and the cyberstalker.

(5) Crime scene characteristics

Examine crime scenes and cybertrails for distinguishing features (e.g., location, time, method of approach, and choice of tools) and try to determine their significance to the cyberstalker. The aim of this stage is to gain a better understanding of the choices that the cyberstalker made and the needs that were fulfilled by these choices.

(6) Motivation

Make sure that you ascertain what personal needs the cyberstalking was fulfilling. Be careful to distinguish between intent (e.g., to exert power over the victim or to frighten the victim) and the personal needs that the cyberstalker's behavior satisfied (e.g., to feel powerful or to retaliate against the victim for a perceived wrong). The aim of this stage is to understand the cyberstalker well enough to narrow the suspect pool, revisit the prior steps, and uncover additional evidence.

(7) Repeat

You should interview the victim repeatedly if the identity of the cyberstalker is still not known. The information that investigators have gathered might help the victim recall additional details or might suggest a likely suspect to the victim. To assist investigators to carry out each of these stages in an investigation, additional details are provided here.

9.6 CYBERSTALKING VICTIMS

Like most traditional crimes, cyberstalking knows no boundaries. Anyone can become a stalking victim, whether it is random or predicated on poor judgment when one releases personal information on the Internet. Even though most of the evidence is anecdotal, it strongly suggests that the majority of cyberstalkers are men and the victims are women; however, there have been several highly publicized cases of females stalking men and same-sex stalking (Reno, 1999). Unlike male stalkers, female stalkers are more inclined to stalk and harass ex-partners and less likely to stalk strangers. Female stalkers are also more likely to target other females in the hopes of establishing an intimate relationship with the victim. Female stalkers are very similar to males in regard to demographic profiles and psychiatric status; however, males are more likely to have a history of criminal offending or substance abuse (Purcell et al., 2001).

As noted, virtually anyone can become a victim, but certain demographic groups are more at-risk than others such as women, juveniles, newcomers to the Internet, and other particularly vulnerable groups. In a 2002 study conducted by the online victim advocacy group, Working to Halt Online Abuse, 71% of cyberstalking victims were women and 59% of that group had some type of previous relationship with the stalker (Hutton and Haantz, 2003). A prior relationship, whether real or perceived, seems to be the catalyst for cyberstalking, particularly when the victim attempts to end the relationship (Reno, 1999).

Interestingly, a 2001 research study concluded that 61% of the cyberstalking victims were Caucasian followed by Asians with 3.9% and African Americans with 1.6%. One should approach these findings with a degree of caution since the survey data was confined to the United States with only a minimal number of respondents. However, several follow-up studies have revealed similar findings in that the majority of victims are Caucasian women between the ages of 18 and 30 (McFarlane and Bocij, 2003).

Nearly four out of five victims are females and females are eight times as likely to be the stalking victims of ex-partners or acquaintances (Hutton and Haantz, 2003). Due to the different levels of online harassment, some victims may not report the harassment to law enforcement for one reason or another. It has been speculated that the majority of cyberstalking victims do not report being victimized for one of two reasons. First, the victim may feel that the behavior is not serious enough to warrant the attention of the police or second, the victim does not believe that law enforcement will take the matter seriously. Sadly, when a victim does report a cyberstalking incident to law enforcement, many law enforcement agencies simply advise the victim to come back if the perpetrator confronts them or makes a threatening statement offline. In response to being stalked, some cyberstalking victims may experience abrupt changes in sleep and eating patterns, nightmares, hypervigilance, anxiety, helplessness, and fear for safety. Hypervigilance is often associated with post-traumatic stress disorder to describe a symptom whereby the victim when in a state of fear, lashes out inappropriately through aggressive and, at times, violent behavior (Bocij, 2005). Very rarely do brief episodes of stalking cause distress in the victim; however, there have been a number of stalking incidents that have extended for weeks, months, or even years. The frequency of such communication greatly increases the risk of a potential physical assault. Victimization may also lead to vandalism but not necessarily vandalism in the traditional sense of the term. Vandalism is typically associated with traditional stalking; however, vandalism can also take place in cyberspace as well. For instance, vandalism may be used to damage the victim's personal computer data with the assistance of a computer virus or Trojan horse program as mentioned earlier. As mentioned, there are a number of Internet websites out there in cyberspace that will happily provide interested parties with information on a victim.

9.7 TECHNIQUES

Cyberstalkers use a variety of techniques. They may initially use the Internet to identify and track their victims. They may then send unsolicited email, including hate, obscene, or threatening mail. Live chat harassment abuses the victim directly or through electronic sabotage (for example, flooding the Internet chat channel to disrupt the victim's conversation). With newsgroups, the cyberstalkers can create postings about the victim or start rumors that spread through the bulletin board system. Cyberstalkers may also set up a web page on the victim with personal or fictitious information or solicitations to readers. Another technique is to assume the victim's identity online, such as in chat rooms, for the purpose of sullying the victim's reputation, posting details about the victim, or soliciting unwanted contacts from others. More complex forms of harassment include mail bombs (mass messages that virtually shut down the victim's email system by clogging it), sending the victim computer virus, or sending electronic junk mail (spamming). There is a clear difference between the annoyance of unsolicited email and online harassment. Unsolicited email is to be expected from time to time. However, cyberstalking is a course of conduct that takes place over a period of time and involves repeated, deliberate attempts to cause distress to the victim. People who do not have access to the Internet, or who choose not to go online, are not immune to cyber-based crime. Databases of personal information available on the Internet can enable a stalker to trace a victim's username to their real name, address, telephone number, and other personal information, or can enable a stalker to impersonate the victim online. The offender can then harass the victim on the computer via email or at home through the mail, telephone calls, or even by appearing at the victim's home or workplace. Telecommunication technologies also make it much easier for a cyberstalker to encourage third parties to harass and/or threaten a victim. For example, in the first successful prosecution under California's new cyberstalking law, prosecutors in the Los Angeles District Attorney's Office obtained a guilty plea from a 50-year-old former security guard who used the Internet to solicit the rape of a woman who rejected his romantic advances. The defendant threatened his 28-year-old victim, who had never been online and did not even own a computer, by impersonating her in various Internet chat rooms and online bulletin boards, where he posted, along with her phone number and address, messages that she fantasized about being raped. On at least six occasions, sometimes in the middle of the night, men knocked on the victim's door offering to rape her in response to the Internet "personal ad." The defendant pleaded guilty in April 1999 to one count of stalking and three counts of solicitation of sexual assault. As a result of the stalker's actions, the victim was eventually forced from her apartment, lost her job, suffered significant weight loss, and developed a fear of going outside of her residence. Most of the cyberstalking cases that have been prosecuted did not involve technically complex forms of stalking, and email was simply being used as an alternative form of communication. However, this is not always the case. The availability of anonymizing software provides a high degree of protection for stalkers seeking to cover their tracks more effectively. Examples of these types of technologies are "anonymous re-mailers," which automatically shield the sender's identity with pseudonyms and send the email through servers that instantly erase digital tracks to prevent later access by anyone, even law enforcement. Another example is Stratfor's Shredder, a software program for Windows 95 that acts like an electronic paper shredder that automatically overwrites deleted files, including all the routine computer backups. The more complex software and computer technologies become, the easier it is for cyberstalkers to operate anonymously, and the more difficult it is for law enforcement to investigate and collect enough evidence to support prosecutions. In order to address cyberstalking, it is critical to understand stalking in general. In many cases, cyberstalking is simply another phase in an overall stalking pattern, or it is regular stalking behavior using new technological tools. Therefore, strategies and interventions that have been developed to respond to offline stalking can regularly be adapted to online stalking situations. There are federal, state, and local criminal justice agencies which have begun to focus on stalking, and some have recently developed special task forces to deal with cyberstalking.

Cyberstalking crime could be defined as a tool bound crime that can be realized as an offense. The use of special means such as the Internet and the cyberspace is essential so that without the Internet, the harassment is not embedded within the definition of cyberstalking. Although, the occurrence is possible everywhere in the cyberspace, there are some places and tools which are considered to be more appropriate for the crime of cyberstalking.

9.7.1 Social Networks

Although social networking websites open a wide window to the socialization, at the same time, they are precursors for various crimes against women, especially in the cyberspace. The legal and psychological research on the risky functions of the cyberspace and consequent effects has proved that social networking is far more dangerous than chat rooms. Social networking users may spread cruel rumors about others on a social website that can be seen by hundreds of victims' Internet friends. Social networks could cause a number of online harassments hatred talks in the cyberspace, cyberbullying, and morphed images (Citron, 2009).

These social networks are able to easily attract teenage girls as well as women because they feel that the risk of anonymous sexual predators or privacy problems is less than the real world. However, most of the users are oblivious to the fact that their identity could be exploited by malicious intent and thus they are likely exposed to offline sexual assault, identity theft, online harassment, Internet infidelity, and victimization.

9.7.2 Email

Research findings indicate that a cyberstalker uses email messages more than any other means of electronic communication to harass and intimidate victims (Petrocelli, 2005). Emails allow offenders to send successive harassment, threatening, hateful email messages with vile images, video or audio. In some cases, cyberstalkers have used victims' email addresses and other personal information for subscription or purchase of books, magazines, or other Internet services without the knowledge or consent of the victims. Unfortunately, there are a number of websites that allow users to create emails applying minimum personal information for free. Although the site asks for user-identifying information, it rarely confirms the authenticity of the personal data provided. This makes the efforts of law enforcement much more difficult. Moreover, some email servers intentionally remove identifying information for a little fee and make it extremely difficult for law enforcement to track intruders' emails. Many cyberstalkers join such services or use money orders or other forms of payment to prevent being identified. An intelligent cyberstalker frequently uses computer software to send continuous numerous messages regularly or randomly. In addition, such an offender is likely to use anonymous emails that are mostly impossible to track (Reno, 1999). The invention of spyware has allowed stalkers to purchase programs with low prices. Such software programs are specifically designed to inform the offenders from when the victims are online (Petrocelli, 2005).

9.7.3 Chat Rooms and Discussion Forums

Chat rooms and discussion forums are usually websites in which Internet users post their opinions and comments on one or more topics. However, forums could also be a place for cyberstalkers to send personal information about the victim, including names, addresses, phone numbers, email addresses, and confidential information (Petrocelli, 2005).

Cyberstalkers often enter discussion boards, chat rooms, and the like, for attention or mere companionship (Stephens, 1995). Once contact has been initiated, the cyberstalker will continue to befriend the victim. In many cases, the cyberstalker perceives that a "relationship" exists when one does not. In other words, the cyberstalker truly believes that a relationship exists even though the victim may have innocently responded to an offender's question in a chat room or discussion board (Stephens, 1995). However, if the offender believes that the relationship has been jeopardized in any way, the cyberstalker may launch into a full-fledged campaign to ruin the victim's reputation, financial credit, or personal identity (Stephens, 1995).

Discussion forums are typically a place for Internet users to post opinions and comments on one or more subjects. However, discussion boards can also be a place for cyberstalkers to postharmful, negative personal data about the victim, including the victim's name, address, phone number, email address, and other confidential information. The term cybersmearing is used to refer to the posting of embarrassing or humiliating rumors about the victim in a chat room, newsgroup, or bulletin board (Bocij and McFarlane, 2003). The most common form of cybersmearing is the posting of false sexual innuendos about the victim (Petrocelli, 2005). This online verbal abuse can also take the form of chat harassment or what is commonly referred to as flaming, in the cyber world, in which the victim is belittled or demeaned in a live public forum (The National Center for Victims of Crime, Cyberstalking2004).

9.8 RELEVANT CASE STUDIES

Case study 1: Amy Boyer

Amy Boyer was a 20-year-old student in her final year of a dental hygiene course. Amy was widely regarded as a well-liked and highly inspired young lady, as evidenced by the fact that she was supporting her studies by working two part-time jobs. In October 1999, Liam Youens committed suicide shortly after he shot 20-year-old Amy Boyer as she left work. While investigating the murder a number of disturbing facts emerged. Youens had (i) been unknown to Amy, been following her movements for more than 4 years, (ii) obtained confidential information about Amy from various Internet services including her Social Security number and her work address, (iii) kept a diary detailing his long obsession about Amy on his website and how he had been watching her for years, and (iv) outlined his plan to murder Amy on his website. The written detailed plan was carried out exactly as described.

Case study 2

Cynthia Armistead-Smathers of Georgia received obscene emails from the account of Richard Hillyard. She then began receiving messages sent through an anonymous remailer (an online service that masks the sender's identity). The messages included phrases, such as "You'd better watch your back,"

"Let's get it on bitch," and "I'm your worst nightmare." After Hillyard's Internet service provider (ISP) canceled his account, Armistead-Smathers began receiving messages from the Centers for Disease Control and Prevention in Atlanta where Hillyard worked. She then received thousands of messages from men who had seen a posting of a nude woman (presumed to be Arrnistead-Smathers), which listed her email address and offered prostitution during the Olympics. Out of fear, she moved three times that year, changed her phone number frequently, and began to carry a licensed concealed weapon.

The police informed her that there was little they could do until she received an anonymous message from someone saying that he had followed her 5-year-old daughter and her from the post office box to their home. Hillyard was charged with stalking and later acknowledged getting into an online argument with Arrnistead Smathers but denied sending the message.

Case study 3

Jake Baker, a student at the University of Michigan, was arrested by FBI agents on February 9, 1995, and charged with "transmitting threats across state lines" to a pseudonymous Arthur Gonda. The charge came about after it was discovered that Baker had posted an erotic fantasy on the Internet in which he raped and tortured a character with the same name as one of Baker's real-life classmates. The charges were later revised to making a "threat to injure another person," but in the meantime, Baker had been suspended from the university, and his story had made headlines around the world. Baker was eventually acquitted, in part because his story was determined to be assertive and did not constitute a threat.

Case study 4

In the United States' first successful prosecution of a hate crime on the Internet, Richard Machado, a former student at the University of California, Irvine, was convicted of violating the civil rights of 59 mostly Asian students by sending threatening email messages (signed "Asian hater"). His message stated, "I personally will make it my [life's work] to find and kill everyone [sic] of you personally. OK. That's how determined I am. Do you hear me?" He threatened to kill them if they did not withdraw their enrollment from school. Initially, a jury was deadlocked nine to three in favor of acquittal. After serving a year in jail and undergoing a second trial, he was fined $1,000 and was given 1 year of probation, which prohibited his use of the university computer laboratories. His attorney argued that the threat was a "classic flame" (online slang for an angry message that is more annoying than harmful). However, many disturbed recipients of the email message were prepared to arm themselves with pepper spray, became suspicious of strangers, and refused to go out alone in the dark.

Case study 5

Andrew Archambeau was charged with the misdemeanor of stalking a school teacher whom he had met on a video dating service. After 5 days, the teacher realized that she was not interested in pursuing a relationship. Archambeau, however, persisted and sent her (the teacher) approximately 20 email messages. When the emails were traced to Archambeau, he responded that his "caller ID" showed that someone from her area was ringing and hanging up and that he perceived it as her shy manner of expressing interest. She denied the claim and went to the police after he left a message on her answering machine saying that he had watched her leaving work.

He argued that pursuing his romantic interest via email was nonthreatening, because email messages can be ignored by the recipient. However, Michigan's anti-stalking law prohibits nonconsensual contact via electronic communications. Archambeau pleaded no contest to the charges and was sentenced to a year's probation and ordered to undergo a psychiatric evaluation.

REFERENCES

1. Bocij, P., & McFarlane, L. (2003). Seven fallacies about cyber stalking. *Prison Service Journal*, *149*(1), 37-42.
2. Bocij, P., & McFarlane, L. (2003). Cyber stalking: defining the invasion of cyberspace. *Forensic Update*, *1*(72), 18-22.
3. Clemmitt, M. (2006). Cyber socializing. *CQ Researcher*, *16*(27), 1–34.
4. Citron, K. (2009). Cyber civil rights. *Boston University Law Review*, *89*, 61-125. Retrieved from http://ssrn.com/abstract=1271900
5. Ogilive, E. (2000). *Cyberstalking, trends and issues in crime and criminal justice*, no. 166. Canberra: Australian Institute of Criminology.
6. Petrocelli, J. (2005). Cyber stalking. *Law & Order*, *53*(12), 56-58.
7. Reno, J. (1999). *1999 report on cyber stalking: A new challenge for law enforcement and industry*. Retrieved April 1, 2018, from http://www.usdoj.gov/criminal/cybercrime/cyberstalking.htm

CHAPTER 10

CONTENT-RELATED CYBERCRIMES

"Cybercrime is the greatest threat to every company in the world."

—Ginni Rometty, Chair, President and CEO, IBM

CONTENTS

Cyber terrorism is tempting for terrorist group as they would require less people, money and fewer resources. Moreover, it enables the terrorist to remain anonymous, since it is being carried out far away from actual place or victim. Also, it enables terrorists to conduct their operations with little or no physical risk to themselves. Cyber terrorism consists of physical terrorism and cyber terrorism. Cyberterrorist is exploiting technology via the Internet to implement their terrorist purposes. This chapter is an attempt to provide a glimpse on cybercrime in society. Each section covers content that is considered illegal, including child pornography, hate speech/xenophobic material, and cyber terrorism. Case studies are given for each subsection except cyber terrorism. Also, legal measures sanctioned by international organizations are highlighted.

10.1 CHILD PORNOGRAPHY

Child pornography is a form of child sexual exploitation. Federal law defines child pornography as any visual depiction of sexually explicit conduct involving a minor (persons less than 18-years old). Images of child pornography are also referred to as child sexual abuse images. Federal law prohibits the production, distribution, importation, reception, or possession of any image of child pornography. A violation of federal child pornography laws is a serious crime, and convicted offenders face fines severe statutory penalties.

The treatment of children as sexual objects has existed through the ages, and so too has the production of erotic literature and drawings involving children. However, pornography in the modern sense began with the invention of the camera in the early 19th century. Almost immediately, sexualized images involving children were produced, traded, and collected. Even so, child pornography remained a restricted activity through most of the 20th century. Images were usually locally produced, of poor quality, expensive, and difficult to obtain. The relaxation of censorship standards in the 1960s led to an increase in the availability of child pornography, and, by 1977, some 250 child pornography magazines were circulating in the United States, many imported from Europe. Despite concern about the extent of child pornography, law enforcement agencies had considerable success in stemming the trafficking of these traditional hard copy forms. However, the advent of the Internet in the 1980s dramatically changed the scale and nature of the child pornography problem and has required new approaches to investigation and control.

Internet child pornography is unlike most crimes local police departments handle. Local citizens may access child pornography images that were produced and/or stored in another city or on another continent. Alternatively, they may produce or distribute images that are downloaded by people thousands of miles away. An investigation that begins in one police district will almost certainly cross jurisdictional boundaries. Therefore, most of the major investigations of Internet child pornography have involved cooperation among jurisdictions, often at an international level. However, within this broader scheme, local police departments have a crucial role to play. By concentrating on components of the problem that occurs within their local jurisdictions, they may uncover evidence that initiates a wider investigation. Alternatively, they may receive information from other jurisdictions about offenders in their districts. Because of the increasing use of computers in society, most police departments are likely to encounter Internet child pornography crimes. Therefore, it is important that all police departments develop strategies for dealing with the problem. Larger departments or districts may have their own dedicated Internet child pornography teams, but smaller ones do not, and the responsibility for daily investigations will fall to general-duties officers. It would be a mistake to underestimate the importance of local police in detecting and preventing Internet child pornography offenses. One study found that 56% of arrests for Internet child pornography crimes originated from non-specialized law enforcement agencies.

Figure 10.1: Picture depicting a child accessing illicit web content.

Source: https://euranetplus-inside.eu/internet-providers-should-should-do-more-to-tackle-child-pornography/

10.1.1 Victims of Child Pornography

It is important to distinguish child pornography from the more conventional understanding of the term pornography. Child pornography is a form of child sexual exploitation, and each image graphically memorializes the sexual abuse of that child. Each child involved in the production of an image is a victim of sexual abuse.

While some child sexual abuse images depict children in great distress and the sexual abuse is undisputable, other images may depict children that seem complacent. However, just because a child appears complacent does not mean that sexual abuse did not occur. In most child pornography cases, the abuse is not a one-time event, but rather ongoing victimization that progresses over months or years. It is common for producers of child pornography to groom victims, or cultivate a relationship with a child and gradually sexualize the contact overtime. The grooming process fosters a false sense of trust and authority over a child in order to desensitize or break down a child´s resistance to sexual abuse. Therefore, even if a child appears complacent in a particular image, it is important to remember that the abuse may have started years before that image was created.

Furthermore, victims of child pornography suffer not just from the sexual abuse inflicted upon them to produce child pornography, but also from knowing that their images can be traded and viewed by others worldwide. Once an image is on the Internet, it is irretrievable and can continue to circulate forever. The permanent record of a child´s sexual abuse can alter his or her life forever. Many victims of child pornography suffer from feelings of helplessness, fear, humiliation, and lack of control given that their images are available for others to view in perpetuity. Unfortunately, emerging trends reveal an increase in the number of images depicting sadistic and violent child sexual abuse, and an increase in the number of images depicting very young children, including toddlers and infants.

10.1.2 Components of the Problem

The problem of Internet child pornography can be divided into three components namely the production, distribution, and downloading of images. In some cases, the same people are involved in each stage. However, some producers and/or distributors of child pornography are motivated solely by financial gain and are not themselves sexually attracted to children.

(1) Production

This involves the creation of pornographic images. Collectors place a premium on new child pornography material. However, many images circulating on the Internet may be decades old, taken from earlier magazines and films. Images may be produced professionally, and, in these cases, often document the abuse of children in third world countries. However, more commonly, amateurs make records of their own sexual abuse exploits, particularly now that electronic recording devices such as digital cameras and webcams permit individuals to create high quality, homemade images. With the advent of multimedia messaging mobile phones, clandestine photography of children in public areas is becoming an increasing problem.

(2) Distribution

This involves the uploading and dissemination of pornographic images. These images may be stored on servers located almost anywhere in the world. Distribution may involve sophisticated pedophile rings or organized crime groups that operate for profit, but in many cases, is carried out by individual amateurs who seek no financial reward. Child pornography may be uploaded to the Internet on websites or exchanged via email, instant messages, newsgroups, bulletin boards, chat rooms, and peer to peer (P2P) networks. Efforts by law enforcement agencies and ISPs to stop the dissemination of child pornography on the Internet have led to changes in offenders' methods.

Child pornography websites are often shut down as soon as they are discovered, and openly trading in pornography via email or chat rooms is risky because of the possibility of becoming ensnared in a police sting operation (e.g., undercover police entering chat rooms posing as pedophiles or as minor children). Increasingly those distributing child pornography are employing more sophisticated security measures to elude detection and are being driven to hidden levels of the Internet.

(3) Downloading

This involves accessing child pornography via the Internet. The images do not need to be saved to the computer's hard drive or to a removable disk to constitute downloading. In some cases a person may receive spam advertising child pornography, a pop-up link may appear in unrelated websites, or he may inadvertently go to a child pornography website (e.g., by mistyping a keyword). In most cases, however, users must actively seek out pornographic websites or subscribe to a group dedicated to child pornography. In fact, it has been argued that genuine child pornography is relatively rare in open areas of the Internet, and, increasingly, those seeking to find images need good computer skills and inside knowledge of where to look. Most child pornography is downloaded via newsgroups and chat rooms. Access to websites and online pedophile groups may be closed and require paying a fee or using a password.

10.1.3 The Law and Child Pornography

To date, this is the only conviction for virtual child pornography in the Netherlands, and it remains to be seen whether in future cases courts will adopt this court's using the perspective of a minor to interpret the term "realistic." In January 2010, another computer-related activity in relation to child pornography was criminalized in the Netherlands, by an Act (Staatsblad 2009, 544) that implemented the Lanzarote Convention (CETS 201). Art. 240b DCC was extended with the criminalization of intentional obtainment of access to child pornography by means of a computer or communications service.

The main reason for the expansion is that the Internet increasingly allows the "consumers" of child pornography to watch it online without storing the pictures, thereby effectively circumventing the act of criminal possession of child pornography. A crucial threshold for criminal liability in this respect is "intentional" (or, in the convention's terms, "knowingly"): to prevent users from being held liable if they only accidentally come across child pornography while surfing the net, the prosecution will have to prove that the obtaining access was done purposefully. The Explanatory Memorandum suggests that intentionality can be proven, for example, by the user paying for access, by the name of a hyperlink clicked on by the user, or by the user revisiting a website on which he has seen child pornography on a first visit. As the legislator adopted the term "intentionally" (opzettelijk) rather than "deliberately" (welbewust)—which had been advised by the Public Prosecutor—the lower threshold of intention applies, that is, "conditional intention" (voorwaardelijk opzet): someone is criminally liable if he knows that an act on the Internet can lead to his accessing child pornography and he nonetheless takes a substantial risk that this will occur.

Child pornography laws in Japan prohibit and outlaw child pornography. The production, sale, distribution, and commercialization of child pornography is illegal under Article 7 of the Act on Punishment of Activities Relating to Child Prostitution and Child Pornography, and the Protection of Children and is punishable by a maximum penalty of 5 years in prison and/or a fine of ¥5,000,000. Possession of child pornography with any intent of distribution and sale is also illegal.

Manga artists and anime directors have argued that it is dangerous to try to define child pornography when it comes to artwork, drawings, and animation when regarding hentai due to it being highly ambiguous, and have cited freedom of expression to prevent it from being abused. For example, they argued that even in the anime and manga series Doraemon, the scene of the schoolgirl Shizuka Minamoto taking a bath might be misinterpreted as "child pornography." Arts depicting underage characters (lolicon and shotacon) and photography of underage models (junior idol) remain controversial in Japan.

The law in England on child pornography predates the cybercrime convention and did not specifically mention computers. Section 1 (1) of the Protection of Children Act 1978 as amended by the Criminal Justice and Public Order Act 1994 makes it an offence. In addition, Section 160 of the English Criminal Justice Act 1988 provides inter alia as follows;

(a) to take, or permit to be taken, an indecent photograph of a child (a person under the age of 16); or

(b) to distribute or show such indecent photographs or pseudophotographs; or

(c) to have in his possession such indecent photographs or pseudophotographs with a view to their being distributed or shown by himself or others.

By virtue of the amendment made by the 1994 Act, the term "photograph" includes data stored on a computer disk or by other electronic means which are capable of conversion into a photograph, including graphic images (Section 7.4 (b)). The test, therefore, is that if data can be converted into an indecent image it will be deemed a photograph for the purposes of the section.

In New Zealand, the legislation does not specifically define child pornography. However, material that promotes or supports the sexual exploitation of children and young persons are considered "objectionable" and is illegal. Such material need not involve the sexual exploitation of real children in order to be objectionable. Cartoons, fictional text, "morphed" images and pictures of adults dressed to appear as young persons can be found objectionable. The jurisprudence has clarified that photographs of nude children in sexual poses can be considered objectionable (child erotica), even where there is no sexual activity.

Other countries still have not adopted the legal framework to transpose into national legislation the provisions of the Protocol. This is the case of Paraguay, which ratified the protocol and has a draft law that would transpose the protocol's provisions into national law.

The penal code of Norway defines pornography as sexual depictions of an offensive nature or that in other ways has a degrading effect on people, or are brutalizing, including sexual depictions during which use is made of children, corpses, animals, violence, and compulsion. It then defines child pornography as sexual depictions in moving or still pictures of persons under the age of 18 or those who are depicted as under the age of 18.

In the Dominican Republic, child pornography is understood as all representation, through any means, of children, boys and girls, and adolescents engaged in explicit sexual activities, real or simulated, or any depiction of the genitals of children and adolescents for primarily sexual purposes.

In terms of means of representation of child pornography, some laws are broader in scope. For example, in Barbados, legislation refers to "photographs," while in Belgium representation can be through "media and visual objects of any kind."

South Africa has a comprehensive definition of child pornography that addresses explicitly its manifestations on the Internet. The Films and Publications Act No. 34 of 1999 and 2004 states: "Child pornography includes any image, however, created, or any description of a person, real or simulated, who is, or who is depicted or described as being, under the age of 18 years: (a) engaged in sexual conduct; (b) participating in, or assisting another person to participate in, sexual conduct; (c) showing or describing the body, or parts of the body, if such a person in a manner or in circumstances which, within context, amounts to sexual exploitation, or in such a manner that it is capable of being used for the purpose of sexual exploitation." The Act defines a publication as including "computer software which is not a film" as well as "any message or communication, including a visual presentation, placed on a distributed network including, but not confined to, the Internet." The visual presentation is intended as "a drawing, picture, illustration, painting, photograph or image or any combination thereof, produced through or by means of computer software on screen or a computer printout."

10.1.4 Types of Offenders

Sexual attraction to children is known as pedophilia. However, an interest in Internet child pornography may be best thought of as falling along a continuum rather than in terms of a hard and fast distinction between pedophiles and non-pedophiles. People can behave very differently on the Internet than they do in other areas of their lives. Interacting anonymously with a computer in the safety of one's own home encourages people to express hidden thoughts and desires. Offenders vary in the strength of their interest in child pornography, as well as in the level of severity of the pornographic image to which they are attracted. From a psychological perspective, based on a typology of general pornography users, the following categories of Internet child pornography users are suggested;

(1) Recreational users: They access child pornography sites on impulse, out of curiosity, or for short-term entertainment. They are not seen to have long-term problems associated with child pornography use;

(2) Vulnerable users: They are defenseless individuals who have developed an interest in child pornography, but may not have done so had it not been for the Internet;

(3) Sexual compulsives: They have a specific interest in children as sexual objects and seek out child pornography.

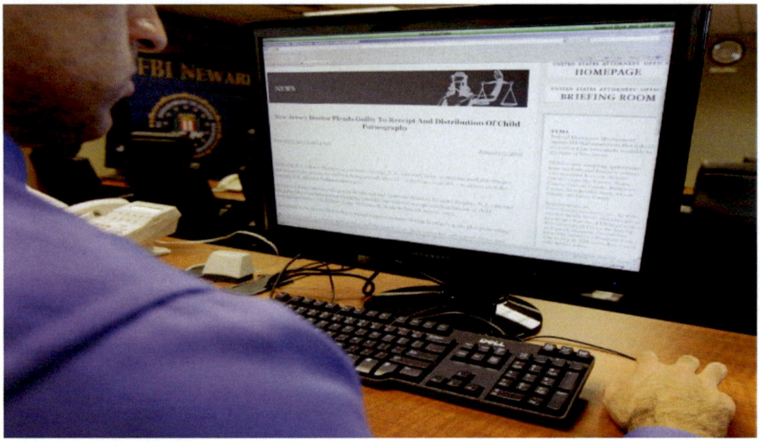

Figure 10.2: An FBI agent working on a computer. *Source: http://www.nj.com/news/index.ssf/2012/12/a_depraved_world_fbi_agents_wa.html*

10.1.5 An Offending Typology

Variations among offenders translate into different patterns of Internet behavior. Offenders vary in the level of their involvement in Internet child pornography, the degree of networking in which they engage with other offenders, their expertise in employing security strategies to avoid detection, and the extent to which their Internet behavior involves direct sexual abuse of children. The following typology of child pornography offending has been suggested;

(1) Browsers: Offenders who stumble across child pornography but knowingly save the images. They are not involved in networking with other offenders and do not employ security strategies to avoid detection. Their browsing is an indirect abuse of children.

(2) *Secret fantasizers:* Offenders who create digital images (e.g., through morphing) for private use to satisfy personal sexual desires. These offenders do not network with other offenders, do not employ security strategies, and their private fantasies are an indirect abuse of victims.

(3) *Non-secure collectors*: These are offenders who seek child pornography in non-secure chat rooms (i.e., chat rooms that do not employ security barriers such as passwords) and other open levels of the Internet. They are involved in relatively high levels of networking, and, by definition, do not employ security strategies.

Their collecting behavior is an indirect abuse of children. Because of the non-secured nature of their activities, there are limits to the number and nature of the images they can collect.

(4) *Trawlers*; These are offenders who seek child pornography on the web through open browsers. They may engage in minimal networking, but they employ few security strategies and their trawling is an indirect abuse of victims.

(5) *Physical abusers*: These are offenders who sexually abuse children and for whom an interest in child pornography is just part of their pedophilic interests. They may record their own abuse behaviors for their personal use, in which case, from a legal standpoint, the possession of pornography is secondary to the evidence of their abusive behavior that it records. They may or may not network. By definition, a physical abuser directly abuses victims and his security depends upon the child's silence.

(6) Secure collectors: Offenders who are members of a closed newsgroup or other secret pedophile ring. They engage in high levels of networking and employ sophisticated security measures to protect their activities from detection. Their collecting behavior is an indirect abuse of children. Because they occupy hidden levels of the Internet, they have access to a wide range of images.

They may engage in obsessive levels of collecting, which not only involves amassing huge numbers of images but also carefully cataloging and cross-referencing them.

As with other types of collections, they may expend considerable effort in obtaining rare and highly prized images. The collection may become an end in itself.

(7) *Groomers*: These are offenders that develop online relationships with children and send pornography to children as part of the grooming process. Grooming involves direct abuse of children. They may or may not be involved in wider networking with other offenders, but their contact with children exposes them to risk of detection. The child may tell someone about the relationship, or the offender may be unwittingly communicating with an undercover police officer.

(8) Distributors: Offenders involved in disseminating abuse images. In some cases, they have a purely financial interest in child pornography. More often, offenders at any of the above levels

who share images may be classified as distributors. Thus, the extent of a distributor's networking, his level of security, and whether he engages in direct abuse of children depends upon the level at which he is operating.

(9) *Producers*: They are the offenders who record the sexual abuse of children for the purpose of disseminating it to others. The extent of their networking varies depending on whether they are also distributors. Again the producer's direct abuse of the victim compromises his security.

10.1.6 Sources of Digital Evidence

Computers and their associated services retain a considerable amount of evidence of their use. Resolute, computer savvy offenders may take precautions to cover their tracks, but many offenders will have neither the foresight nor the necessary expertise to do so and will leave a trail of incriminating evidence.

(a) The offender's computer: Downloaded images saved on a computer's hard drive are the most obvious evidence of pornography use. However, there are also more subtle records that technicians can locate when examining a suspect's computer. For example, log files show who was logged into the computer and when; modem logs record when a computer was connected to the Internet; web browser history entries show an offender's online activity; and email and chat logs reveal online communication with cohorts or potential victims. Note, however, that seizure of a suspect's computer requires specialized expertise, and, if handled incorrectly, may result in the loss of critical evidence.

(b) ***Hand-held devices*** An increasing number of devices contain components of a computer (referred to as embedded computer systems) and can be used in child pornography. These devices include digital cameras, PDAs, and mobile phones. For example, digital cameras can be used to record abuse; the files can then be easily uploaded to the Internet. Similarly, in addition to voice conversations between perpetrators, mobile phones increasingly permit the recording, storing, and transmitting of digital images. These devices may have incriminating digital records stored on their memory cards.

(c) ***Servers*** Different servers may provide information with which to track pornography use. ISP authentication servers record customer account details against IP addresses (authentication logs), which can then be used to identify users. FTP and web servers used to upload and download electronic files have logs that record users' IP addresses, what files were accessed, and when. Similarly, email servers retain logs of customer use. Local area network servers may be used to store collections of pornography for personal use. Individuals may use local servers connected to their work computers so that searching a suspect's work server may reveal hidden collections of pornography.

(d) ***Online activity*** Purpose-built or commercially available digger engine software allows law enforcement personnel to monitor online activity and identify the IP addresses of chat room contributors. Although online operations can yield conclusive digital evidence of an offender's involvement in Internet child pornography activities, officers should be careful not to become overzealous and engage in entrapment.

10.1.7 Effects of Child Pornography

With the increasing acceptance of the Internet over the last 20 years, the recent menace of child pornography is a threat to the absolute innocence of children. It is agreed that pictures portraying the children in a sexually explicit manner is wrong because the children have no idea of the results of being represented sexually. Communities have reached a decision that children should remain sexually innocent and never be exposed to the sexual exploitation of adults.

In legal pornography, studies have shown a strong relationship between so-called deviant sexual behaviors with the regular viewing of pornographic images and videos. It is established that adults who watch legal porn are more likely to practice what they have seen in pornographic films with their actual life sexual partners. Legal pornography accommodates sexual fantasy in such a way that adults are free to have sexual fantasies of other adults. However, when that practice is translated to child pornography, it could have severe social consequences.

Many social experts and criminologists have conducted studies that revealed that pedophile and child rapists are often inspired by child porn. This causal link is significant in sustaining the criminality of child pornography. Many jurisdictions offer stricter sentences for child molesters who were caught with child pornography as well. The trend is substantial enough to present a distinct problem in the incidence of child molestation. The illegality of child porn is, therefore, a precautionary measure.

The lives of these children, who have been endangered to instances of pornography, are incessantly reminded of the awful experience during their sexual exploitation because the illegal pornographic images are published and distributed among a secret network of sexual predators.

The security of the innocence of children is the major concern of the entire community and should not be accepted in any way because child porn is particularly damaging because the abuse stays longer than the first exploitation. Even after the pornographic contents are deleted or otherwise destroyed, the psychological effects on the child's upbringing are very prominent. The circulating images of child porn are plagues for victims lost in a state of reminiscence. There have even been cases in which a victim tries to seek restitution from everyone who downloaded the child porn image.

Child pornography is a major social problem because it is a crime that does not only affect the loved ones of the victim; it is an anti-social behavior that adversely affects the entire community. As such, punishments are unarguably severe for owners, producers, and distributors of child porn. Neither the government nor the society should ever tolerate this crime and the perpetrators of this crime should not be granted impunity.

10.2 HATE SPEECH

The primary difficulties of developing a legal response to racism are questions of how to explain it. The absence of commonly accepted definitions is not surprising, because the race itself is a social construct, without practical basis.

The concept of race is still used in political instruments and contemporary laws to determine the difference between people's perceptions based on physical and social groups such as nationality, ethnicity, and national origin. It follows that racism is used as an umbrella to talk about a combination of values, behavior, and attitudes that exclude people based on their ethnicity, race, cultural practices, indigeneity, national origin, in some cases, religious belief.

Hate speech whether through language, images or symbols are the obvious demonstrations of racism. Its guideline is said to be warranted on the grounds, well-being, and safety, as well as group harm to the target community who may construe such expressions as a sign of xenophobia and victimization. Racism is said to have engulfed moral failure to treat others equally, fairly and decently. The legal measure was taken on "hate speech" is a public restriction on the attitudes that impede the value of multiculturalism and the equality associated with liberal democracy. Violation of this shared cost makes racial insults "a universal wrong."

Understanding the crime of racism contradicts two additional complications. The first is the application of the term "racism" to the expression of prejudice toward overlapping features such as ethnicity, language, nationality, immigration status or tribal religions. Without modulating the distinct etiologies of various forms of discrimination, the line between these foundations of discrimination can be easy to cross over. For example, Arab Australians reported about the discriminatory conduct directed toward them could be based on the postulation that they are Muslims thereby creating an imbalance between race and religion for xenophobic victims. Second, it is difficult to distinguish expression of racism that requires prohibition and that which does not or, to put this in another way, the question of how to strike a balance between freedom of expression and protection from racist speech. Liberal democracies have taken a diversity of nuanced methods, which are grounded in diverse historical, institutional and political frameworks. At the end of the spectrum is the United States that eradicated trend that emanated after the war thus limiting freedom of expression to protect national minorities by passing judgment against racism. However, still with limits, the United States has reinforced its protection around the liberty to express provocative speech supported by the interpretation of the First Amendment. This issue was boldly stated in 2016 as there was a post-election racial discrimination which succeeded the election of Donald Trump as president (see Figure 10.3). On the contrary, the jurisdictions of the European Union have slowly but steadily extended the protection of human rights by restricting the views of racists' perceptions over the last few decades. This has been shown by France, which has a strong legislative approach, and in recent years there had been a considerable number of high ranking prosecutions for hate speech.

The introduction of new technologies such as digital or automotive technology generates new ways to commit crime and new ways to duck detection. The legal principles on these challenges exist in a region known as cybercrime. In applying legal policies to online hate speech, we must have a good understanding of cybercrime and the collaboration between the Internet and the law.

Figure 10.3: Post-election Hate Speech as captured by NBC news.

Source: https://www.nbcnews.com/nightly-news/video/hate-speech-is-on-the-rise-following-u-s-presidential-election-824559171837

10.2.1 Case Study

The Appeal Court Amsterdam (November 17, 2006, LJN AZ3011) convicted a defendant for publishing discriminatory statements about Jews and homosexuals on a website. The publication of statements like "yet another of those daylight-shirking lawless Jews" and "so even today Jews still act like beasts" were unreasonably offensive. The Court considered the Internet to be a wonderful means for exercising freedom of expression, but reasoned that there are limits to what is acceptable for publication on the Internet, given that anyone can publish, without any obstacle, texts that are hurting and offending to others while such publication does not serve any respectable aim. The defendant's argument that the website was a "mildly provocative, amusingly stinging" means of attracting readers' attention to his column about Mel Gibson's The Passion of Christ was rejected; the court reasoned that the debate could equally well be conducted without the grievous passages. Hence, the defendant was convicted to a fine of 500 euros and a suspended sentence of 1-week imprisonment with 2 years' probation.

10.2.2 International Law on Hate Speech

(a) European Framework

The following is the definition contained in the 1997 Recommendation of the Committee of Ministers of the Council of Europe: "…the term 'hate speech' shall be understood as covering all forms of expression which spread, incite, promote or justify racial hatred, xenophobia, anti-Semitism or other forms of hatred based on intolerance, including: intolerance expressed by aggressive nationalism and ethnocentrism, discrimination and hostility against minorities, migrants and people of immigrant origin.

Nor was a narrower definition provided by the carefully prepared 2002 recommendation of the Council of

Europe's Commission against Racism and Intolerance (ECRI), which was issued as Recommendation No. 7." 18. The law should penalize the following acts when committed intentionally:

(a) public incitement to violence, hatred or discrimination,

(b) public insults and defamation or

(c) threats against a person or a grouping of persons on the grounds of their race, color, language, religion, nationality, or national or ethnic origin;

(d) the public expression, with a racist aim, of an ideology which claims the superiority of, or which depreciates or denigrates, a grouping of persons on the grounds of their race, color, language, religion, nationality, or national or ethnic origin;

(e) the public denial, trivialization, justification or condoning, with a racist aim, of crimes of genocide, crimes against humanity or war crimes;

(f) the public dissemination or public distribution, or the production or storage aimed at public dissemination or public distribution, with a racist aim, of written, pictorial or other material containing manifestations covered by paragraphs 18 a), b), c), d) and e);

(g) the creation or the leadership of a group which promotes racism; support for such a group; and participation in its activities with the intention of contributing to the offenses covered by paragraph 18 a), b), c), d), e) and f);

(h) racial discrimination in the exercise of one's public office or occupation.

(b) United Nations

The UN Human Rights Committee has considered it necessary to include provisions that directly concern hate speech in its recommendations on the application of Articles 19 and 20 of the Covenant. These provisions are in addition to the general principles mentioned in the preceding paragraph:

46. States parties should ensure that counter-terrorism measures are compatible with paragraph 3. Such offences as "encouragement of terrorism" and "extremist activity," as well as offences of "praising," "glorifying," or "justifying" terrorism, should be clearly defined to ensure that they do not lead to unnecessary or disproportionate interference with freedom of expression….

48. Prohibitions of displays of lack of respect for a religion or other belief system, including blasphemy laws, are incompatible with the Covenant, except in the specific circumstances envisaged in article 20, paragraph 2, of the Covenant. Such prohibitions must also comply with the strict requirements of article 19, paragraph 3, as well as such articles as 2, 5, 17, 18 and 26. Thus, for instance, it would be impermissible for any such laws to discriminate in favor of or against one or certain religions or belief systems, or their adherents over another or religious believers over non-believers.

Nor would it be permissible for such prohibitions to be used to prevent or punish criticism of religious leaders or commentary on religious doctrine and tenets of faith.

49. Laws that penalize the expression of opinions about historical facts are incompatible with the obligations that the Covenant imposes on States parties in relation to the respect for freedom of opinion and expression. The Covenant does not permit general prohibition of expressions of an erroneous opinion or an incorrect interpretation of past events. Restrictions on the right of freedom of opinion should never be imposed and, with regard to freedom of expression, they should not go beyond what is permitted in paragraph 3 or required under article 20.

10.3 CYBERTERRORISM

Cyber terrorism is defined by U. S. Federal Bureau of Investigation as a premeditated attack against a computer system, computer data, programs and other information with the sole aim of violence against clandestine agents and subnational groups. In 2004, the FBI (Lourdeau) redefined cyber terrorism as "a criminal act perpetrated by the use of computers and telecommunications capabilities, resulting in violence, destruction and/or disruption of services, where the intended purpose is to create fear by causing confusion and uncertainty within a given population, with the goal of influencing a government or population to conform to a particular political, social or ideological agenda" (FBI, 2004). The main aim behind cyber terrorism is to cause harm and destruction. Cyber terrorism is the convergence of cyberspace and terrorism. It refers to unlawful attacks and threats of attack against computers, networks, and the information stored therein when done to intimidate or coerce a government or its people in furtherance of political or social objectives. Further, to qualify as cyberterrorism, an attack should result in violence against persons or property, or at least cause enough harm to generate fear. Attacks that lead to death or bodily injury, explosions, or severe economic loss would be examples. Serious attacks against critical infrastructures could be acts of cyberterrorism, depending on their impact. Attacks that disrupt non-essential services or that are mainly a costly nuisance would not. Numerous scenarios have been suggested. In one, a cyber-terrorist attacks the computer systems that control a large regional power grid. Power is lost for a sustained period of time and people die. In another, the cyberterrorist breaks into an air traffic control system and tampers with the system. Two large civilian aircraft collide. In a third, the cyberterrorist disrupts banks, international financial transactions, and stock exchanges. Economic systems grind to a halt, the public loses confidence, and destabilization is achieved. Cyber terrorists are state-sponsored and non-state actors who engage in cyber-attacks to pursue their objectives. Transnational terrorist organizations, insurgents, and jihadists have used the Internet as a tool for planning attacks, radicalization and recruitment, a method of propaganda distribution, and a means of communication, and for disruptive purposes. While no unclassified reports have been published regarding a cyber-attack on a critical component of U. S. infrastructure, the vulnerability of critical life-sustaining control systems being accessed and destroyed via the Internet has been demonstrated. The cyber-terrorist is assumed to be professional, creative, and very clever. They will seek unorthodox and original methods to accomplish their goals. Individuals who are well-schooled in traditional information security techniques are not well suited to being a cyber-terrorist, simply because they have been exposed to or trained in classic security techniques and doctrine. The cyberterrorist will seek to accomplish their mission by techniques not mitigated by classic security mechanisms (Petrović, R., 1999).

Terrorists leave traditional way of fighting with classical weapon and other weapon but also they introduce the use of sophisticated high technology which shows that they become "modern" warriors who take apace with technology development. When computer terrorism is in question, nowadays, there is real danger about information resources especially in global information networks, which means that if they are exploited by the terrorists, global information network can become effective weapon for cyber-attacks. Also, it gives terrorists opportunities for combating in a way which previously they can only dream about it.

Figure 10.4: A terrorist in a gas mask holding his hand up to a digital image. *Source: https://www.postonline.co.uk/insurer/3362111/pool-re-expands-cover-to-include-physical-damage-from-cyber-terrorism*

10.3.1 Cyberspace as a New Terrorism Arena

With a stroke of a keyboard, one can facilitate identity theft, computer viruses, hacking, malware usage, destruction, and manipulation of data. This use of the computer with a computer as a target, paint the "traditional" picture of cyber terrorism. As hacking into a computer has occurred since the early 1980s, there is now a convergence of terrorism and cyberspace, with the attack launched against Internet-connected systems and computers to generate fear. With our computer-dependent society, it is easy to cause havoc within the anonymity of cyberspace. Cybersecurity has increased worldwide with businesses, governments and individual vulnerable to remote attack and misuse of data. Cybersecurity experts are worried about the crippling of major infrastructure and perhaps a nations' power system with a tap of a mouse. Information and communications technology permeate much of the world's critical infrastructure and strengthen the global economy. Many are not winning this new war of cyber terrorism.

Terrorists have moved into cyberspace to facilitate traditional forms of terrorism such as bombings. They use the Internet to communicate, coordinate events, and advance their agenda. While such activity does not constitute cyber terrorism in the strict sense, it does show that terrorists have some competency using the new information technologies. Even in democracies, however, there are limits to what terrorists can post on the Net. After a group of anti-abortionists put up a website terrorizing doctors who performed abortions, a federal jury ordered the pages be taken down and damages of more than $ 100 million paid. The Nuremberg Files site had listed the names of about 200 abortion providers under the heading of "baby butchers." Readers were invited to send in such personal details as the doctors' home addresses, license plate numbers, and the names of their children. Three doctors whose names appeared on the list were killed, and after each, the doctor's name was promptly crossed out. Doctors named on the site testified that they lived in constant fear and used disguises, bodyguards, and bulletproof vests. In ordering the site down, the federal jury said the site and "wanted" posters amounted to death threats against the doctors.

Many terrorists are using encryption to conceal their communications and stored files, compounding the difficulties of providing effective counter-terrorism. Hamas, for example, reportedly has used encrypted Internet communications to transmit maps, pictures, and other details pertaining to terrorist attacks. Ramsey Yousef, a member of the international terrorist group responsible for bombing the World Trade Center in 1994 and a Manila Air airliner in late 1995, encrypted files on his laptop computer. The files, which the US government officials decrypted, contained information pertaining to further plans to blow up eleven commercial airliners in the Far East owned by the United States.

The Aum Shinrikyo cult, which gassed the Tokyo subway in March 1995, killing 12 people and injuring 6,000 more, also used encryption to protect their computerized records, which included plans and intentions to deploy weapons of mass destruction in Japan and the United States.

10.3.2 War against Cyber Terrorism

International cooperation in order to confront cyber terrorism has different form of relationship between government and law enforcement agencies. The cooperative efforts are divided into three types: international and global effort, multilateral and multinational effort and regional effort.

(1) Effort from International and Global Organization

(a) United Nation

United Nation is the lead organization which involves in the coordination and cooperation relating to the problem of international terrorism. In their resolutions, they require the member states to promote the multilateral consideration of existing and potential threats in the field of information security, as well as possible measures to limit the threats. These resolutions have the same motive to improve the cybersecurity awareness at both the international and the national levels. However, following the tragedy of September 11, the Security Council resolution 1373 moves forward to fight against terrorism. The aim of this resolution is to counterterrorism effort. This resolution provides an internationally recognized definition of terror for the first time which seems to provide an inclusive ban on all forms of violence that international target civilian, regardless of the motive, as well as calls on countries to prosecute terrorists.

(b) Interpol

The basement of Interpol is to prevent and combat international crime even where diplomatic relations do not exist between particular countries and it works on the gaps between the legal framework and criminal phenomena. Interpol has created an anti-terrorism section in September 2002 in the wake of alarming of international terrorist attack which is called Fusion Task Force (FTF). The primary objectives are to: identify active terrorist groups and their membership, solicit, collect and share information and intelligence, provide analytical support, enhance the capacity of member countries to address the threats of terrorism and organized crime. Interpol has identified public safety and terrorism as a priority crime area, and countries can benefit from Interpol's unique position in the international law enforcement community in the fight against terrorism.

(2) Effort from Regional Organization

(a) European Union

After the terrorist attack on Madrid, the European Union and its members promise to do everything in their power to combat all forms of terrorism. Therefore, the European council approves the decision of the European Parliament to declare 11 marches as European day commemorating the victim of terrorism. By December of 2004, European council calls on member state to ratify the convention on the mutual assistance in criminal matters, its protocol and the three protocols to Europol convention. Also, their framework implements in other aspect such as traffic data by the service provider, cross-border pursuit, exchange of information on conviction for terrorist offences, etc. the council adopted necessary measures for council regulation to identify new and applicable function for the Schengen information system (SIS).

(3) Effort from Multilateral and Multinational Organization

(a) The Commonwealth Nations

Commonwealth nation main task is to harmonize their laws of its member states. It creates the Model Law on Computer and Computer-Related Crime and had a great impact on the domestic legislation. It expands criminal liability including reckless liability for the offences of interfering with data, interfering with computer systems, and using illegal devices. Also, it covers the problem of dual criminality by condemning the act which has done by offender oust side his territorial nationality, if he does an offence under a law of the country where the offence was committed. Another task of the commonwealth is to consider the legal mutual legal assistant between Commonwealth member and also between Commonwealth member and non-commonwealth. The Commonwealth law minister proposes to the member state to take the convention on cybercrime as a basis for mutual legal assistance between Commonwealth member states and the non-Commonwealth States.

(b) The G8 Forum

The G8 Forum is an informal forum and so it lacks an administrative structure compare with international organization. The group of G8 was originally formed in 1975 with six members and it was known as the G6. Canada then joined in 1975 and Russia became a formal member in 1998. The leaders from the United States, United Kingdom, France, Germany, Japan, Canada, Italy, and Russia have been meeting annually since 1975 to discuss issues of importance, including crime and terrorism, and the information highway.

Figure 10.5: A working meeting of the G8 Summit held in Northern Ireland (2013). *Source: http://en.kremlin.ru/events/president/news/18358*

(c) Council of Europe Convention on Cybercrime

The Council of Europe's Convention on Cybercrime was developed in 2001 to address several categories of crimes committed via the Internet and other information networks. It is the first and only international treaty on this issue, and its primary goal is to "pursue a common criminal policy aimed at the protection of society against cybercrime, especially by adopting appropriate legislation and fostering international cooperation." The Convention provides a general framework for developing comprehensive national legislation against cybercrime as well as international cooperation between State Parties to this treaty. In order to make this Convention more effective, it needs to expand beyond its current relevance and application to Europe. However, the Convention only addresses "crimes committed via the Internet and other computer networks, dealing particularly with infringements of copyright, computer-related fraud, child pornography and violations of network security" (Convention on Cybercrime, n.d.) and does not specifically include cyber terrorism. To be an effective mechanism, cyber terrorism must be included.

To date, countries are signatories to the convention and of these—including the United States—have ratified it. Signatories to the convention must define criminal offenses and sanctions under the domestic laws for four categories of computer-related crimes as listed out above.

The convention also requires signatories to establish domestic procedures for detecting, investigating and prosecuting computer crimes, as well as collecting electronic evidence of any criminal offense. It also requires that signatories engage in international cooperation to the farthest extent.

There has been a debate about whether there should be a global standard—be it the Convention or a different entity—for dealing with cybercrime. Some have suggested that a global convention could help countries harmonize their legislation on cybercrime. One argument, in this case, is that similar legislation across countries could enhance international cooperation since a number of countries base mutual legal assistance on the notion of "dual criminality," wherein an action that is illegal in one country is also considered a crime in the other. Others, however, have expressed reservations about supporting a global standard for combating cybercrime.

10.3.3 Effective Law Enforcement

There remain many challenges for law enforcement agencies in relation to cyber terrorism. The rapid advancement of computer technology has increased the frequency and impact of cyber terrorism worldwide. These cyber terrorists continue to operate in a borderless environment with the knowledge that there is no single international legislation. Governments have varying technical competencies to deal with cyberterrorist acts and the coordination among law enforcement authorities are restricted by foreign policies and political ideologies. Law enforcement agencies around the world are also limited by resources in relation to funding and personnel trained in cyber terrorism. This, in turn, raises the issue of developing a secure mechanism for transferring and sharing information on cyber threat data to law enforcement agencies. One could argue that the current international legislative environment provides very limited or no deterrence for perpetrators committing cyber terrorism. In order for countries to counter cyber terrorism, it is critical for governments, their respective law enforcement agencies and industry to stop working in silos. The coordinated international action is the only way to tackle this global issue which is affecting countries on an increasingly greater scale. A cultural shift needs to occur among all governments, IT, law enforcement and legal sectors. Law enforcement agencies and industry need to cooperate to improve the sharing of information especially in identifying and alerting new and emerging threats, including modes of attack. A comprehensive education and awareness program for lawyers, judiciary and the public on cyberterrorism could also contribute to a higher likelihood of cyber terrorism prosecution. Industry and enforcement agencies must also increase and improve their understanding of the legal process and requirements for evidence collection and presentation in the judicial process. This will facilitate more accurate systemized investigations and will lead to more reliable information being brought before courts.

REFERENCES

1. Casey, E. (2004). *Handbook of computer crime investigation: Forensic tools and technology*. Elsevier Academic Press. Retrieved April 4, 2018, from https://epdf.tips/queue/handbook-of-computer-crime-investigation-forensic-tools-amp-technology.html
2. Convention on cybercrime – summary. (n.d.). Retrieved April 4, 2018, from http://conventions.coe.int/Treaty/en/Summaries/Html/185.htm Council of Europe
3. Johnson, T. (2006). Forensic computer crime investigation. Boca Raton, Florida: CRC, Taylor & Francis.
4. Marcella, A, & Menedez, D. (2008). *Cyber forensics: A field manual for collecting, examining, and preserving evidence of computer crimes*. Auerbach Publications: Florida.
5. Nelson, B, Phillips, A., & Steuart, C. (2010). *Guide to computer forensics and investigations*. Cengage Learning.
6. Taylor, M., & Quayle, E. (2003). *Child pornography: An internet crime*. London: Brunner-Routledge.

BIBLIOGRAPHY

1. Ackerman, E. (1997). When obsession turns ominous. *U. S. News & World Report*, *123*(20), 43.
2. Baryamureeba, V., & Tushabe, F. (2004). The enhanced digital forensic investigation process model. *Digital forensics research workshop (DFRWS)*. Baltimore: CiteSeer.
3. Beebe, N., & Clark, J. (2004). A hierarchical, objectives-based framework for the digital investigations process. *Digital forensics research Workshop (DFRWS)* (pp. 147-67). Baltimore, St. Paul: West Publishing Company.
4. Beebe, N. (2009). Digital forensic research: the good, the bad, and the unaddressed. *IFIP Advances in Information and Communication Technology, 306,* 17-36.
5. Bellovin, S. M. (1989 April). Security problems in the TCP/IP protocol suite. *Computer Communications Review, 19*(2), 32-48.
6. California Penal Code 5 646.9 (West 1999).
7. Carvey, H. (2001). *NT Incident Response Investigation and Analysis Information Security Bulletin, 6*(5), 35-44.
8. Hendren, J. (1997, May 25). Online harassment bill gains momentum. *Los Angeles Times*. p E4.
9. Casey, E. (2004b). Network traffic as a source of evidence: tool strengths, weaknesses, and future needs. *Digital Investigation, 1*(1), 28-43.
10. Casey, E., Daywalt, C., Johnston, A., & Maguire, T. (2009). Network investigations. *Digital forensics and investigation*. Boston: Elsevier.

11. Chaikin, D. (2006). Network investigations of cyber attacks: the limits of digital evidence. *Crime, Law and Social Change, 46*, 4-5.
12. Comer, D. (1995). *Internetworking with TCP/IP volume* I: *Principles, protocols, and architecture* (3rd ed.). Upper Saddle River, NJ: Prentice Hall.
13. (Eds.). *Information security management handbook.* (pp. 601-614) New York: Auerbach.
14. Espiner, T. (2006). *Mobile phone forensics 'hole' reported.* Retrieved August 18, 2008, from URL http://news.zdnet.co.uk/hardware/0,1000000091,39277347,00.htm
15. Halder, D., & Jaishankar, K. (2008). Cybercrimes against women in India: problems, perspective and solutions. *TMC Academic Journal*, *3*(1), 48-62.
16. Hassan, B. (2005). *The rights and security in cyberspace*. Tehran: Abrar Contemporary Institute of International Studies.
17. Held, G., & Hundley, K. (1999). *Cisco security architecture* (p. 26). New York: McGraw-Hill.
18. Henry, P., & De Libero, G. (1996). *Strategic networking*: *from LAN and WAN to information superhighways*. Massachusetts: International Thomson Publishing Company.
19. Hutton, S., & Haantz, S. (2003). *Cyberstalking*. Retrieved from http://www.nw3c.org
20. Hua, T. (1998, May 5,). Ex-student sentenced for hate e-mail. *Los Angeles Times,* p. A24.
21. Jansen, W. (2005). *Mobile device forensic software tools*. Paper presented at the Techno Forensics 2005, Gaithersburg, MD, USA.
22. Maharaj, D. (1997, December 2). U.S. to retry man in hate e-mail case. *Los Angeles Times,* p. A3.
23. Malin, C., Casey, E., & Aquilina, J. (2008). *Malware forensics*. Syngress.
24. McGraw, G., & Felten, E. (1996). *Java security*: *hostile applets*, *holes and antidotes*. New York: John Wiley & Sons.
25. Meloy, J. (1996). Stalking (obsessional following): a review of some preliminary studies. *Aggression and Violent Behavior, 1*(2) 147-162.
26. Meloy, J. (1998). *The psychology of stalking: clinical and forensic*

perspectives. San Diego: Academic Press.

27. McCarthy, P. (2005). *Forensic Analysis of Mobile Phones*. (Unpublished bachelor of computer and information science (honors) degree). Adelaide: University of South Australia.
28. Meloy, J., & Gothard, S. (1995). Demographic and clinical comparison of obsessional followers and offenders with mental disorders. *American Journal of Psychiatry*. *152*, 258-63.
29. Mishra, R.C. (2001). *Crime trends and criminal justice*. Delhi: Author's Press.
30. Morley, D. (2008). *Understanding computers in a changing society* (3rd ed., pp. 196-199). Course technology Cengage learning.
31. Morris, R. (1985, February). *A weakness in the 4.2BSD UNIX TCP/IP software*. Computing Science Technical Report 117, AT&T Bell Laboratories.
32. Neumann, P. (1995). *Computer-related risks*. New York: ACM Press.
33. Plonka, D. (2000). *FlowScan: A network traffic flow reporting and visualization tool.* Usenix.
34. Pica, G. (2011). *Criminology* (A. H. Najafi Abrandabadi, Trans. 2nd ed.). Mizan Publication.
35. Reiter, L. (1998, May 5). Stamp out e-mail harassment. *The Record,* p. LO9.
36. Reno v. American Civil Liberties Union, 521 U. S. 844 (1997).
37. Reuben, R. (1997). The court logs on: Decency act decision may change the nature of the internet. *American Bar Association Journal, 83*, 42.
38. Sableman, M. (1995). Responsibility on the net: Home grown or imposed? *Saint Louis Journalism Review, 26*, 11.
39. Stephens, G. (1995). *Crime in cyberspace*. *Futurist, 29*(5), 24-29.
40. Shelley, G., Cashman, T., & Vermaat, M. (2004). *Discovering computers: A gateway to information*. Boston: Thomson.
41. Vacca, J. (2002). *Computer forensics computer crime scene investigations*. Revere, MA: Charles River Media.
42. Yeschke, C. (2003). *The art of investigative interviewing* (2nd ed.). Boston: Butterworth Heinemann.
43. Ziembhca, S. (1998, May 26). Will County focusing on internet criminals. *Chicago Tribune,* p. 1.

INDEX

G

H

I